AN EDUCATOR'S GUIDE

Schoolwide Positive Behavioral Interventions and Supports

INTEGRATING ALL THREE TIERS

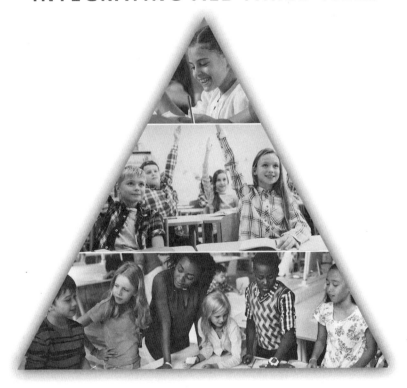

JASON E. HARLACHER   BILLIE JO RODRIGUEZ

MARZANO Research

555 North Morton Street
Bloomington, IN 47404
888.849.0851
FAX: 866.801.1477

email: info@MarzanoResearch.com
MarzanoResearch.com

Visit **MarzanoResearch.com/reproducibles** to download the free reproducibles in this book.

Printed in the United States of America

Library of Congress Control Number: 2017906378

ISBN: 978-0-9903458-7-9

Text and Cover Designer: Laura Cox

Marzano Research Development Team

Director of Content & Resources

Julia A. Simms

Editorial Manager

Laurel Hecker

Marzano Research Associates

Mario Acosta

Tina H. Boogren

Toby Boss

Robin J. Carey

Bev Clemens

Michelle Finn

Douglas Finn III

Jane Doty Fischer

Jeff Flygare

Laura Hack

Jason E. Harlacher

Tammy Heflebower

Lynne Herr

Mitzi Hoback

Jan K. Hoegh

Proficiency Scale Analyst

Christopher Dodson

Editorial Assistant / Staff Writer

Jacob Wipf

Jeanie Iberlin

Bettina Kates

Jessica McIntyre

Diane E. Paynter

Kristin Poage

Cameron Rains

Tom Roy

Mike Ruyle

Roberta Selleck

Julia A. Simms

Gerry Varty

Phil Warrick

David C. Yanoski

Bill Zima

Acknowledgments

The content of this book comes from a variety of sources, including research, our personal experience working in schools, our work as trainers of Schoolwide Positive Behavioral Interventions and Supports (SWPBIS), and an array of organizations that train on SWPBIS and offer examples of schools using SWPBIS on their respective websites. We want to explicitly thank the following organizations, as their examples and work are referenced throughout this book.

- ▲ Florida PBIS (now FLPBIS: MTSS)
- ▲ Colorado Department of Education, RTI/PBIS Unit (now MTSS)
- ▲ Midwest PBIS
- ▲ MIBLSI
- ▲ Washoe County School District
- ▲ Springfield Public Schools
- ▲ Maryland PBIS
- ▲ Nevada PBIS
- ▲ PBIS Technical Assistance Center
- ▲ RTI Innovations Conferences

On a personal note, I have to thank my classmates, professors, and colleagues within the field, beginning with my time in Davis School District in Farmington, Utah. I was a new intern in school psychology, and it was there that my close friend and colleague Heidi shared her use of the Principal's 200 Club at one of her schools. That was my first introduction to the idea of SWPBIS, although we didn't call it that at that time. That idea was one of the reasons I enrolled at the University of Oregon as a doctoral student. It was at Oregon that my passion for improving schools grew, and it was there that I had the honor of being an advisee of Dr. Kenneth W. Merrell. Although he left us many years ago, I carry his influence with me to this day. He taught me to always focus on the student and the school, and along with my other professors, I learned the value of changing the system in order to impact behavior. It is my hope that this book answers a need of practitioners for not just the conceptual knowledge of SWPBIS, but also its practical application. As ecological behaviorists, my classmates, colleagues, and I are always asking "What does it look like?" and I hope this book can answer that in respect to SWPBIS.

—Jason Harlacher

For me, the journey into positive behavior support and schools began with an amazing child, Corey, who taught me how to think about the world differently. After learning on my feet the value of stating expectations positively rather than saying what not to do, I was lucky enough to establish mentors, peers, and colleagues who have helped me grow in my understanding of behavior and the systems that can positively influence outcomes for all. My journey has included both purposeful and serendipitous turns, and I am thankful for those who saw potential in me, for those who challenged me to think differently about how the world works, and for those who gave me the chance to try out my work in the real world. Through these experiences, I have gained an understanding of what SWPBIS can look like. I hope this book will be a resource for those who, like me, are passionate about making changes that can have a large, positive impact on outcomes for students.

—Billie Jo Rodriguez

Marzano Research would like to thank the following reviewers:

Melani Amaris
Manager, Student Services
San Jose Unified School District
San Jose, California

Susan Bruhl
Director of Student Support Services
Addison Northeast Supervisory Union
Bristol, Vermont

Kelly McNabb
District PBIS Coach
Cobb County School District
Marietta, Georgia

Laura Mooiman
Program Specialist for PBIS
Napa Valley Unified School District
Napa, California

Table of Contents

Reproducible pages are in italics.

About the Authors

Jason E. Harlacher, PhD, is a consultant, researcher, and adjunct professor with over twelve years of experience in education. He works full time as a Multi-Tiered System of Supports (MTSS) Specialist with the Colorado Department of Education (CDE). Prior to joining CDE, Dr. Harlacher worked as a school psychologist, a response to intervention (RTI) consultant, and the state director for positive behavior support of Nevada (now Nevada PBIS). He is the sole author of *Designing Effective Classroom Management* and a coauthor of *Practitioner's Guide to Curriculum-Based Evaluation in Reading*. He presents nationally on schoolwide prevention models and has published articles on RTI, social-emotional learning, and classroom interventions. Dr. Harlacher earned a bachelor's degree in psychology from Ohio University, a master's degree in school psychology from Utah State University, and a doctorate in school psychology from the University of Oregon.

Billie Jo Rodriguez, PhD, NCSP, BCBA, is a practicing school psychologist, district positive behavior support coach, and adjunct professor with over eleven years of education experience. She currently works for Springfield Public Schools and teaches coursework in special education and school psychology at the University of Oregon. She has sixteen peer-reviewed publications in refereed journals as well as ten additional publications in the areas of Multi-Tiered System of Supports, (MTSS), functional behavior assessment and support planning, and Positive Behavioral Interventions and Support (PBIS). Prior to joining Springfield Public Schools as a school psychologist and Positive Behavior Support coach, Dr. Rodriguez worked as an assistant professor in school psychology at the University of Texas at San Antonio and as a behavior specialist for Clackamas Education Service District. Dr. Rodriguez has served on a team coordinating Tier Two and Three PBIS supports for a state-funded Oregon Department of Education grant, has served on the Oregon Coaches' Network, and has participated in the Texas Behavior Support network. Dr. Rodriguez presents nationally in the areas of MTSS, functional behavior assessment and intervention development, and PBIS. She earned a bachelor's degree in psychology from the University of Central Arkansas, a master's degree in special education from the University of Oregon, and a doctorate in school psychology, also from the University of Oregon.

About Marzano Research

Marzano Research is a joint venture between Solution Tree and Dr. Robert J. Marzano. Marzano Research combines Dr. Marzano's fifty years of educational research with continuous action research in all major areas of schooling in order to provide effective and accessible instructional strategies, leadership strategies, and classroom assessment strategies that are always at the forefront of best practice. By providing such an all-inclusive research-into-practice resource center, Marzano Research provides teachers and principals with the tools they need to effect profound and immediate improvement in student achievement.

Introduction

Greyson Cole Elementary School is a midsize school nestled in a small neighborhood on the outskirts of Reno, Nevada. Tumbleweeds regularly blow through the parking lot, and one can see the crisp Nevada landscape from its windows. It's not uncommon for a neighborhood dog to find its way to the playground during recess.

Like most schools, Greyson Cole Elementary School has its share of student problem behavior. Teachers manage behaviors that range from students running in the hallways to students fighting with each other. During one school year, the staff completed 397 major discipline referrals—documenting fighting, bullying, or property damage—and 434 minor discipline referrals—documenting tardiness, noncompliance, and minor acts of disrespect (Harlacher, 2011). Not surprisingly, such behavior extends to the buses, where over five hundred citations were given out during the same school year. In fact, inappropriate student behavior was so out of control that bus drivers occasionally turned the bus around to return to the school. Such referral rates paint a somewhat chaotic setting where time is often spent on managing behavior instead of on delivering instruction.

What are options for schools such as this one to respond to problem behavior? They could certainly adopt a zero-tolerance policy and use suspension as a means of restoring order, but zero-tolerance policies are largely ineffective for lowering misbehavior rates and for improving school climate (Advancement Project & Civil Rights Project, 2000; American Psychological Association Zero Tolerance Task Force, 2008; Costenbader & Markson, 1998; Tobin, Sugai, & Colvin, 1996). Perhaps identifying students with chronic problem behavior and developing interventions for those students could work, as school-based interventions are an effective means for managing student behavior (Bowen, Jenson, & Clark, 2004; Rathvon, 2008). However, the interventions themselves can be taxing for teachers to implement consistently, decreasing effectiveness (Kratochwill, Elliott, & Callan-Stoiber, 2002; Kratochwill & Shernoff, 2004; Noell, Duhon, Gatti, & Connell, 2002; Wolery, 2011). Additionally, teachers don't always have access to the resources they need for such interventions, such as technical assistance and training manuals, and the heavy use of individualized interventions creates a fragmented, piecemeal system that is inefficient (Merrell, Ervin, & Peacock, 2012; Peacock, Ervin, Daly, & Merrell, 2010). Schools and teachers need a more preventative, effective, and comprehensive approach to discipline. Enter Schoolwide Positive

Behavioral Interventions and Supports (SWPBIS). SWPBIS is a preventative framework that uses increasingly intensive layers of support to prevent problem behavior, create a positive school climate, and improve the overall social and academic competence of students (Sailor, Dunlap, Sugai, & Horner, 2009).

Greyson Cole Elementary School implemented SWPBIS as part of a districtwide implementation initiative (Harlacher, 2011). The results were positive after just one year of implementation, as the number of minor referrals dropped by 43 percent. The reduction in referrals was an estimated sixty-two hours of time back to teachers and students (185 referrals at twenty minutes of instructional time each). The number of major referrals dropped by 29 percent, gaining back an estimated twenty-eight hours of administrative time (112 referrals at fifteen minutes of administration time). The effect on the referrals generated from students while on the school buses was startling—they went from over five hundred to only sixteen, a reduction of 97 percent. This school isn't alone. A middle school just down the road implemented SWPBIS as well and found a reduction of 70 percent in major referrals (677 to 200) and a 46 percent drop in suspensions (243 to 156; Harlacher, 2011). Other schools have experienced similar results with SWPBIS, both at the elementary level (Horner et al., 2009) and the secondary level (Bohanon et al., 2006; Simonsen et al., 2012). The results of SWPBIS implementation can be dramatic.

Overview of This Resource

Within *An Educator's Guide to Schoolwide Positive Behavioral Interventions and Supports*, we describe SWPBIS in depth and provide practitioners and school-level personnel with a comprehensive resource. Whether you're a principal in a school plagued by behavioral issues, a teacher who wants to know more about SWPBIS, a coach working with teams to implement positive behavior support strategies, or a district-level coordinator faced with improving school climate, you can use this book as a resource. Although there are resources available on SWPBIS, some of them are technical and target researchers, while others only focus on one aspect of SWPBIS, and still others are too conceptual and not detailed enough for practitioners. This book fills the void in the literature by providing a comprehensive SWPBIS overview and specific, practical advice for school personnel and practitioners. It provides the theoretical background of SWPBIS and the tangible aspects of it, so readers will know the *why* behind SWPBIS as well as what it looks like in practice. Because this book is comprehensive, we also envision it being helpful for university personnel and for educators in training.

We wrote this book based on the SWPBIS research from experts that included Robert Horner, George Sugai, Heather Peshak George, Don Kincaid, Wayne Sailor, Glen Dunlap, and Kent McIntosh, as well as our personal experience working with school teams to implement it. We provide a clear description of the model, what SWPBIS looks like in practice, and what steps schools can take to implement it successfully.

How to Use This Book

We have provided a wealth of information in this book, as we wanted to detail SWPBIS conceptually and what it looks likes in practice. We hope this book serves as a guide for those just starting out with their SWPBIS journey and for those who are experienced with SWPBIS. To that end, this book contains explicit information on the theoretical basis of SWPBIS, as well as numerous examples and discussion of what implementation looks like in practice in both elementary and secondary schools. We also provide questions that school teams can ask to evaluate both the impact of their SWPBIS framework and the quality of implementation of the framework. This book also contains sections devoted to the necessary data and the critical systems needed for successful implementation. In short, this is a comprehensive and practical book that provides content on many things related to SWPBIS.

We begin the book with an overall description of SWPBIS and its theoretical underpinnings in chapter 1, including a summary of the research supporting its use at the elementary and secondary levels. We also present the four key elements of SWPBIS—(1) outcomes, (2) practices, (3) systems, and (4) data—and describe the model's tiered nature. We then cover each subsequent tier—Tier One in chapter 2, Tier Two in chapter 3, and Tier Three in chapter 4—detailing what each tier looks like in practice by describing each of the four key elements. We include examples of what schools have done for each tier, and we discuss using the Problem-Solving Model for each tier at both the systems and student level. Chapter 5 explains how to put SWPBIS into action, and we discuss the systematic approach needed in order to implement SWPBIS for sustainability. We also provide direction for school personnel on where to start. Chapter 6 describes two case summaries, one of which details SWPBIS at an elementary school and the other at a secondary school. Each of the chapters ends with a summary of the most important information, and the epilogue brings things to a close. We end the book with two appendices. Appendix A is a template for a menu of Tier Two interventions; appendix B is a functional behavior assessment interview. We have collected educators' accounts of SWPBIS implementation for your benefit as well—you'll find their comments throughout the book in special feature boxes.

Ideally, readers will progress though each chapter sequentially, but we understand each reader's background and experience impacts informational needs. Those new to SWPBIS will want to start with chapter 1, but those who want specific information on a given tier can jump ahead to that chapter (chapters 2 to 4). For those looking just for information on how to implement SWPBIS, they can skip to chapter 5. For those who need a concrete example of the whole model, chapter 6 provides that.

Overview of Schoolwide Positive Behavioral Interventions and Supports

A school is primed for academic success if its students regularly engage in appropriate behaviors and require minimal discipline time. As we like to say about students and behavior, "If they're not listening to directions, they're not listening to instruction." This is the aim of using Schoolwide Positive Behavioral Interventions and Supports (SWPBIS) in schools: to create a safe, orderly environment with a positive school climate that enables students to achieve social and academic success. Within this chapter, we explore SWPBIS's research base and theoretical background, after which we discuss the four key elements and the Problem-Solving Model.

Positive Behavioral Interventions and Supports (PBIS) is about building effective environments and using evidence-based practices that teach and encourage appropriate behaviors to replace undesired behavior (Carr et al., 2002). Accordingly, PBIS applied to the entire school is *schoolwide PBIS*. This creates a framework for all students that uses a broad range of strategies for teaching positive behaviors while also preventing and reducing undesired behavior, thus creating a system of supports within the school (Sailor et al., 2009). This system of supports is often referred to in the broader sense as Multi-Tiered System of Supports (MTSS), which incorporates social behavior systems (for example, SWPBIS) as well as academic systems (for example, response to intervention; Buffum, Mattos, & Weber, 2009; Jimerson, Burns, & VanDerHeyden, 2007). We refer to SWPBIS as a framework that can be applied as a stand-alone framework or as the behavior support side of MTSS (McIntosh & Goodman, 2016). We also use the terms *model* and *framework* interchangeably, as both refer to the broad, tiered structure of SWPBIS.

SWPBIS provides all students with universal instruction, called Tier One, using instructional and behavioral principles to teach a handful of schoolwide behavioral expectations (for example, be safe, be respectful, be responsible). This foundational level serves a preventative function to mitigate problematic behavior, and at least 80 percent of the students' needs are met with universal instruction alone (George, Kincaid, & Pollard-Sage, 2009; Horner, Sugai, et al., 2005). A range of increasingly intensive and evidence-based supports are available for students who need more direct support for behavioral concerns, which allows school teams to match each student's needs with a corresponding level of support and intervention. An additional 10 to 15 percent of students require supplemental, targeted support called Tier Two (also referred to as *targeted support*), and 3 to 5 percent require intensive, individualized support called Tier Three (also referred to as *indicated support*; Sugai & Horner, 2009). As illustrated in figure 1.1, SWPBIS creates a healthy, functioning school in which all students' needs are met. It is important to understand that figure 1.1 represents a healthy system and is the ideal outcome of implementing SWPBIS. Some schools may serve populations in which most students may initially appear to need Tier Two or Tier Three supports; however, once the foundational systems and supports are in place, such schools can achieve outcomes that represent a healthy system (that is, at least 80 percent of students' needs are met with Tier One alone, no more than 10 to 15 percent require Tier Two, and no more than 5 percent require Tier Three; Bohanon et al., 2006; Netzel & Eber, 2003). Whereas some schools may find that that 40 percent of their students are at risk for academic or behavioral failure, over time, SWPBIS will likely decrease the number of students who are at risk (Greenwood, Kratochwill, & Clements, 2008). See table 1.1 for a summary of SWPBIS.

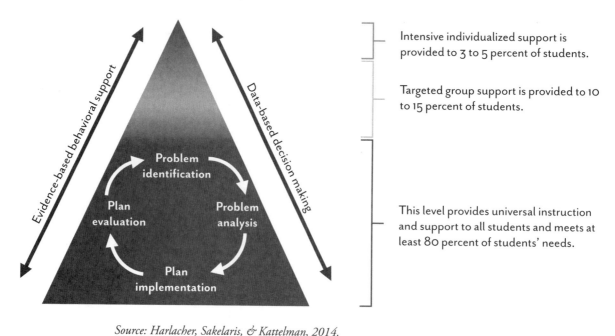

Intensive individualized support is provided to 3 to 5 percent of students.

Targeted group support is provided to 10 to 15 percent of students.

This level provides universal instruction and support to all students and meets at least 80 percent of students' needs.

Source: Harlacher, Sakelaris, & Kattelman, 2014.

Figure 1.1: SWPBIS framework.

SWPBIS is a responsive, efficient system of supports in which the intensity of support and services increases as students receive supports that are higher up in the triangle. To ensure their needs are met, teachers screen all students at least two to three times per year to identify those who may be at risk for behavioral difficulties (students already identified at risk are monitored with similar tools). Teachers provide students with support, and their progress is regularly monitored to ensure that support is effective (Horner, Sugai, Todd, & Lewis-Palmer, 2005; Sailor et al., 2009). Every teacher proactively assesses students' needs, provides instruction, and then monitors its impact on every student; the entire school uses

Table 1.1: SWPBIS Summary

Instruction	Group Size	Frequency and Duration
Tier One		
Three to five positively stated expectations; teaching and reinforcement of those expectations; consistent procedures for responding to misbehavior	Whole school, taught in various formats (for example, at an assembly, in classroom, and so on)	Initial teaching; reteaching and recognition provided throughout school year; instructional boosters provided as needed, based on data
Tier Two		
Targeted group, interventions to supplement Tier One with goal of displaying schoolwide expectations with increased instruction in explicit skills, increased opportunities to practice and receive feedback	Small group or 1:1 Designed to reach groups of students but not always delivered in a group setting	Occurs daily or weekly, depending on intervention Duration determined by student's progress, but typically no longer than twenty weeks
Tier Three		
Intensive instruction that includes small-group, 1:1, and wraparound services Individually designed	1:1 or small group, depending on intervention	Varies by student, but usually daily occurrence Longer duration relative to Tier Two

Source: Adapted from Harlacher et al., 2014.

this approach. Such processes create a fluid system that emphasizes evidence-based practices and data for decision making (Horner, Sugai, et al., 2005; Sailor et al., 2009). Consequently, SWPBIS is a continuous-improvement system. It requires school teams to regularly examine both the impact and the implementation of individual interventions *and* the system itself (Newton, Horner, Algozzine, Todd, & Algozzine, 2009).

However, SWPBIS is about more than just teaching behavioral expectations to students; SWPBIS focuses on creating supportive environments (Sugai & Horner, 2009). The most obvious way school teams do this is through its facilitation of social competence by directly teaching behavioral expectations and prosocial skills (Sugai & Horner, 2009). For example, school teams teach students the schoolwide expectations (such as be respectful and be safe), and they may also receive instruction on related prosocial skills (such as having empathy and working cooperatively). Additionally, the school team sets up an environment where students are more likely to succeed and to engage in prosocial behaviors (and learning) rather than problematic behaviors. The language adults use is geared toward the expectations (for example, "When we listen to others, that's a way of being respectful"), structures can change in the environment (such as adjusted schedules or a modified layout of a common area), and the ratio of feedback for appropriate behavior to redirects for misbehavior increases as students are acknowledged often for displaying prosocial behavior. This differs starkly from approaches that focus on *within-child problems*, where the focus is only on students and adjusting their behaviors. Because of its focus on prosocial skills and the setting in which those skills occur, SWPBIS impacts the school's overall climate, culture, and safety. In turn, students experience more positive social outcomes, develop lifelong skills, and face improved academic learning opportunities (McKevitt & Braaksma, 2008; Sugai & Horner, 2009).

> "PBIS is the foundation for our school community; not only does it bring students and staff together, but it also incorporates families. Using PBIS helps us to consistently see students actively engaged in all aspects of their school day. When students are aware of the expectations set for them, they consistently rise to meet them. This system helped us create an uplifting environment in school where students and teachers alike feel successful."
>
> —Nikki Matthews, fourth-grade education teacher, Walterville Elementary School, Springfield, Oregon (personal communication, May 13, 2016)

Next, we will delve into the research base for SWPBIS, its theoretical background, its four key elements, and the Problem-Solving Model.

Research Base for SWPBIS

To date, over twenty-one thousand schools in the United States use SWPBIS (National Technical Assistance Center on Positive Behavioral Interventions and Supports [NTACP-BIS], n.d.). Behind SWPBIS is a long history of effective results. In fact, Robert Horner, George Sugai, and Timothy Lewis (2015) provided a list of over one hundred references that have explored the effects of SWPBIS, including evaluation studies and randomized controlled studies. We summarize some of the results here.

The implementation of SWPBIS is associated with decreases in office discipline referrals and instances of problem behavior (Algozzine et al., 2008; Algozzine, Wang, et al., 2012; Bradshaw, Mitchell, & Leaf, 2010; Curtis, Van Horne, Robertson, & Karvonen, 2010; Horner et al., 2009; Muscott, Mann, & LeBrun, 2008), decreases in both in-school and out-of-school suspensions (Bradshaw et al., 2010; Curtis et al., 2010; Muscott et al., 2008; Netzel & Eber, 2003; Scott, 2001; Simonsen et al., 2012), and increases in feelings of school safety from both students (Metzler, Biglan, Rusby, & Sprague, 2001) and staff (Horner et al., 2009). One study found that students in schools using SWPBIS had better emotion regulation, fewer concentration problems, and more prosocial behaviors than in schools that did not (Bradshaw, Waasdorp, & Leaf, 2012). Teachers also reported feeling more confident in handling discipline and feeling less burnout from the school day (Ross, Romer, & Horner, 2012), and the model was associated with improvements in the organizational health of the school (Bradshaw, Koth, Bevans, Ialongo, & Leaf, 2008; Bradshaw, Koth, Thornton, & Leaf, 2009).

Studies have found associations between the use of SWPBIS and increases in academic achievement, albeit modest (Bradshaw et al., 2010; Horner et al., 2009; Muscott et al., 2008). The association between SWPBIS and achievement is logical, as schools have reported gaining back hours and days of instructional time because of decreases in absences, tardies, and suspensions (Caldarella, Shatzer, Gray, Young, & Young, 2011; Taylor-Greene et al.,

1997). One middle school reported gaining back over 222 hours from reductions in office referrals and over 640 days due to decreased absences (Caldarella et al., 2011).

Perhaps most appealing is that the work to implement the model is an efficient process, as schools with positive results have received two to three days of initial training and a few follow-up trainings prior to implementing the model (Bradshaw et al., 2012; Mass-Galloway, Panyan, Smith, & Wessendorf, 2008). The actual process of teaching the schoolwide behavioral expectations to students is also very efficient. Susan Taylor-Greene and colleagues (1997) reported spending a half day at the beginning of the year and a few booster sessions during the year for their model, which resulted in nearly a 50 percent reduction in referrals. Paul Caldarella and colleagues (2011) reported using monthly twenty-minute lessons throughout the school year to teach students the expectations and certain social skills, which resulted in large reductions in referrals and absences.

The benefits of SWPBIS are not exclusive to one setting or type of school, as beneficial results occur in early education settings (Fox & Hemmeter, 2009; Frey, Boyce, & Tarullo, 2009; Muscott et al., 2008), elementary schools (Bradshaw et al., 2010; Bradshaw et al., 2012; Horner et al., 2009), middle schools (Metzler et al., 2001; Taylor-Greene et al., 1997), and high schools (Mass-Galloway et al., 2008; Muscott et al., 2008; Simonsen et al., 2012). The findings also include rural settings (Curtis et al., 2010) and urban settings (Bohanon et al., 2006; Netzel & Eber, 2003). Given these findings, it is evident that SWPBIS is a well-researched and evidence-based practice that benefits a variety of students and settings (Horner, Sugai, & Anderson, 2010).

Theoretical Background

Six principles serve as the theoretical and conceptual background of SWPBIS (Sugai & Horner, 2009).

- ▲ Principle 1.   Use of behavioral principles
- ▲ Principle 2.   Use of a proactive and preventative approach to discipline
- ▲ Principle 3.   Focus on instruction and matching support to student need
- ▲ Principle 4.   Use of evidence-based practices
- ▲ Principle 5.   Use of data-based decision making
- ▲ Principle 6.   Focus on a schoolwide perspective

The following sections address each in order.

Principle 1: Use of Behavioral Principles

SWPBIS's historical roots are grounded in behaviorism and applied behavior analysis (Sugai & Horner, 2009). Behavioral principles are used because of their effectiveness in achieving valued outcomes and facilitating healthy development in students (Sugai & Horner, 2009; Shinn, Walker, & Stoner, 2002). Table 1.2 (page 10) provides a brief summary of key terms and concepts related to behaviorism. Students are taught prosocial skills and then acknowledged for using those skills with reinforcement methods, and various strategies are used to manage, prevent, and decrease unwanted behavior (Sugai & Horner, 2009; George, Kincaid, & Pollard-Sage, 2009).

Table 1.2: Key Terms and Concepts for Behaviorism

Term	Definition
Setting Events	People, events, or conditions that precede the behavior (but are temporally distant) and temporarily affect the value of a reinforcer
Antecedent	Event that occurs before a behavior; the trigger to the behavior
Behavior	The observable and measurable act
Consequence	Event or result that occurs after a behavior, influencing the likelihood of the behavior occurring again in the future
Reinforcement	A consequence event that *increases* the likelihood of a behavior occurring again; it strengthens the behavior
Punishment	A consequence event that *decreases* the likelihood of a behavior occurring again; it weakens the behavior

Source: Alberto & Troutman, 2013; Baer, Wolf, & Risley, 1968; Skinner, 1953, 1976; Watson, 1913; Wolery, Bailey, & Sugai, 1988.

A *behavior* is an observable and measurable act, such as a student raising her hand. Behavior occurs within a context, so each behavior is preceded by *antecedent* that triggers the behavior. In this case, a teacher asking a question in class is the antecedent. Behavior is then followed by a *consequence*, which can either make the behavior more likely to happen in the future (which is called *reinforcement*) or make it less likely to happen in the future (which is referred to as *punishment*). For example, if a teacher calls on a student, that may serve as reinforcement. However, if the student is called upon, gives a wrong answer, and his or her classmates laugh, the student may not raise her hand in the future when the teacher asks a question, thus resulting in punishment for raising her hand. *Setting events* temporarily affect the value of a reinforcer, making them more or less desirable. In this case, a setting event may be that the student had a fight with a classmate and therefore the desire to be called upon is stronger now (the student really wants the teacher's attention, in this case). Another example that perhaps we can all relate to is online shopping! When you receive an email coupon, that is an antecedent that triggers the behavior of online shopping. The consequence is reinforcement, as you are rewarded with new clothes at a discounted price (thanks to that coupon). A setting event could be that someone made fun of your clothes last week, making new clothes more desirable.

Additionally, educators and school teams that use SWPBIS consider the environment and contextual influences to identify antecedents and setting events for certain behaviors (Crone & Horner, 2003; Sugai & Horner, 2009). Rather than assuming problems are housed solely within an individual, the SWPBIS approach examines the school context to determine how the environment contributes to the problem (Carr et al., 2002; Crone & Horner, 2003). As such, school personnel will consider the setting and the conditions that are contributing to or causing the identified problem, be it with the systems in place, certain processes, the environment, the behavior of staff, another student, or a group of students (Crone & Horner, 2003; George et al., 2009; Sailor et al., 2009). Such an approach places the ability to change behavior in the hands of the educators, as they can identify alterable variables related to behavior that can be adjusted accordingly.

"When you plant lettuce, if it does not grow well, you don't blame the lettuce. You look for reasons it is not doing well. It may need fertilizer, or more water, or less sun."

—Thich Nhat Hanh, Buddhist monk, author, and peace activist

Principle 2: Use of a Proactive and Preventative Approach to Discipline

The use of SWPBIS focuses on a proactive and preventative approach to discipline and behavior management. Instead of assuming that students know the prosocial behaviors needed to succeed in school, school teams and staff using SWPBIS create core behavioral expectations that are applicable across the entire school and proactively teach the expected behaviors rather than waiting until misbehavior occurs. Instead of other service delivery models that provide support after an incident (Carr et al., 2002; Netzel & Eber, 2003), students are taught a reasonable number of expectations at the beginning of the school year to get all of them on the same page regarding how to be successful across school settings.

The use of SWPBIS focuses on provisions of support early on to prevent problems from becoming more severe. In practice, school teams using SWPBIS will screen students throughout the year to identify those in need of support before their misbehavior becomes a chronic issue. School teams also analyze school-level data on a regular basis to identify problem areas and make environmental changes before they become larger problems. The overall approach is to provide support quickly and early, and to identify areas of concern in the school environment and adjust them immediately (George et al., 2009).

Principle 3: Focus on Instruction and Matching Support to Student Need

This principle behind SWPBIS is elegant: teach behavior in the same manner as academics (Darch & Kame'enui, 2004; Horner, Sugai, et al., 2005). Just as students learning academic skills need practice and opportunities to demonstrate those skills, so do they with behavioral skills (Darch & Kame'enui, 2004; Horner, Sugai, et al., 2005). To teach students expectations, school teams that use SWPBIS adopt an instructional approach that involves modeling, practice, and feedback. Accordingly, the staff make a conscious choice to shift from a reactive, punitive approach for discipline to a proactive, reinforcement-based approach (Carr et al., 2002; Netzel & Eber, 2003; Horner, Sugai, et al., 2005). The staff view misbehavior as an opportunity to reteach, not as a chance just to punish the student. Instead of using only punishment strategies to manage misbehavior, SWPBIS focuses on teaching and reinforcing behavioral expectations first. Punishment strategies (such as time-out or loss of privileges) are used second, and only when other options are exhausted and when data support their use. Misbehavior is an opportunity to reteach.

Along with an instructional approach to social behavior, school teams that use SWPBIS focus on creating a match between a student's current skills and corresponding level of support. A range of strategies to teach and encourage appropriate behavior is used to both mitigate the impact of misbehavior and avoid it altogether. The entire school is organized to create universal supports for all students (that is, Tier One), and increasingly intensive layers of instruction are used for students who require more support (that is, Tiers Two and Three). The range of supports ensures that each student's needs are matched with an appropriate level of support, and data are used to monitor if each student's support is effective. Bear in mind that students who need additional support receive Tier Two or Three *in addition to* Tier One and do not receive Tier Two or Tier Three *instead of* Tier One. The tiers are layers of support that are added on top of each other. The provision of Tier Two or Three does not supplant a lower tier; instead, it supplements it.

Principle 4: Use of Evidence-Based Practices

SWPBIS places a premium on strategies and approaches that have evidence supporting their effectiveness. It does this to ensure that students have the best chance at making progress and reaching identified goals. Practices that have documented evidence of their impact are used, and practices that do not have evidence or are shown to be ineffective are discarded. However, even though there is evidence to support the use of certain practices, educators do not assume they will be effective for every student and situation. Instead, implementation of SWPBIS involves regularly gathering and analyzing data to ensure that the practices are implemented as intended and that they are in fact having an impact in any given school context (George et al., 2009).

Principle 5: Use of Data-Based Decision Making

Too often educators make decisions with limited data, don't have the necessary data needed, or ignore the data available (Mandinach, 2012; Merrell et al., 2012; Reschly, 2008). To avoid these situations, SWPBIS involves regularly collecting and analyzing data for decisions. The focus on data creates a continuous-improvement cycle in which practices are implemented, information is gathered, and formative and summative decisions are made to ensure the practices are achieving the desired results (Newton, Horner, et al., 2009; Shinn, 2008a). This creates an iterative process within SWPBIS in which school teams monitor both the implementation and its impact.

> "It's amazing to watch schools and districts learn to use their data and apply evidence-based practices with high fidelity. Nevada schools went from a designated week of respect to a year of respect!"
>
> —Ashley Greenwald, director of Nevada PBIS, research assistant professor, University of Nevada, Reno, Nevada (personal communication, January 9, 2017)

Principle 6: Focus on a Schoolwide Perspective

A schoolwide perspective means that SWPBIS is used throughout the entire school and that the whole staff work collaboratively to support it. Instead of each teacher managing behavior or issues by him- or herself, the faculty takes a team-based approach. The practices and systems associated with SWPBIS are used in every setting and classroom, and the staff work akin to a pit crew coordinating services to achieve a goal (George, 2009).

A schoolwide perspective also means that issues are considered from a systemic perspective. Whereas school teams will monitor implementation and the impact of supports for individual students, they will also monitor implementation and impact of the entire model, including the collective needs of groups of students (Newton, Horner, et al., 2009). When issues arise or when a student needs support, school teams consider whether the identified problem is indicative of a larger, systemic issue or if it's an isolated problem. Additionally, the school teams create systems that provide efficiency, coherency, and consistency with student discipline. This means that the totality of factors and structures within a school, such as resource allocation, leadership, and processes for accessing support, are aligned to support SWPBIS.

As an example, one team at an elementary school we worked with reviewed its office discipline referral data and identified a large increase in referrals from a handful of students in the afternoon (Harlacher, 2011). Before deciding upon a solution, the team examined additional data and discovered that a lot of sixth-grade students were receiving referrals for behavior during specials time (for example, music). Instead of singling out certain students and developing behavior plans, the sixth-grade staff simply retaught the schoolwide expectations to all sixth-grade students for behavior during music and increased reinforcement during that time. As a result, the number of referrals decreased as the expected behavior during music improved. This team-based approach illustrates the systemic perspective that school teams use with SWPBIS (Sugai & Horner, 2006). Had the team implemented individual plans without considering the system or context, it would not have efficiently or effectively addressed the issue.

The six aforementioned principles comprise the conceptual background of SWPBIS in which the overall goal is to achieve sustainability (McIntosh, Filter, Bennett, Ryan, & Sugai, 2010) and improve the social and academic functioning of all students and the overall climate of the school. These principles highlight the difference between SWPBIS and other behavioral initiatives in schools. SWPBIS is a school reform *framework* that emphasizes evidence-based practices and uses data to help staff make decisions that will prepare students to be productive members of society (George et al., 2009; Horner, Sugai, et al., 2005). See table 1.3 for a list of what SWPBIS is and is not.

Table 1.3: What SWPBIS Is and Is Not

SWPBIS Is . . .	SWPBIS Is Not . . .
A framework for decision making	A packaged program
A systemic and cultural change that is embedded throughout the school and culture	A scripted intervention or something that is added onto existing structures
Data driven	A rigid manual to follow
Preventative and responsive	A temporary solution
Inclusive of all students	Only about extrinsic rewards
A continuum of support using universal and targeted evidence-based practices	Just for students with chronic behavior issues

Source: NTACPBIS, 2010.

Four Key Elements

The principles behind SWPBIS may appear complex, but in practice, SWPBIS consists of four key elements: (1) *outcomes*, (2) *practices*, (3) *systems*, and (4) *data* (see figure 1.2; Sugai & Horner, 2006). These four elements provide a framework for organizing all of the pieces of SWPBIS and allow teams to think through the components they need to have a sustainable SWPBIS model. *Outcomes* are defined as the social, behavioral, and academic outcomes that school teams wish to achieve through the implementation of SWPBIS. *Practices* are the strategies and methods used to support students in displaying prosocial behavior, and the *systems* are processes and procedures put into place to support the staff in implementing those practices and gathering the necessary data (Sugai & Horner, 2006). *Data* are the clear pieces of information used to monitor implementation of the system, monitor its impact, and determine if the identified outcomes are achieved. As seen in figure 1.2, the outcomes should promote social competence and academic achievement. Staff then gather data to support decision making to determine the extent to which the students are reaching outcomes are effective, that the practices teachers implement to support students' behavior in achieving the outcomes, and that the systems are in place to support staff with implementing the designated practices and gathering the necessary data to make decisions.

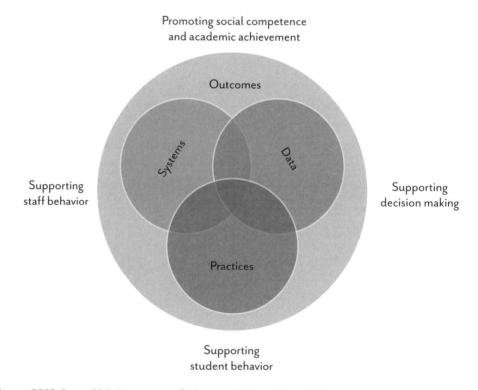

Source: PBIS Center, U.S. Department of Education, Office of Special Education, 2017.

Figure 1.2: Four key elements of SWPBIS.

George Sugai, a professor at the University of Connecticut and leading researcher in SWPBIS, is credited with an analogy to help think about these elements. If you consider going on a vacation, the *outcome* is the destination. Sometimes we take trips to a faraway or new destination, and other times we take trips that are closer and more familiar. *Practices* can be related to the way we drive. Some of us are "Sunday" drivers who like to take our time along the way, making lots of stops and taking in all the scenery. Others are like delivery truck drivers who only stop when the service station is on the right side of the road because it is more efficient than crossing traffic to stop for services on the left side of the road. In our vacation analogy, *systems* can be thought of as the car we drive to our destination. A reliable mode of transportation versus a car that continually breaks down and needs service makes a huge difference in whether we are likely to arrive at the destination. The data make up the map or GPS information we use to get to the destination. It is important that the information we use to determine how to arrive at our vacation destination is accurate (updated with detours and construction information) to increase the precision of our decision making about which routes to take. Similarly, the more complex the route to the destination, the more data we are likely to need. These four key elements interact with each other and are the salient features that comprise the SWPBIS framework. When all four elements are in place within a school, teams can develop a sustainable SWPBIS framework (McIntosh, Horner, & Sugai, 2009; Sugai & Horner, 2006).

Outcomes: Promoting Social Competence and Academic Achievement

Prior to implementing SWPBIS, school teams will identify the specific and relevant outcomes that they want to achieve with implementation. Outcomes are the "academic and behavior targets that are endorsed and emphasized by students, families, and educators" (NTACPBIS, n.d.). As Robert Horner, George Sugai, Anne Todd, and Teri Lewis-Palmer (2005) described:

> Schools are expected to be safe environments where students learn the academic and social skills needed for life in our society. The basic goals of any system of schoolwide [PBIS] must be to provide the behavioral assistance needed to achieve those [outcomes]. (p. 365)

To that end, school teams identify their desired outcomes and define those in measurable manners. All students, staff, and parents decide upon and value these outcomes (Sugai & Horner, 2006). One way to frame the outcomes is to consider them as goals of implementation; what do teams want SWPBIS to achieve?

Schools will identify long- and short-term outcomes of using SWPBIS. Long-term outcomes are overarching and global outcomes that are often distal; they take months or years to achieve, such as improved academic performance or increased safety within the school. Short-term outcomes are more immediate and pressing goals, and they are typically reached within a few weeks or within the semester or quarter. For example, schools may identify a short-term outcome of reducing referrals among sixth-grade students or increasing attendance of students during the second semester. The outcomes can also be organized across tiers. For example, a Tier One outcome is to ensure that at least 80 percent of students have zero to one office referrals or that all Tier Two interventions are provided with at least 90 percent fidelity.

As an example, a PBIS team at XYZ Elementary School implemented SWPBIS to improve the overall climate within its school and to decrease student problem behavior. During implementation, it identified a need to examine behavior during recess. The team wanted to decrease disrespectful behavior that occurred when students were lining up from recess to come inside. It set a goal to reduce office referrals by 50 percent over a two-month period. This reduction in office referrals was the outcome the team monitored to determine if they had been successful. The intervention involved special recess positive tickets that students got for lining up appropriately. Students took those tickets back to the classroom, and at the end of the week, the class with the most tickets for this behavior got an extra recess (and the teacher got an extra fifteen minutes to herself because extra recess was given during another recess period, so someone other than the classroom teacher was responsible for supervision). When the team reviewed the outcome of this intervention, it met the goal of reducing the office referrals by at least 50 percent. In addition, teachers and staff reported an increase in focused instruction and acknowledgment for lining up appropriately and respectfully transitioning in from recess. The classroom teachers also reported that the focus on appropriate behavior at recess reduced time spent responding to "tattling" and other inappropriate recess behaviors (students still being frustrated when they came into the classroom, and arguments extending into the classroom), resulting in shorter, more pleasant transitions and increased instructional time immediately following recess (Rodriguez, 2015).

Identifying the outcomes that school teams wish to achieve provides an organizing framework to make decisions about the data schools will gather, the practices they use, and the systems they need to put into place. For example, if a school team identifies increases in attendance as a valued outcome, one would expect that school to examine data on attendance rates throughout the school year. When faced with decisions about which professional development to conduct, this school team would select trainings related to attendance and truancy rather than trainings unrelated to attendance. Although decisions about professional development are often made because of mandates and priorities from district leadership, having clearly defined outcomes assists schools in determining which practices to adopt and which ones not to adopt. In short, any school that uses SWPBIS needs to define its purpose and outcomes for using the model.

Practices: Supporting Student Behavior

As school teams identify the outcomes they want to achieve and the data they need to gather, they also decide upon the practices needed to achieve those outcomes. The practices refer to the strategies and methods used to improve student behavior and prevent undesired behavior. This is the instructional piece of SWPBIS that is organized into tiers. Tier One is universal support provided to all students, and it's designed to foster prosocial behavior and decrease occurrences of inappropriate behavior. In practice, it consists of identifying schoolwide expectations, teaching them to all students, and providing a high rate of reinforcement for meeting these expectations. It also includes establishing a continuum of procedures for managing undesired behavior.

At Tier Two, students continue to take part in the Tier One practices but are also provided more intensive support based on a common need through additional instruction and reinforcement of the schoolwide expectations (Hawken, Adolphson, MacLeod, & Schumann, 2009). Designed to be provided quickly and efficiently, Tier Two consists of a range of interventions that may include social skills instruction, frequent check-ins with school staff, or before- and after-school programs.

At Tier Three, teachers provide students with individualized and intensive instruction in addition to the prosocial climate and supports (Scott, Anderson, Mancil, & Alter, 2009). The interventions reduce the severity of problem behaviors and enhance prosocial behaviors, and they are multifaceted. The coordination and delivery of Tier Three often entails academic and behavioral supports and is function based (Crone & Horner, 2003). This can include school-based supports, school-home components, and community supports.

Systems: Supporting Staff Behavior

To ensure that practices are implemented well and that the staff can gather the necessary data to inform outcomes, school teams also consider the systems and procedures they need to adjust or put into place to support the staff.

Systems change is often one of the more complex aspects of the SWPBIS elements because it typically involves adjustments that are more difficult to see, and it requires administrative leadership and strong buy-in to change many moving parts that have become engrained habits within the school (Bohanon & Wu, 2014). For example, schools may need to adopt new processes and programs for office discipline referral data recording, entry, and management that allow staff to have meaningful information, which enables them to determine the effectiveness of a practice. Changing this one aspect of the SWPBIS system to better assess outcomes will require a thoughtful data-revision process. The team will:

- ▲ Reassess what data are collected for each office discipline referral form
- ▲ Design the form and consider how teachers can feasibly complete it (such as a half sheet that recess attendants can carry and has less information than a full sheet, or checkboxes rather than blanks to maximize efficiency)
- ▲ Determine which information other staff and parents receive, who communicates office referral to other staff and parents, and how the communication occurs
- ▲ Determine the program for data entry and management
- ▲ Decide logistics for who will input the data into the program and when the data will be entered
- ▲ Determine which team will review the data and how often
- ▲ Assess the impact of the changes and monitor whether the referral procedures are being followed accurately

There are numerous considerations for just one tiny aspect of SWPBIS. Another example could involve an administrator providing time in the master calendar for schoolwide teaching of expectations following a school break. This often involves adjusting multiple schedules as well as dealing with protecting instructional time for teachers to meet certain academic mandates. For the individual chapters on the tiers (chapters 2, 3, and 4), we discuss the specific systems that need to be in place. Here is a summary.

At Tier One, school teams put systems in place that include establishing a representative team to guide implementation, securing funding and resources, training and coaching staff to obtain and maintain their buy-in for SWPBIS and ensure that they understand Tier One, and having clear data procedures that include ongoing use of data to screen students and to monitor implementation. At Tier Two, similar systems include establishing personnel and a team to oversee Tier Two supports; dedicating roles for staff to support Tier Two; training and coaching; and communicating with students, families, and staff on those supports; as well as ongoing use of data to support decision making related to implementation and impact. At Tier Three, systems include a specialized behavior support team; access to behavioral expertise; procedures for identifying students who need additional support; and communicating with families, students, and staff; as well as ongoing use of data to support decision making related to the implementation and impact of Tier Three (Horner et al., 2010).

Data: Supporting Decision Making

Once school teams identify the outcomes that they want to achieve, they then identify the data needed to measure progress toward those outcomes. School teams will identify specific sources of data, which we discuss in subsequent chapters, but school teams use data to answer two questions for all aspects of SWPBIS: (1) Are practices implemented with fidelity and (2) What is the impact of those practices? *Implementation* is the act of applying a certain practice, whereas *implementation fidelity* is the extent to which a practice is implemented as intended (also referred to simply as *fidelity*; Hosp, 2008; Wolery, 2011). *Impact* (synonyms include *outcome* or *effect*) is the benefit of that practice. To have the necessary data to answer questions about implementation and impact, school teams gather four types of data—(1) fidelity, (2) screening, (3) diagnostic, and (4) progress monitoring.

Are Practices Implemented With Fidelity?

Fidelity data gauge the extent to which practices are being implemented as intended. There are a variety of methods for measuring fidelity, but often observations of the practices, questionnaires about the practices, or checklists of the components of a practice help to document and check fidelity (Kovaleski, Marco-Fies, & Boneshefski, n.d.; Newton, Horner, et al., 2009; Newton, Todd, et al., 2009). By measuring (and ensuring a high degree of) fidelity, educators can be confident that a lack of desired outcomes is the result of an ineffective practice (in other words, even though the practice was implemented accurately, it still didn't reach the desired outcome). Accordingly, they can also be confident that when a desired outcome is reached, it is because educators implement the practice with fidelity. If educators do not measure fidelity, they are lacking information as to the extent to which educators were using the practice correctly and they may misattribute failure to reach the outcome to the practice itself when fidelity is actually the culprit (Harlacher et al., 2014). Additionally, sometimes low fidelity might tell a team that a practice is not a good fit for a particular context, and the team can discuss whether certain modifications to the practice (retraining, providing additional resources, and so on) will achieve desired outcomes or whether it should consider a new practice or intervention. Fidelity measures are used for each solution implemented and for each level of support (Tier One, Tier Two, Tier Three). Fidelity measures calculate the overall implementation of the tiers of SWPBIS and implementation of individual interventions.

To provide an analogy for the importance of measuring fidelity, consider a person who wants to lose weight. This person sets a goal to lose eight pounds in one month by attending yoga four times per week. After one month, this person has lost four pounds. Without knowing if the person followed the exercise plan, it's difficult to determine which is at fault— the fidelity or the plan. If the person did yoga four times per week and still did not reach the goal, we can assume the plan was not effective. However, if the person only did yoga two times per week, then we can't know if the exercise plan would have worked or not—it wasn't followed. Conversely, if the person met the goal and did not measure fidelity, we can't be sure what led to the weight loss. Was the person lucky, or did the plan actually work?

When fidelity isn't met and the goal isn't met, we must adjust fidelity and then try again. If fidelity is met, we can conclude the plan didn't work. Figure 1.3 illustrates the logical conclusions when examining a goal and fidelity. By ensuring that practices are implemented with fidelity, decision makers can determine the extent to which practices are effective in achieving goals.

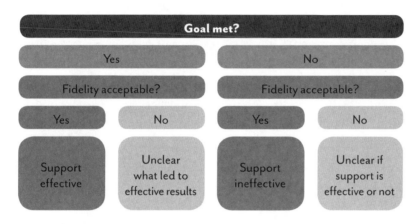

Figure 1.3: Logic of fidelity and decision making.

Screening data identify those students who are at risk (Hosp, 2008). Office discipline referrals (ODRs) are commonly used within SWPBIS (Irvin, Tobin, Sprague, Sugai, & Vincent, 2004), but schools may also screen using social and behavioral assessments (Anderson & Borgmeier, 2010; Hawken, et al., 2009). School teams also use screening data to understand the extent to which the overall system is healthy—at least 80 percent of the student population is responding to Tier One universal supports and are low risk for chronic problem behaviors, 10 to 15 percent seem to have some risk and are responding to Tier Two interventions, and about 5 percent need additional individualized supports. If the SWPBIS system is not healthy, the screeners can help teams identify where to target additional Tier One supports for all students. If the system appears healthy, the screeners can help determine students who may need additional support (Hawken et al., 2009).

Once a team identifies a problem (for example, too many referrals on the playground) or when students are determined to need additional support, it uses *diagnostic* data to determine why the problem is occurring. Whereas screeners are brief measures of general outcomes, diagnostic tools take longer to administer; they dig into the context of the problem and provide extensive data on why the problem is occurring. For example, XYZ Elementary examined additional detailed office discipline referral data on specific behavior types, when the problems occurred, who got the referrals, and why there were numerous referrals occurring on the playground. From this additional information, the team could identify a reasonable solution. For individual students, teachers gather information on the purposes or functions of a behavior so the school staff can examine them to determine the reason behind the behavior. Schools commonly use ODRs to provide more detailed information on a student's behavior, but the school staff may also use request-assistance forms or brief interviews with staff or students that will help identify the functions of behavior (Hawken et al., 2009). For some students, the staff may conduct a *functional behavior assessment*, an extensive assessment process designed to ascertain why a problem behavior is occurring and determine the environmental triggers and responses to that behavior (Crone & Horner, 2003).

What Is the Impact of These Practices?

Following the use of screening and diagnostic tools, teachers monitor the impact of solutions to the problem to ensure it is meeting the desired outcome. In *progress monitoring*, staff collects data to determine if support is effective while it is occurring to make formative decisions (Hosp, 2008). Schools use an array of methods and sources to monitor solutions, such as permanent products, daily behavior tracking cards, attendance, and ODRs (Rodriguez, Loman, & Borgmeier, 2016). The previous example (where XYZ set a goal to reduce playground lining-up referrals by 50 percent) demonstrates progress monitoring. The team set a goal to reach by two months, but it reviewed data every two weeks to determine the impact of their solution—providing tickets for lining up and free recess intervention—and to modify if needed. For progress monitoring the impact of supports for individual students, teachers can often use a screening tool as a progress-monitoring tool; for example, teachers use ODRs to screen students and to examine progress. However, there may be situations where the nature of the behavior will determine the exact method used for its monitoring. For example, a student with aggressive behavior may be monitored using methods that are more explicit and detailed than ODRs. Additionally, the intensity of monitoring changes for individual students depends on which level of support they are receiving. All students are essentially monitored using screening tools throughout the year, but students in Tiers Two and Three will have more intensive monitoring (Harlacher et al., 2014; Horner, Sugai, et al., 2005).

Table 1.4 summarizes how the four elements look at each tier.

Problem-Solving Model

One of the features of SWPBIS that separates it from other schoolwide models or other approaches to discipline is its reliance on data to make decisions (Horner, Sugai, et al., 2005; Sugai & Horner, 2006). To ensure that data are used accurately and efficiently, school teams use the *Problem-Solving Model* (PSM). The PSM is a four-step model used to define problems in clear and concise terms and then identify a targeted solution to solve that problem (Good, Gruba, & Kaminski, 2002; Reschly, 2008; Shinn, 2008a; Tilly, 2008). The four stages of the PSM are: (1) Problem Identification, (2) Problem Analysis, (3) Plan Identification and Implementation, and (4) Plan Evaluation (see figure 1.4, page 22). Whereas we can view the four key elements (outcomes, practices, systems, and data) as an organizing framework for schools to achieve sustainability and effectiveness with SWPBIS, we can view the PSM as the engine that drives the elements. As school teams use the PSM to identify and solve problems, they will consider each of the four key elements at various steps of the PSM.

Table 1.4: Key Elements of SWPBIS

	Outcomes	Practices	Systems	Data
Tier One	Improvements in school climate and safety, discipline, student behavior, and academic outcomes	Identification of three to five positively stated expectations Procedures to actively teach those expectations Strategies to reinforce expectations and desired behavior Strategies to manage unwanted behavior	Leadership team (team-based approach) Secured resources and funding Training and coaching Data use and procedures	Screening* Progress monitoring Fidelity
Tier Two	Prevention of chronic behavior issues and improvements in students' social-emotional skills and behavior Students receiving support reach goals and do not require support long-term.	Targeted interventions designed to supplement school-wide expectations Are based on collective needs of groups of students Are efficient and effective (less than 30 minutes per week per staff member) Provides more teaching, practice, and feedback on school-wide expectations	Tier Two team (team-based approach) Secured resources and funding Training and coaching Data use and procedures (efficient processes to select, match, and provide support to students)	Brief diagnostic Progress monitoring Fidelity
Tier Three	Chronic behavior issues are lessened in intensity and severity. Improvements in students' social-emotional skills and behavior.	Individually designed, intensive instruction Designed to remediate chronic issues Provides more teaching, practice, and feedback on schoolwide expectations and other identified behaviors/skills	Tier Three team (team-based approach) Secured resources and funding Training and coaching Data use and procedures (clear processes to identify, assess, and provide support to students)	Diagnostic Progress monitoring Fidelity

*Teachers administer screening to all students but use the results to identify students who may need Tier Two or Tier Three support.

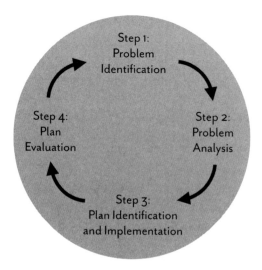

Figure 1.4: The Problem-Solving Model.

Problem Identification

The first step of the PSM is Problem Identification. During this step, educators answer the question, What is the problem? Educators define the problem in observable and measurable terms that indicate the gap between the observed results and the expected results. In doing so, the educators clarify the magnitude of the problem and then determine whether there actually is a problem. For example, a team may identify that only 65 percent of students are receiving zero to one office referrals when at least 80 percent of students should have zero to one referrals. In this situation, there is a problem; 10 percent is a large enough magnitude. Conversely, if 75 percent of students are receiving zero to one referrals, the school may decide that 5 percent is not a large enough gap to indicate a problem. Once educators identify an initial problem, they can proceed to step 2.

Problem Analysis

If a problem is deemed worth solving, then school teams spend time analyzing the problem and answer the question, Why is the problem occurring? Whereas step 1 points out that a problem exists, step 2 entails gathering more information on the context of the problem. During step 2, Problem Analysis, educators gather or examine any additional data needed to answer all five Ws and one H.

1. *What* is the problem?
2. *When* is it occurring?
3. *Where* is it occurring?
4. *Who* is engaged in the behavior?
5. *Why* is it occurring?
6. *How often* is the behavior occurring?

Note that *why* refers to the functions of behavior, such as getting or getting away from attention, tangible objects or events, or sensory issues. It is also helpful to answer the *why* question last because the context of a behavior influences the function of the behavior. All of the gathered information paints a detailed picture of the problem, which in turn allows educators to make a summary statement. A *summary statement* defines the problem and indicates what, where, who, when, why, and how often the behavior is occurring (O'Neill, Horner, Albin, Sprague, & Storey, 1997; University of Oregon, 2011). This information also further quantifies the problem and provides parameters for a goal.

Developing a summary statement for the behavior involves moving from a general problem statement to a precise problem statement (Newton, Horner, 2009; University of Oregon, 2011). Precise problem statements are critical because they allow teams to develop efficient and targeted solutions (University of Oregon, 2011). While a general problem statement alerts someone that there's a problem, it is vague and nondescript. With a precise problem statement, detailed information about the problem is included. In essence, going from a general problem statement to a precise problem statement is going from step 1 to step 2 of the PSM (see table 1.5).

Table 1.5: General Versus Precise Problem Statements

General	Precise
Noise in the hallway	In the last month, there have been fifteen office referrals for inappropriate language or disrespect in the hallway. The problem typically occurs during the transitions to and from lunch, and the majority of referrals are fifth graders. The most common function of behavior is peer attention.
High rate of ODRs	We have had twice as many ODRs during the month of October as we had in the month of September. The majority of ODRs are happening in the classroom and on the playground across grade levels. Noncompliance is the most common problem behavior in the classroom and it typically results in work avoidance; physical aggression is the most common problem behavior on the playground and results in peer attention or obtaining items.
Student disruption very high	There have been twenty instances of minor disruption occurring during the last fifteen minutes of our classes across grade levels before lunchtime in the last four weeks. Peer attention maintains the disruption.
Kids so mean; tease and bully each other	Three students have received ten referrals this month for bullying others. They are sending mean text messages and spreading rumors about other students to get peer attention.
Twice as many referrals in January compared to December	The doubling in referrals from December to January has occurred in all grades for being late to class. The motivation is peer attention, as they talk to each other in between classes.

It's important that educators ensure precise problem statements by confirming that they include information on the five Ws and one H. Missing any one of those pieces of information can result in a less than precise solution (University of Oregon, 2011). For example, if a general problem statement indicates noise in the hallway, a school team may enlist an intensive solution for the problem (for example, all educators reteach expectations to students). However, if the precise problem statement for *noise in the hallway* indicates that the issue occurs only after lunch and involves a handful of students, then the solution is more targeted and less intensive (educators only reteach expectations to a handful of students). Once educators develop a precise problem statement, they can proceed to the next step of the PSM to identify a solution.

Plan Identification and Implementation

Step 3 is Plan Identification and Implementation, during which educators answer the question, What can be done to solve the problem? This step includes identifying a goal and designing a plan (which can also be viewed as solution) to reach that goal.

The plan is designed to be comprehensive, is based on principles of behaviorism, and includes these six components.

1. **Prevention:** What changes to the context can educators make to avoid the problem?
2. **Teaching:** What replacement behaviors will educators teach?
3. **Recognition or reinforcement:** How can teachers provide rewards for the desired behavior?
4. **Extinction:** How can teachers prevent the undesired behavior from being rewarded?
5. **Consequences:** What are efficient punishment strategies for the undesired behavior (if data indicate the need for punishment strategies)?
6. **Evaluation of implementation and impact:** How will teachers measure fidelity and impact (Newton, Horner, et al., 2009)?

Creating a comprehensive solution ensures that there are strategies to prevent the behavior, strategies to teach new replacement behaviors, strategies to reinforce the new behavior and prevent the old behavior from occurring, and strategies to monitor the implementation (that is, fidelity) and impact of the solution. Once teachers develop and implement a solution or plan, the team actively monitors and evaluates the plan during the next step of the PSM.

Plan Evaluation

In step 4, Plan Evaluation, educators answer the question, Did it work? by monitoring the plan's implementation and impact (Newton, Horner, 2009). During this stage, educators examine the data and make decisions regarding continued use of the plan. If fidelity of implementation is good, educators can then make decisions about continuing, fading out, intensifying, or altering the current plan. If the fidelity is not good, then educators can have discussions about how to improve fidelity, and they continue the plan before they make decisions about its impact.

The PSM provides an organizing framework for educators to identify and solve problems. The four steps allow school teams and individual educators to (1) initially identify a problem, (2) understand the context and reasons the problem is occurring, (3) develop a plan to solve the problem, and (4) monitor the impact and implementation of that plan for the problem (Newton, Horner, et al., 2009; Shinn, 2008a). Table 1.6 illustrates the steps of the PSM.

Table 1.6: PSM Steps

Step of the PSM	Example
1. Problem Identification	There have been fifteen office referrals (observed level) for inappropriate language or disrespect in the hallway in the last month, and there should be no more than two during that time (expected level).
2. Problem Analysis	A majority of fifth graders are being loud and saying inappropriate or disrespectful things to each other during the transitions to and from lunch each week in order to obtain peer attention.
3. Plan Identification and Implementation	The plan will include: (1) prevention of the problem behavior by reteaching "being respectful" and then asking teachers to stand in hallway and use active supervision to prompt students; (2) teaching the desired behavior by reteaching "being respectful" and teaching students to say hello to each by waving, giving a high five, or saying hello appropriately; (3) recognition or reinforcement of the desired behavior by providing students PBIS tickets for appropriate behavior and saying hello appropriately; (4) extinction of the problem behavior by prompting students to perform an appropriate way of saying hello to each other when loud or inappropriate; (5) using consequences by having students stop and wait until hallways are clear before they can proceed if they display the problem behavior; and (6) evaluation of implementation and impact by tracking impact by examining referrals and tracking implementation by counting the number of teachers who use active supervision during transition times.
4. Plan Evaluation	Meet in one week to examine data on implementation (for example, rating of adherence to the plan on a scale of 1–3) and impact (such as office referrals).

Problem Solving for Systems Versus Students

Within the context of the PSM, SWPBIS teams can examine problems on a systems level as well as problems on a student level. Systems-level problem solving examines the system as a whole, whereas student-level problem solving focuses on groups of students or individual students. A matrix illustrates how school teams can consider implementation and impact data on both of those levels (see table 1.7). We discuss specific questions and answers for each tier in their respective chapters.

Table 1.7: Problem-Solving Questions Between the Tiers

	Implementation	Impact	
	Fidelity	Systems Level	Student Level
Tier One	Is Tier One being implemented with fidelity?	Do we have a healthy model at Tier One?	Are there groups of students displaying undesired behavior?
Tier Two	Is Tier Two being implemented with fidelity?	Do we have a healthy model at Tier Two?	Which students require Tier Two supports?
Tier Three	Is Tier Three being implemented with fidelity?	Do we have a healthy model at Tier Three?	Which students require Tier Three supports?

Summary

SWPBIS is a schoolwide framework designed to improve school climate and discipline while also setting the foundation for academic and social-emotional outcomes (Sailor et al., 2009). The model is based on proactively teaching students schoolwide expectations and is housed in behavioral and instructional principles. The model enlists four key elements to ensure its effectiveness and sustainability—(1) outcomes, (2) practices, (3) systems, and (4) data—and educators use the PSM to solve problems and drive the connection among the key elements. We explore the details of each tier separately within the next several chapters and provide examples of SWPBIS for each of the elements.

2

Tier One

Tier One consists of universal supports provided to every student in the building and is the foundation of SWPBIS (George et al., 2009). Tier One is the behavioral and social-emotional learning curriculum that educators provide to each student. Every student has access to the curriculum and teachers actively instruct the curriculum using instructional principles and behavior theory. When students receive additional supports above and beyond Tier One, they still continue to receive Tier One supports (additional supports supplement Tier One, they don't supplant it). If there are gaps within Tier One, the additional tiers will be less effective, so it's important that teams build an effective Tier One before designing and implementing the upper tiers (Greenwood et al., 2008). We summarize Tier One specifics in table 2.1.

Table 2.1: Tier One Summary

Tier One Is . . .	Tier One Is Not . . .
Universal supports for all students	Just for a few students nor is it removed when students receive additional support
The active teaching and reinforcement of schoolwide expectations	Hoping students learn the schoolwide expectations on their own
Use of active feedback and encouragement for students to display the expectations	Ignoring students when they display the expectations because "they should just do them"
Use of a range of strategies to discourage undesired behavior	The sole use of punishment when students misbehave, nor is it reactionary and punishment based
The foundational piece of the framework	Something that can be skipped
Used and supported by all staff	Only used by a few staff

We have organized this chapter along the four key elements within the context of Tier One of SWPBIS, beginning with identifying outcomes. We then present the practices for Tier One before discussing the systems essential to it. We then discuss commonly used data within Tier One, and we end the chapter by discussing the application of the PSM at Tier One for systems and students. Throughout the chapter, we provide examples of the elements in practice for Tier One and provide extensive case summaries of an elementary school and of a secondary school in chapter 6 to illustrate clear examples of SWPBIS across all three tiers.

Outcomes

Within this section, we share outcomes that schools may identify for Tier One when using SWPBIS. Educators can identify outcomes for fidelity of implementation and for impact of Tier One. Outcomes provide the overall purpose of Tier One for the school and represent what the school wants to achieve with implementation of the model.

The school should ensure that the Tier One elements are implemented with fidelity. After all, if Tier One isn't being implemented, it's difficult to expect to obtain any outcomes of impact. Schools will regularly check their implementation of Tier One to ensure they are implementing its key elements well. We commonly measure these elements by using a published fidelity measure with a designated fidelity criterion. (We discuss these measures later in the Data section, page 52.)

When considering the impact of Tier One, it is difficult to identify common outcomes across schools because each school will contextualize SWPBIS for its sites and identify outcomes that are specific to it. However, one common goal is to create a healthy system in which most students' needs are met through universal instructional supports alone. As such, schools using SWPBIS will examine their disciplinary data and determine if their SWPBIS system is healthy and effective in meeting the needs of most of the students. One marker of a healthy SWPBIS system is one in which at least 80 percent of students have zero to one office discipline referrals for major behaviors, no more than 15 percent have between two and five referrals, and no more than 5 percent have six or more referrals (Horner, Sugai, et al., 2005). If a school's data do not approximate these percentages, then efforts go toward improving the system as a whole to achieve such percentages.

Schools using SWPBIS are not limited to disciplinary data for outcomes. They can also review various data such as truancy, attendance, academic achievement, perceptions of safety, and the number of suspensions and expulsions, particularly between student subgroups (such as racial or ethnic groups, gender, or students with disabilities) and decide what outcomes or goals make sense for its site. For example, a school may discover that students with disabilities are suspended twice as often as students without disabilities, leading to a goal of creating more equity with suspension practices. Additionally, schools using SWPBIS may survey their staff or community members (such as parents or guardians) to gather information on concerns about school climate and discipline as well as identifying relevant outcomes.

Schools using SWPBIS will identify long-term and short-term outcomes for Tier One. Long-term outcomes are significant and distal outcomes regarding the use of SWPBIS that take time to achieve (for example, over the course of one or more school years), such as improvement in school climate. Short-term outcomes are immediate outcomes that are often achieved within the context of the school year, such as a reduction in referrals during lunchtime. Long-term outcomes (like improving school climate) are decided early on, but various short-term outcomes (like reducing office referrals from the hallway) will arise as the school implements and monitors the model.

Having determined the outcomes they wish to achieve with SWPBIS, schools can then turn to the exact practices they'll implement for Tier One in order to reach those outcomes.

Practices

The practices for Tier One include identifying and teaching three to five common school-wide expectations to students, along with implementing methods to reward students for displaying the expectations and to decrease problem behavior (we also refer to *problem behavior* as undesired or unwanted behavior; George et al., 2009; Horner, Sugai, et al., 2005). We discuss each of the following practices of Tier One next.

1. Identifying schoolwide expectations
2. Teaching expectations
3. Reinforcing expectations
4. Responding to undesired behavior

Identifying Schoolwide Expectations

At the foundation of Tier One are a handful of schoolwide expectations that are taught to all students (George et al., 2009; Horner et al., 2005). *Expectations* are general descriptions of desired behavior that apply to all students and all settings (George et al., 2009). The expectations are positively stated (that is, tell students what to do instead of what not to do), involve action words, and use developmentally and culturally appropriate language. They are limited to no more than five because additional expectations become redundant and burdensome for students and staff to remember (McKevitt & Braaksma, 2008).

Perhaps the most common expectations schools use are Be Safe, Be Respectful, Be Responsible because safety, respect, and responsibility cover a wide range of desired behavior in schools (Lynass, Tsai, Richman, & Cheney, 2012). Teams can organize their expectations into acronyms (PAWS: be Prompt, Accept responsibility, Work hard, Show respect) or mnemonics (The 3 Bs: Be Safe, Be Respectful, Be Responsible; Lynass et al., 2012), which help students remember the expectations. Visuals can also prompt and remind students, such as *Gimme Five* and holding up one's hand open to signify the five expectations—Be Respectful, Be Responsible, Follow Directions, Keep Hands and Feet to Yourself, Be There and Be Ready (Taylor-Greene et al., 1997). We have included sample expectations here.

- ▲ Respect Ourselves, Respect Others, Respect Property (Netzel & Eber, 2003)
- ▲ Be Respectful, Be Responsible, Be Academically Engaged, Be Caring (Bohanon et al., 2006)
- ▲ GRIT: Goals, Respect, Integrity, and Teamwork (Houghton-Portage Township Schools, n.d.)
- ▲ RISE: Respect Individuals, Self, and the Environment (PBIS Maryland, n.d.)
- ▲ Be REAL: Responsible, Engaged, Appropriate, Learner (Fenton Community High School, n.d.)
- ▲ STAR: Safe, Teachable, Accept Responsibility, Respect (McKevitt & Braaksma, 2008)

Once educators have identified expectations, the educators concretely define common settings in the school (George et al., 2009; McKevitt & Braaksma, 2008). This is depicted in a matrix with the expectations listed across the columns (or rows) and the common settings listed in the rows (or columns). Table 2.2 has a sample matrix. Within each cell of the matrix, each expectation is explicitly defined as a set of rules for that particular setting. Whereas expectations are broad descriptions of behavior, rules are explicit, specific descriptions of behavior (George, 2009; Lynass et al., 2012). Rules are positively stated, expressed in simple language, limited to five per setting, more detailed than expectations, and applicable only to certain settings (George et al., 2009).

Table 2.2: Sample Matrix of Expectations and Rules for Common Settings

Location	Expectations		
	Be Safe	Be Respectful	Be Responsible
Arrival and Dismissal	Use the doors on the right. Dismount bicycle or wheels once you reach the concrete.	Use an indoor voice once inside. Let those in front of you go first.	Gather up your materials. Follow the school dress code. Be on time to school.
Commons and Cafeteria	Stay seated until dismissed. Eat your own food.	Use table manners. Talk quietly.	Bring your lunch or money to buy lunch. Throw away trash.
Hallways	Walk facing forward on the right-hand side. For stairs—keep right hand on the rail, left hand holds materials.	Use an indoor voice. Be mindful of students learning in their classrooms. Keeps hands, feet, objects to self.	Keep hallways, stairways, and pods clean. Go directly to where you're going.
Bathrooms	Allow only one person in a stall. Wash hands with soap and water.	Give others privacy. Keep trash and water off floor.	Wash hands, flush. Return promptly to class.

Each school using SWPBIS will have a schoolwide matrix for the entire school, and some sites may choose to include a classroom setting within their matrix so that universal rules are established for classrooms. However, some schools may wish to have individual classroom matrices (George et al., 2009; Simonsen & Myers, 2015). In this situation, teachers will individually (or in grade-level or department-level teams) create their own matrices. Instead of settings, teachers will define common routines within their classrooms such as morning entry, lining up, independent seatwork, and using a hall pass (see table 2.3). The classroom matrices are used at the elementary level, but secondary schools may opt for a classroom row as part of their schoolwide matrix. This is because older students may not need as much explicit instruction for classroom routines as younger students (McKevitt & Braaksma, 2008).

Table 2.3: Sample Matrix of Classroom Expectations and Rules

	Be Safe	Be Respectful	Be Responsible
Class Entry	Walk quietly into the room and find a seat. Hands, feet, objects to self.	Talk with level 1 voice.	Have only the appropriate materials out for class.
Hallway Pass	Sign out and take a pass. Walk facing forward. Keep hands and feet to self. Look out for opening doors.	Use level 0 voice. Mind your own business.	Go directly to and from the location of your pass.
Independent Work	Use materials appropriately. Keep hands, feet, and objects to self.	Work quietly. Raise hand to have needs met.	Complete your own work. Make sure your name is on your materials and assignments.
Group Instruction	Keep chair legs on floor. Keep hands, feet, and objects to self.	Raise hand to speak and wait patiently. Follow teacher directives.	Be prepared and ready to participate.
Dismissal	When dismissed, stand up, push in chair, and wait for person in front of you to leave before you go.	Be sure your area is clean. Hold the door for the person behind you.	Write down homework in your planner. Put materials away neatly.

Some schools may also create matrices for other major settings or events, such as a school event (for instance, assemblies) or for those who play sports (see table 2.4). Additionally, schools may opt to include teacher responsibilities as part of their expectations, listing what teachers can do to prompt and reinforce students' use of the expectations for each setting or routine (for example, use active supervision, stand by the entrance and greet students as they enter your classroom).

Table 2.4: Sample Matrix of Expectations and Rules for Athletics at a Secondary School

	Respect	Achievement	Honor
Practice	Arrive on time with all needed equipment, listen to coaches' directions, use appropriate language; display positive sportsmanship.	Push yourself and encourage teammates to excel; work hard to always do your best.	Show team spirit on and off the field.

continued ➔

	Respect	Achievement	Honor
Competition	Show positive sportsmanship; solve problems cooperatively; have positive interactions with others on and off the field.	Set and reach for both individual and team goals; encourage your teammates.	Suit up in clean uniforms; represent your school with excellent conduct.
Eligibility	Show up on time for every practice and competition; follow school and team rules consistently.	Earn passing grades; attend school regularly (only excused absences).	Show team pride in and out of the school; set a positive example for others.
Lettering	Show up on time for every practice and competition; compete 100 percent.	Demonstrate academic excellence.	Show team pride; suit up in clean uniform and attire; cheer for teammates.
Team Travel	Take care of your own possessions; leave places as nice as you found them (including disposing of your own trash); be where you are directed to be.	Complete your assignments missed for team travel; do your best.	Demonstrate positive behavior to represent your school well; cheer for teammates; show you are proud.

Source: Adapted from Lewis, n.d.

Each teacher should be free to individualize the exact strategies within the classroom to fit his or her needs. However, the practices and strategies should align with the schoolwide practices, as creating a disconnect between classroom practices and the schoolwide practices can confuse students. When considering classroom practices, school teams can consider the following five evidence-based practices that are connected to high-quality classroom management (note the overlap with schoolwide Tier One practices; Harlacher, 2015). In doing so, teams can further ensure the effectiveness of their Tier One supports.

1. Identify and teach classwide expectations. These should be linked to the schoolwide expectations.
2. Maximize structure and routine. Students should be taught procedures to get their needs met and the classroom should be physically and temporally predictable.
3. Use a variety of active engagement strategies. Students are engaged with instruction through a variety of means, such as peer-to-peer responding, unison responses, small groups, discussions, and projects.
4. Use a range of strategies to reinforce behavior. Teachers can use a variety of means from social to tangible to verbal reinforcement to provide students feedback on the desired behaviors in the classroom.
5. Use a range of strategies to manage misbehavior. Teachers can use a variety of means to manage misbehavior, such as active supervision, reteaching, conferencing with students, and modeling desired behavior.

Additionally, ensuring strong classroom management increases the likelihood that students who need additional supports, such as Tier Two or Tier Three, will benefit from them. By providing effective Tier One and classroom management practices, school teams can be confident that additional supports layered on top of Tier One will be effective. We discuss this more in the next chapter, but it's important that a strong foundation of effective practices is evident within classrooms.

Teaching Expectations

Once educators define the expectations and create the matrix, they explicitly teach the expectations to students. They create lesson plans that include explicit modeling and teaching of the expectations in the actual setting, examples and nonexamples of the expectations, follow-up or extension activities, a plan to remind or prompt students for the expectations, and a monitoring plan (Langland, Lewis-Palmer, & Sugai, 1998; McKevitt & Braaksma, 2008). See table 2.5 for a lesson format.

Table 2.5: Lesson Format for Teaching an Expectation

Step	Description
Step 1: Identify the expectation.	The staff identify the expectation to be taught for this lesson.
Step 2: Provide a rationale for teaching the expectation.	The staff indicate a rationale for why the expectation is important.
Step 3: Define a range of examples.	The staff teach students the expectation using a range of examples and nonexamples to illustrate how the expectation looks and does not look in the school.
Step 4: Describe activities or role playing for practice of expectation.	The staff list activities to provide extended practice for students to demonstrate the expectation.
Step 5: List methods to prompt expectation.	The staff list ways that students will be prompted or reminded to follow the expectation.
Step 6: Describe how staff will assess student progress.	The staff list ways that they will monitor student progress (for example, lesson impact).

To teach expectations, schools typically have some sort of kickoff event during which they introduce the expectations and SWPBIS model to students (McKevitt & Braaksma, 2008). Following an introductory assembly, the staff teach the expectations in the actual setting and involve the adults who are naturally part of the setting (for example, cafeteria staff teaching lunchroom expectations). Susan Taylor-Greene and colleagues (1997) described an efficient method in which an assembly is held to introduce the program to students, and then fifteen- to thirty-minute lessons are held at each of six common locations: (1) classroom, (2) hallway, (3) gym, (4) cafeteria, (5) commons area, and (6) bus. Students rotate through in groups of thirty to sixty and received minilessons on what the expectations looked like for that setting. In the study, the staff was able to teach all 530 students all of the expectations in just one half-day. In addition to assemblies or a rotating schedule described previously, schools can create videos, skits, songs, or poems to teach and illustrate the expectations to students (George, 2009).

Once teachers initially teach the expectations, the school will want to ensure that the expectations are embedded within the school's daily routine through a variety of methods

(George, 2009; McKevitt & Braaksma, 2008). For example, the expectations should be physically visible at the school—for instance, on classroom posters, T-shirts for staff and students, bumper stickers for cars, or hallway banners. School teams can also design ways to embed the expectations into the school's subjects and curricula. Students can read stories in literature and identify the extent to which the characters engage in their school's expectations (George, 2009). Students in a civics class can write letters to the community about how they are learning and displaying their expectations. Mathematics classes can incorporate how many PBIS tickets students earn or develop ways to estimate how many tickets are given out per day or week. The fine arts department can create a play or skit about the expectations or develop artwork depicting the expectations to display around the school.

School teams can partner with local businesses to extend the expectations outside the school; for example, store owners can hand out PBIS tickets or display a PBIS matrix for the store in their business (George, 2009). For example, imagine that a store owner near a small rural high school was having difficulty with high school students loitering and engaging in disruptive behaviors in his store. After learning about the behavioral expectations and the SWPBIS system at the local high school, the owner adopted the same behavioral expectations and SWPBIS system. Not only did he hand out the tickets, but he also provided certain items for sale in exchange for the tickets. This resulted in an increase in appropriate behavior at the store and also increased buy-in for the tickets in the school setting since items at the store were often highly preferred by the students (and often unobtainable since many of the students did not have money to purchase items in the store).

Additionally, schools may have a monthly focus lesson based on one of their expectations (George, 2009; PBIS Maryland, n.d.). For example, if Be Respectful is one of the expectations, schools can tease apart the expectation of respect into other behavioral qualities, such as cooperation, empathy, and understanding culture. A lesson can be created for each of those qualities, and students can receive monthly lessons on those qualities. Finally, schools will want to hold data-driven booster sessions on the expectations as another way to ensure ongoing instruction (George, 2009). For example, looking at data on referral rates can indicate to staff when students will need refreshers on the expectations (for example, after winter break) as well as what expectations, and in which locations, may need reteaching.

Because expectations are taught at the start of a year, school teams will have to consider how to handle new students who enter the school midyear. Teachers can take time to teach the new students the expectations and other aspects of SWPBIS, or the teacher can assign a student or school office staff member to teach the expectations to the new student. Schools can also deal with this issue by planning regular times to review and reteach the expectations (for example, a school may review expectations monthly, so new students will be exposed to the expectations at that time). Capturing all of the creative ways schools embed and extend the expectations is beyond the scope of this chapter. However, school teams should create the expectations with the goal of making them part of the school's culture and ensuring ongoing instruction.

Reinforcing Expectations

After being introduced to the expectations, students will need ongoing acknowledgment and feedback by school staff to facilitate learning of the expectations. Ongoing acknowledgment for adhering to the expectations is an important practice in SWPBIS because it strengthens the prosocial skills and expectations being taught to students (George et al., 2009; Horner, Sugai, et al., 2005). Staff members will provide acknowledgment for students who engage in the expectations at the individual and group level, but they will also host events that reinforce the school culture and climate for all students. The school will create a comprehensive acknowledgment system that includes high-frequency acknowledgment, long-term acknowledgment, group recognition, and noncontingent acknowledgments. First, we describe behavior-specific praise, which is paired with high-frequency acknowledgment.

Behavior-Specific Praise

To provide feedback and acknowledge students' appropriate behaviors, teachers and staff should give behavior-specific praise. *Behavior-specific praise* is instructional because it involves specific feedback about a particular behavior that is provided contingent on performing the behavior (Lewis, Hudson, Richter, & Johnson, 2004; Simonsen, Fairbanks, Briesch, Myers, & Sugai, 2008; Sutherland, Wehby, & Copeland, 2000). Whereas general praise is vague and not attached to a specific behavior (for example, "Good job!" "Way to go!"), behavior-specific praise consists of stating the behavior that the student is displaying and providing feedback that the behavior is desirable: "You did a wonderful job facilitating your group's discussion and making sure everyone contributed. That's a great example of being responsible!" See table 2.6 for examples of specific versus vague praise.

Table 2.6: General Versus Behavior-Specific Praise

General Praise	Behavior-Specific Praise
Wow! You did such a good job!	John, thank you for raising your hand and waiting to be called on before answering.
Marianne, that is great! You're a hard worker!	Marianne, you worked really hard and stayed focused on that assignment. I can tell you put a lot of work into it.
Super!	Everyone contributed, and you all found a way to cooperate. Excellent.
Incredible! Yes!	You're looking at me and following along. That tells me you're listening and that you're ready to work. That's appreciated.
You're so nice!	It's really respectful of you to hold the door for others as we come into the classroom.
Good job!	Thank you for walking in the hall. That is a great way to demonstrate safety.
Thanks!	Wow! You showed responsibility by arriving to class on time with all your materials.

Source: Harlacher, 2015.

Behavior-specific praise is very powerful for changing behavior and increasing rates of prosocial behavior. For example, Kevin Sutherland, Joseph Wehby, and Susan Copeland (2000) studied an increase in behavior-specific praise from once every ten minutes to once every two minutes in a self-contained fifth-grade classroom. This resulted in almost twice as much on-task behavior, rising from 48 percent to 86 percent. Other studies have found increases in on-task behavior and decreases in problem behavior as a result of using more behavior-specific praise in elementary and secondary settings, as well as regular education and special education settings (Allday et al., 2012; Hawkins & Heflin, 2011; Pisacreta Tincani, Connell, & Axelrod, 2011; Rathel, Drasgow, Brown, & Marshall, 2014; Sutherland & Wehby, 2001). Behavior-specific praise serves as a positive, meaningful connection as well as a reminder for expectations (saying, "I love that you were responsible and finished your work neatly and completely" reminds all students who hear this praise of what is expected). Behavior-specific praise can be paired with tangible acknowledgments, which we discuss next.

High-Frequency Acknowledgment

A high-frequency acknowledgment is a small, inexpensive item such as a ticket, token, sticker, or signature that is given to students contingent on displaying the schoolwide expectations (George et al., 2009). The acknowledgments serve a clear functional purpose: they strengthen the learning of the expectations and provide immediate, tangible feedback to students. Additionally, they can serve as visual prompts for staff to regularly provide acknowledgment for engaging in desired behaviors. All staff give high-frequency acknowledgments, including custodial, playground, bus, and cafeteria staff on a daily, regular basis. They provide a steady dose of feedback to students to teach and strengthen the use of the schoolwide expectations.

The type of high-frequency acknowledgments used in schools varies considerably. Many schools use paper tickets, referred to as PBIS tickets. See figure 2.1 for examples. Typically, the ticket has a space for the student's name, the location, and the specific expectation the student displayed that earned the ticket (George et al., 2009).

Figure 2.1: High-frequency acknowledgment tickets.

Paper tickets require money for printing, so other schools have opted to use signatures as a cost-saving measure. In this example, all students carry a daily planner with a cover page that lists the expectations and spaces for signatures (see figure 6.5 in chapter 6, page 168). When staff see a student displaying the expectation, they sign the student's cover page (J. Ancina, personal communication, August 20, 2015). Other high-frequency acknowledgments include stamps, stickers, or recognition posted on a class- or schoolwide board (that is, each classroom posts a symbol or checkmark by students' names to indicate they earned a high-frequency acknowledgment).

There should be clear procedures and policies regarding how to provide high-frequency acknowledgments to students. Time should also be devoted to teaching the staff how to provide behavior-specific praise, as it may be a new skill for some staff. To make the high-frequency acknowledgments most effective, follow these guidelines (George, 2009):

- ▲ Flood students with acknowledgments initially in order to establish buy-in and trust with the system among students.
- ▲ Provide a high ratio of positive acknowledgments to corrections (five praise statements for every one redirect or negative interaction; Flora, 2000; Kern, White, & Gresham, 2007; Reinke, Herman, & Stormont, 2013).
- ▲ Name the expectation that is being acknowledged, and pair it with behavior-specific praise (Smith & Rivera, 1993; Walker, 1979).
- ▲ Focus more on the interaction with the student and the specific behavior acknowledged, and less on the high-frequency acknowledgment. Over time, you'll fade out the high-frequency acknowledgment and use a Behavioral Support Plan (BSP) to acknowledge student behavior. This links the new behavior to intrinsic motivation and natural reinforcement (Akin-Little, Eckert, Lovett, & Little, 2004).
- ▲ Make the acknowledgment unpredictable and variable.
- ▲ Provide acknowledgment on a consistent basis and throughout the day and week.

Provide parameters on how often to pass out the high-frequency acknowledgments to avoid staff burnout (for instance, pass out twenty PBIS tickets to ten random teachers each week in their mailboxes; only those teachers pass out their twenty tickets that week, and each week, ten new teachers will receive tickets).

What you pay attention to is what you get, so spend more time promoting responsible behavior than responding to irresponsible behavior (Beaman & Wheldall, 2000; Brophy & Good, 1986; Thomas, Becker, & Armstrong, 1968; Walker, Ramsey, & Gresham, 2004). If you see misbehavior, be sure to also find appropriate behavior to acknowledge immediately. For example, if you notice a student off-task during independent seat work, find a student who is on task and offer acknowledgment paired with specific feedback for being on task. If the student who was off task gets back on task, acknowledge the on-task behavior.

When providing praise and acknowledgement to students, the staff should strive for a five-to-one ratio of praise to redirects. Teachers who spend more time promoting appropriate behavior than responding to irresponsible behavior are more effective in their teaching and classroom functioning (Beaman & Wheldall, 2000; Brophy & Good, 1986; Thomas et al., 1968; Walker et al., 2004). Specific praise statements have been shown to increase the intrinsic motivation of students (Cameron & Pierce, 1994) and may help the learner develop a feeling of competence (Brophy, 1981; Gottfried, 1983; Swann & Pittman, 1977). Additionally, increases in teacher praise have positive effects on reading achievement (Gable & Shores, 1980) and mathematics achievement (Luiselli & Downing, 1980).

A school can also incentivize the use of high-frequency acknowledgments by providing raffles or rewards for teachers who pass out a certain number of them. At one elementary school, to ensure that the five-to-one ratio of praise to redirect statements was maintained, each teacher was given a packet of PBIS tickets that included five minor behavior slips and twenty-five PBIS tickets. Teachers weren't allowed to obtain more minor behavior slips until all twenty-five of their PBIS tickets were passed out (J. Daily, personal communication, June 14, 2016). Schools can also provide high-frequency acknowledgments for teachers to give each other. For example, a principal might cover a teacher's recess duty once he or she passed out one hundred high-frequency acknowledgments tickets. Another school we worked with rewarded teachers for certain aspects of SWPBIS with movie tickets donated from a local theater.

> "As a result of PBIS, staff and students are committed to working together to create an environment that focuses on positive supports and celebrating student success, and this is energizing for all of us."
>
> —Marietta VanEkereen, special education teacher, Maple Elementary, Springfield Public Schools, Springfield, Oregon (personal communication, April 5, 2016)

Long-Term Acknowledgment

As part of the reinforcement system, students can earn long-term acknowledgments. These are larger prizes or celebrations that students earn for displaying the expectations over a longer period of time or by redeeming a certain number of high-frequency acknowledgments (thus, the long-term acknowledgment is often connected to the high-frequency acknowledgment). A common example is the school store, where students use their high-frequency acknowledgments to buy products such as school supplies, school shirts, magazines, entries in a raffle, and other items of interest (George et al., 2009; Taylor-Greene et al., 1997). The prizes do not always have to be items that cost money. Instead, schools may sell passes, such as a "first in line" lunch pass, permission to listen to music at an appropriate time, or a free or late homework excuse pass in their stores (George et al., 2009; PBIS Maryland, n.d.). Passes can also include a "bring a buddy" option that allows students to bring a friend along to share the pass.

Long-term acknowledgments are also tied to public display of high-frequency acknowledgments. As one example, the Principal's 200 Club is a schoolwide board that uses group contingencies (Jenson, Evans, Morgan, and Rhode, 2006). The school creates a matrix with two hundred numbered squares. When students earn a PBIS ticket, they draw a number and place their name within that square. Over time the board fills up, and when there is a bingo (a consecutive line of tickets in any direction), those students in the line earn an additional group reward. All the names are then taken down and the process starts over. This reward combines high-frequency acknowledgments, long-term acknowledgements, and a group contingency.

Long-term acknowledgments can also take the form of social rewards, such as reading a list of names of students who have earned a certain number of high-frequency acknowledgments over the school's public announcement system or providing time with a staff member. Some schools give students personalized *self-manager badges*, which signal that they display the expectations consistently. The self-manager badge can then be tied to other privileges, such as lining up first, choosing certain activities, or even having access to a parking space or lot for the day or week (Harlacher, 2011). Students can also earn phone calls or positive referrals home to indicate to parents that their student is doing well at school. See table 2.7 for additional examples of long-term acknowledgment.

Table 2.7: Long-Term Acknowledgments

Reward	Description
Admission to Events	Student can use high-frequency acknowledgments as "money" to purchase admission to dances or sporting events.
Announcement	Announce student's name over the loud speaker and congratulate him or her on displaying the expectations.
Classroom Display	Students who earn a set number of tickets can have a sticker or image pasted on the classroom's wall. Over time, several students contribute stickers or images, creating a collage.
Pancake Breakfast	Students with a certain number of high-frequency acknowledgments attend a pancake breakfast held before school. Parents and community members are invited to attend as well.
Passes	Students can buy passes that allow them to do things like sit in the teacher's chair for a set time, job shadow someone in the school, be first in line, or use their cell phone or iPod.
Schoolwide Display	Randomly draw students, and display information about them on a billboard or within a school trophy case.
Table at Lunch	Students earn the ability to sit at a decorated table in the lunchroom.

Source: Kendyl Depoali Middle School, n.d.; George, 2009; Harlacher, 2011

Group Recognition

Group recognitions are events or acknowledgments that groups of students can earn (Alberto & Troutman, 2013; Kazdin, 1975; Litow & Pumroy, 1975). Specific grade levels, lunch period groups, or classes may be acknowledged for their success in engaging in appropriate behaviors.

Group recognition can be planned or spontaneous. If planned, students are aware of the reward in advance and can prepare for it. For example, a school may offer a reward to students if they have 100 percent participation in the state-level achievement test. If spontaneous, the acknowledgment is intermittent and arises based on a problem or need that comes up during the school year; the idea being to provide fresh, fun, and relatively unpredictable rewards to students. For example, a school may identify a problem with tardies halfway through the school year, so they offer students an early release day if the number of tardies is cut in half (within a certain amount of time). Or a teacher may decide to spontaneously reward the students in a classroom for displaying a specified expectation during mathematics instruction one day. Additionally, teachers may offer certain privileges based on behavior they see that day or to students who have earned a certain number of high-frequency acknowledgments that day or week. For example, elementary students who have earned high-frequency acknowledgments that day can line up first before the other students line up, or secondary students can be dismissed a minute or two early from class. See table 2.8 for examples of group recognition.

Table 2.8: Group Recognition

Example	Description
Classroom Rewards	Classrooms or grades can compete against other classrooms or grades for a set criterion (first to earn one hundred tickets, the most high-frequency acknowledgments within a week, and so on), which teachers can track by placing them in a bucket or providing a visual display of the total tickets earned. Classrooms or grades can compete against each other, or groups of students within classrooms can compete.
"Days Without" Tracker	A problem behavior is identified, and a sign that says "days without . . ." is created. If students go a certain number of days without the behavior, they earn a reward.
Free Choice or Free Recess Time	Classroom earns free time or free recess. Teacher can provide tallies for appropriate behavior, with every ten tallies representing a minute. Once one hundred tallies are earned, the class gets ten minutes of free choice or recess.
Golden Trash Can or Plunger	The cleanest classroom or bathroom earns a golden trash can or plunger for the day or week.
Grade-Level Pajama Day	The grade with the fewest referrals for a specific behavior gets to wear pajamas for the day and watch a movie.
Homework Hold Out	If class meets goal for homework or assignment completion, students may earn the opportunity to have a "homework hold out" where they do not have homework on a night that it would usually be assigned.
Marble Jar	A classroom has a jar with a line drawn on it. As students display expectations, the teacher places a marble in the jar. When the marbles reach the line, the class earns a reward (for instance, a dance party, a popcorn party, or the teacher doing something silly).
Music During Lunch	Music is played softly during lunch to control the noise level. Students can hear the music only if they speak relatively quietly.
Teacher Fun	Students can work for fun rewards, such as duct-taping the principal to the wall, using a dunk tank on a teacher, and so on.

Source: Kendyl Depoali Middle School, n.d.; George, 2009; Harlacher, 2011; Springfield Public Schools, n.d..

Noncontingent Acknowledgments

Noncontingent acknowledgments are rewards or events that are provided to enhance the positive culture and climate associated with the school. These positive experiences are for all students in the school, and students do not have to meet a specific behavioral goal to receive this type of acknowledgment. They can range from simple to complex, and the teachers deliver them at regularly scheduled intervals regardless of the person's behavior (Alberto & Troutman, 2013). An example of a simple noncontingent acknowledgment is making an effort to give students positive attention when they arrive at the classroom or regularly during the day without a student needing to meet a specific behavioral expectation. A complex example is a field day where a school celebrates what it means to be a member of the school and plays field games, with all students invited to participate regardless of behavioral successes.

Responding to Undesired Behavior

In addition to creating practices to identify, teach, and reinforce expectations, schools also determine the practices they will use to document and manage undesired behavior. The steps in creating a coherent system for managing undesired behavior are to:

1. Define major versus minor problem behaviors
2. Identify strategy levels for responding to undesired behaviors
3. Develop a response process

Define Major Versus Minor Problem Behaviors

Teachers may have different levels of acceptability of behaviors, which in turn can lead to one teacher referring many students for fairly minor infractions and another teacher referring students for only serious infractions (George et al., 2009; Todd, Horner, & Tobin, 2006). The result is inconsistency in discipline among the teachers, the administration, and even the students. To ensure a more coherent, clear system, the administration and school team first define minor versus major behaviors (George et al., 2009; Greenwood et al., 2008). Classroom teachers manage *minor behaviors*—those that are disruptive yet not serious, such as running in the hallways, distracting others from working, being off task, or misusing technology (for instance, texting in class). Minor behaviors may still be documented on a minor referral form, but they do not require administrator involvement to solve the problem. Administrators (principal or vice principal) manage *major behaviors* which are those that are unsafe and warrant immediate attention and action, such as physical aggression, bullying, or certain acts of defiance. Schools also identify crisis behaviors or situations, such as firearm possession or drug possession, that require immediate action because of the threat such behaviors pose.

Obtaining agreement on crisis behaviors is more straightforward because of their nature, but obtaining agreement among staff for major versus minor behaviors can be challenging (George, 2009; McKevitt & Braaksma, 2008), particularly for behaviors that can have major or minor versions (for example, disrespect, noncompliance, or disruption). Prior to implementation of SWPBIS, it is likely that different teachers have different ideas of what is acceptable and not acceptable in the classroom. Getting the staff to agree on minor versus major behaviors can be an iterative process, so school teams should be prepared to revisit the definitions of problem behaviors a few times before establishing consensus (George et al., 2009). School teams can also conduct activities in which the staff review referrals from their own school and discuss if the behavior is a minor or major behavior, or they can have staff develop definitions on their own and compare them to reach agreement. The result of such a process should be a graphic or a chart that lists the minor and major behaviors. Staff might decide to include a definition of the behaviors like you see in table 2.9 (page 42) and list crisis behaviors as well.

Table 2.9: Minor Versus Major Behaviors

Minor Behaviors	Definition	Example
Defiance	The student willfully does not follow or respond to adult requests within five seconds of receiving them.	Student ignores a 1:1 direction to begin his or her worksheet.
Disrespect	The student is rude to a teacher or speaks in a condescending or contentious manner.	The student makes a sarcastic comment and rolls his or her eyes.
Disruption in class	The student engages in behavior that interrupts a lesson or activity, such as untimely noisemaking, roughhousing, or sustained out-of-seat behavior.	The student throws crumpled-up paper across the room.
Inappropriate language	The student communicates using vulgar or derogatory speech, gestures, or writing.	The student utters a curse word.
Tardiness	The student arrives late to class or is not seated when the bell rings.	The student is not in his or her seat when the bell rings.
Major Behaviors	**Definition**	**Example**
Fighting and other physical aggression	The student pushes, shoves, hits, kicks, or is in some way violent toward a classmate.	A student punches another student.
Harassment and bullying	The student harasses or bullies a peer by making rude comments, fighting, spreading rumors, or otherwise targeting the peer with malicious intent.	A student writes a false and mean rumor about a student in a notebook.
Property misuse and vandalism	The student intentionally uses property or materials in a destructive or improper manner.	The student is writes in a school textbook.
Repeated tardiness	The student is tardy two times in one week.	The student is late to class on Monday and Tuesday.
Stealing	The student takes something or has something that does not belong to him or her.	The student steals another student's electronic device.

Source: Todd et al., 2006.

Identify Strategy Levels for Responding to Undesired Behaviors

Following identification of the minor versus major behaviors, the school team and staff identify options for how the staff can or should respond to minor, major, and crisis behaviors. This response begins with preventative and antecedent strategies as well as reinforcement-based and instruction-based methods (that is, reteaching the desired behavior; note that the desired behavior has likely been taught previously as part of the schoolwide teaching of expectations) before progressing to punishment-based methods. Additionally, the strategies or responses to behavior can be organized based on how frequently a behavior occurs (for example, more intensive involvement is specified for repeat behaviors).

For example, teachers may provide a brief error correction for the first minor misbehavior. To provide error correction, a teacher labels the misbehavior that the student is engaging in, reminds him or her of the expectation, models it, and asks him or her to demonstrate it. ("Jacob and Laura, I see you are off task by talking to each other instead of working. Remember that to be respectful during independent work time, we work quietly and stay focused on our task. [*Briefly models working quietly, holding pencil, eyes on own paper.*] Please show me that.") Then the teacher provides acknowledgment when students comply. ("Thank you for working quietly and being responsible.") The error correction is brief and instructional, and afterward everyone continues with his or her day; the teacher holds no grudge and displays no reluctance to acknowledge the students for appropriate behavior after the incident. The teacher then makes a concentrated effort moving forward to use prompts, active supervision, and increased praise for appropriate behavior.

For future occurrences of the same behavior, the teacher response becomes more intensive. For the second offense, the teacher response may involve reteaching the desired behavior and using more antecedent and reinforcement strategies. For a third offense, the teacher may use punishment strategies in addition to antecedent and reinforcement strategies, such as reteaching again and assigning a time-out or loss of a privilege.

A school can provide a general list of strategies for managing minor behavior to teachers, or it can organize a list of strategies into a hierarchy, such as the example in figure 2.2. The options are limited for the first and second occurrence before offering more choices for the third occurrence of the behavior. This is by design to communicate to teachers the schoolwide plan for managing minor behavior. Bear in mind that this is just an example; schools may wish to include more or fewer options to respond.

	Response	Antecedent Strategies	Consequence Strategies
First incident	Error correction	Prompts or cues	Increase praise
Second incident	Reteach expectation Student conference	Choose one: ☐ Prompts or cues ☐ Precorrection ☐ Seating change ☐ Curricular modification ☐ Opportunity to practice ☐ Instructional choice ☐ Other:	Choose one: ☐ Active supervision ☐ Increased reinforcement ☐ Structured game ☐ Peer or partner ☐ DRL ☐ DRO ☐ DRA or DRI ☐ Other:
Third incident	Reteach expectation Practice new skill Parent conference	Choose one or two: ☐ Prompts or cues ☐ Precorrection ☐ Seating change ☐ Curricular modification ☐ Opportunity to practice ☐ Instructional choice ☐ Other:	Choose one or two: ☐ Active supervision ☐ Increased reinforcement ☐ Structured game ☐ Peer or partner ☐ DRL ☐ DRO ☐ DRA or DRI ☐ Other:
Fourth incident	Complete major referral form, send student to office		

Note: DRL = differential reinforcement of lower rates of behavior; DRO = differential reinforcement of other behavior; DRA = differential reinforcement of alternative behavior; DRI = differential reinforcement of incompatible behavior.

Figure 2.2: Strategies organized into a hierarchy.

*Visit **MarzanoResearch.com/reproducibles** to download a free reproducible version of this figure.*

If a student continues to display the same minor behavior despite the use of a variety of classroom-based strategies, it is likely the behavior will constitute a major referral. In this situation, the classroom teacher has exhausted what is reasonable for him or her to use to manage a behavior and now requires support of the administration to manage a particular behavior. Sometimes, schools determine three or four minor behaviors (George, 2009), or a certain number of minor behaviors within a time period (for instance, three minors within four weeks) equate a major behavior referral. However, this process can be confusing for students, parents, and staff. Instead, we encourage teams to document both minor and major behavioral infractions and use that information to make decisions about if or when a repeated minor behavior becomes a major behavior. Teachers can also use this information when determining individual and group problems as part of discipline data review (for example, decision rules are created around major office referrals as well as minor discipline referrals for interventions and other problem-solving supports).

For major behavior, school administration will determine options for responses and communicate the range of possibilities to the staff. The response to a major behavior will be more substantial and involved compared to responses to a minor behavior, but the administration will still focus on teaching and strengthening the desired behavior and not just assigning punishment strategies.

Finally, leadership within the school clearly outlines responses to crisis behaviors. Crisis behaviors are ones that pose a danger or threat to the student or others. The immediate response is to secure the safety of the student and others, so typically the staff will notify the office of the behavior and have a lockdown where no one can leave or enter the school. The school's district staff usually determine such procedures.

For students with disabilities or who are on individualized behavior support plans, it is typical that teachers will still document major and minor behaviors for these students according to schoolwide procedures following the process. This is to ensure that discipline behavior data accurately reflect the incidents in the school. Additionally, these data can determine the effectiveness of supports for the individual student. However, the actual response to misbehavior (for example, the consequences and administrative actions) may be individualized, based on team agreement, for what works best for the student and staff who support the student (for instance, a student may not be sent to the administrator office if the plan states that she will cool down in a special location, but the behavioral infraction will still appear on a major referral form).

Develop a Response Process

Following clarity on major versus minor behaviors and identification of strategies to respond to behavior, the *leadership team* (discussed in the next section) organizes that information into a process that clarifies the steps staff members should take when faced with a minor or major behavior. The process specifies how and when to document the behavior, how many minor behaviors must occur prior to that behavior warranting a major office referral, and which behaviors warrant parent communication. Having such a process accomplishes a few things. One, it provides staff with clarity on how they should respond to behavior. Two, it provides consistency within the school as to how all behavior will be managed, which provides predictability to staff and students. Three, the staff know what to expect when the administration or other staff deal with their own students. Sending students to the office, for example, will only lead to a few outcomes, all of which staff can access via some sort of chart or table. Figure 2.3 is an example of a school's discipline process that illustrates all three components of managing misbehavior (for example, identifying minor versus major behaviors, strategies to manage behavior, and a response process).

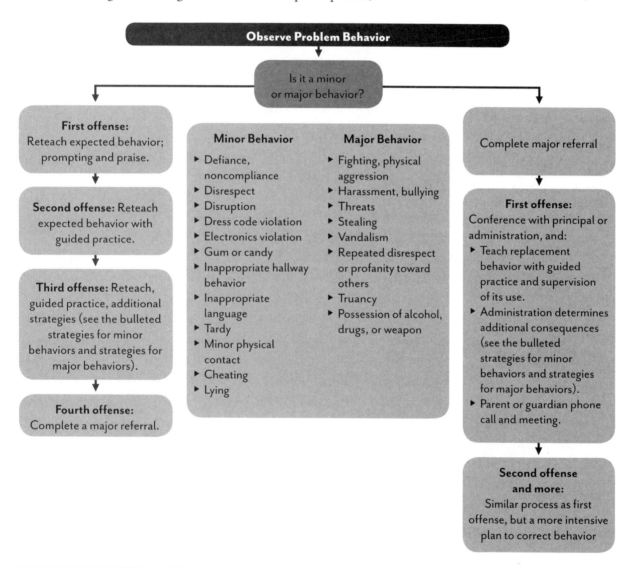

Figure 2.3: Example of a referral process.

Strategies for minor behaviors include:

- ▲ Precorrection
- ▲ Seating changes
- ▲ Cues or prompts
- ▲ An opportunity to practice the skill or behavior
- ▲ Curricular modification
- ▲ Instructional choice
- ▲ Active supervision

- ▲ Increased feedback or reinforcement
- ▲ Differential reinforcement
- ▲ A structured reward plan
- ▲ Peer strategies (including cooperative learning and classwide peer tutoring)
- ▲ Loss of privilege
- ▲ Time-out from reinforcement, recovery room
- ▲ A student conference

Strategies for major behaviors include:

- ▲ In-school suspension
- ▲ Reparative steps (restore room, apologies, and so on)
- ▲ Interventions to teach behavior (Check In–Check Out, social skills, and so on)
- ▲ Referral to community supports
- ▲ After-school or lunch detention
- ▲ An individualized behavior plan
- ▲ Peer mentoring
- ▲ A parent conference and support plan

After determining the practices that schools will use for Tier One SWPBIS, schools then focus on the systems they'll use to support the staff's use of the practices. The systems and practices for Tier One go hand in hand, as the systems will support the staff's use of the specific practices (as well as their ability to gather the necessary data for Tier One). Without clear systems, the staff and students can't access or use the practices needed for SWPBIS.

Systems

Systems for Tier One support the staff in implementing the practices and gathering the necessary data to inform decisions for Tier One. We describe the following four Tier One systems in the subsequent sections.

1. Leadership team
2. Secured funding and resources
3. Training and coaching capacity (understanding by all staff; training on Tier One)
4. Data use and procedures

Leadership Team

An essential foundation for SWPBIS is to establish a *leadership team*. Many schools are familiar with following an initiative that one staff person leads, only to see that initiative fail when said staff member leaves the school (George et al., 2009). To avoid this downfall, SWPBIS uses a team-based approach in which the responsibility of implementing and sustaining SWPBIS is shared among several staff members. In doing so, the team-based approach ensures that all relevant stakeholders are represented, provides a division of responsibility among the team, and creates sustainability of the model (George et al., 2009; Horner et al., 2010).

The leadership team is responsible for overseeing all aspects of the model, and primary responsibilities can be divided into two main categories: (1) *implementation*—designing the model and implementing it to fidelity and (2) *impact*—monitoring and determining the model's effect. Heather Peshak George and colleagues (2009) provide a concrete list of the tasks of the team, which we've reorganized into our two identified categories (see table 2.10). We will also discuss membership and roles, and mission statements.

Table 2.10: SWPBIS Leadership Team's Tasks

Implementation	Impact
Develop an action plan for implementation.	Develop ongoing action plans to ensure that the model and its supports are effective.
Hold regular meetings to discuss implementation (examine fidelity data and action plans).	Hold regular meetings to discuss impact (monitor and analyze existing behavior).
Maintain communication with staff regarding implementation.	Maintain communication with staff regarding impact; report outcomes to staff, parents, and other stakeholders.
Monitor progress toward fidelity goals.	Monitor progress toward desired outcomes.

Source: Adapted from George et al., 2009.

Implementation

The leadership team's task of implementing the model means that the team will be responsible for ensuring that the model is implemented to fidelity. The team begins by building consensus and support for SWPBIS, and then designing the specific Tier One components for their sites; it will design Tiers Two and Three after Tier One is implemented to fidelity. During this time, members will develop what the practices will look like for their school, such as defining the expectations and the referral process, and they will identify the specific systems that the school will use to support staff in implementing the Tier One practices. To determine the specifics of Tier One, the leadership team will obtain staff input and design the model, train staff to implement sections of the model over time, and continually monitor fidelity to ensure that everyone is implementing the model as intended. The leadership team also meets regularly to problem solve any issues that may prevent successful implementation. When problems do arise, the team analyzes the problem and creates an action plan to correct the issue.

Impact

Coinciding with the implementation process is the ongoing evaluation of the impact of Tier One. During implementation, the leadership team will examine pertinent outcome data to ensure that the model is effective. The tasks of examining impact include holding regular meetings to examine data and evaluate progress toward goals, developing action plans to address problems that arise, and communicating outcomes to school staff, parents, and district personnel.

Given these two overarching tasks of the team (implementation and impact), the leadership team will need to meet for one hour at least monthly, and perhaps more in the early stages of implementation, to have sufficient time to check these two tasks. Schools can devote time to examine both implementation and impact during the same meeting (Newton, Horner, et al., 2009), but they may also devote separate meetings to examining implementation when first designing and implementing SWPBIS. Some teams may use a rotating agenda in which they meet twice a month, with one meeting focused on addressing implementation and the second one examining the impact of the model.

Membership and Roles

Each team should assign specific roles, and it's important that the team includes someone with behavior and SWPBIS expertise. This person can fulfill any of the five key roles on the team that we discuss next. Note that PBIS expertise is included on the team, either as a separate role or within one of the roles pictured in figure 2.4 (George et al., 2009; Newton, Horner, et al., 2009).

Figure 2.4: SWPBIS leadership team membership and tasks.

The first role is team leader. This person is responsible for setting the agenda, guiding the team through the agenda items, and generally managing the meeting. Teams have several items to work through, so it's important that the facilitator can move the conversation forward and prevent the discussion from regressing into venting and nonproductive statements.

A minutes recorder is necessary as well. This person is responsible for taking notes, and we emphasize that he or she should record decisions that the team makes and not record everything that its members state. This person reviews the notes, ensures that they make sense, documents action steps and responsibilities, and sends out the minutes to members within twenty-four to forty-eight hours after the meeting (George, 2009). In our experience, teams tend to be more effective if the agenda and minutes are taken electronically and projected onto a screen so the team can see and follow along with the meeting flow efficiently.

A data analyst will gather and organize the data prior to the meeting, but this person should also be savvy with the data-management technology and be able to interpret the data to some degree (George, 2009). Instead of someone who simply puts a graph on a screen, the data analyst should examine the data graphs prior to the meeting and then pull any additional data that the team may want based on the data examined.

A timekeeper is also necessary and is responsible for watching how much time is allocated to each item on the agenda and prompting the team to follow the meeting schedule so that they review all items on the agenda. The timekeeper should be someone who is not afraid to speak up and remind team members of the time at regular intervals throughout the meeting.

Finally, the principal serves as the administrator on the team. The administrator's presence at the meetings is important for two reasons. One, the team may identify solutions that require resources or leadership approval. For example, the team may identify action items that necessitate changes to staff schedules or conversations with certain personnel, so the principal is needed to approve those changes and to allocate resources for the solutions. Second, the principal's attendance indicates the school's commitment and support for SWPBIS within the school. The principal advocates for changes to support the model, makes SWPBIS a priority, and makes it part of the school's overall comprehensive plan for improvement (Horner et al., 2010).

As noted, when considering the roles, the team will want to ensure that it has PBIS expertise on the team as well as someone who understands systems change. A person in any one of the aforementioned roles could provide that expertise or it could be someone in a separate role. Ideally, there is a PBIS coach who is connected to a district-level team. The advantage of accessing a PBIS coach is that the coach can provide an external and somewhat objective lens to the school team. Additionally, the external coach can provide additional examples and resources that may not be easily gleaned without additional perspective. However, a school could implement PBIS without direct support from the district or an external coach (although implementation is likely to be more successful when there is district support).

It is important that the team identifies both a primary person and a backup person to fill each role. Backup people should be prepared to take over the primary person's role at any time should a team member have to miss or leave a meeting; this means backup people should regularly practice their roles even when the primary people are in attendance.

The exact school personnel who sit on the team varies from school to school, but it's recommended that there be a representative selection of members, such as a special education teacher, regular education teachers, and specialists (including educational assistants or unlicensed staff). Ensuring a variety of staff members accomplishes two things. One, this ensures that there are clear liaisons to facilitate communication between the team and all school staff members. Two, a diverse set of members ensures that the team considers various viewpoints and has cultural awareness of others when designing and implementing the model (George et al., 2009).

Mission Statement

One of the first tasks for the leadership team is to develop a mission statement. The mission statement will serve as an organizing framework for the team and the SWPBIS model. The mission statement should reflect the values and purpose of the community and school, and the statements often include the desired long-term outcomes of using SWPBIS (George, 2009). See figure 2.5 for examples of mission statements.

Elementary Schools	Secondary Schools
We believe academic and behavioral student success can be achieved by using a proactive systems approach for creating and maintaining a safe and effective learning environment.	Our mission is to ensure that students have a challenging and rigorous curriculum delivered in a safe, supportive, and respectful environment.
We aim to develop lifelong learners by creating a caring environment that builds character and integrity, promotes prosocial behaviors, and nurtures relationships between home and school.	We facilitate positive behavior change in our students and staff, as well as increasing instructional time, through the development of effective, proactive solutions.

Figure 2.5: Mission statements.

Secured Funding and Resources

Leadership teams should allocate funding and resources to SWPBIS. This is not to say that large amounts of money need to be dedicated to SWPBIS, but teams should allocate some funding for printing (a few hundred dollars), materials, and other related costs (Feuerborn, Wallace, & Tyre, 2013; George et al., 2009; Horner et al., 2010). Schools can also allocate funds to pay for substitutes so that their staff can attend district trainings or national conferences related to SWPBIS, and they can pay for separate work days for the leadership team to work on designing the model. Teams should identify a funding source for implementing SWPBIS and obtain commitment for funding for a minimum of three years (Horner et al., 2014).

Training and Coaching Capacity

Within training and coaching capacity, we have identified two separate processes to consider. First, SWPBIS needs a foundation of understanding, support, and buy-in among staff. The second is initial training and ongoing support on Tier One provided to the staff.

Understanding, Support, and Buy-In Among Staff

A key system is that the leadership team ensures that all staff understand the purpose of SWPBIS and why the school is implementing the model. Without buy-in from the staff, SWPBIS won't be successful (Feuerborn et al., 2013; George et al., 2009). Supporting implementation means that the staff understand the big picture of SWPBIS, that it's a multiyear commitment, and that it may take some time to see all of the benefits from the model. It also includes a communication loop between the leadership team and staff (for instance, schools can have an anonymous questions box or survey the staff throughout the year for feedback).

Initial Training and Ongoing Support on Tier One

As schools implement SWPBIS, the leadership team will need to ensure that the staff have the skills and coaching support to implement it. Initial training for staff will likely involve group sessions or assemblies introducing the staff to the content and the information.

Following that training, the leadership team will want to ensure that the staff receives ongoing and embedded coaching and has access to a support person. For the staff to learn and use the practices associated with SWPBIS, they will need ongoing feedback, support, and coaching of those skills to ensure that they are successful (Reinke et al., 2013). Table 2.11 lists examples of other ways to provide coaching and support to staff members.

Table 2.11: Ongoing Support for Staff

Example	Description
Book Studies	Grade-level or department-level teams read a chapter a month and discuss the application of the content to their school.
Handbook	This is a handbook that illustrates the details of SWPBIS, such as a list of the expectations, the reward plan, and a copy of a referral form.
Monthly Sessions	Staff meetings include fifteen minutes devoted to the teaching or review of skills related to SWPBIS.
Procedures for Incoming Staff	Leaders outline processes for new staff or substitutes, which can include a current staff member leading an orientation or creating a one-page overview of the school's model.
SWPBIS Team Meetings	The leadership team receives support to receive feedback on the efficiency and effectiveness of their meeting processes and procedures as well as for problem solving (as needed).

One final note for providing support and training is for the leadership team itself. If possible, district-level coaches provide support for the leadership team so that it can receive feedback on the efficiency and effectiveness of its meeting processes and procedures. The district-level coaches also provide guidance as the team uses the PSM. Just as the staff are learning new skills, so are members of the leadership team. They will need oversight and support as well.

Data Use and Procedures

Another system is to have clear procedures for data collection and use. Specifically, the leadership team will need to provide clear procedures for gathering relevant data, entering the data, and then using said data. There is no one correct method for gathering, entering, and using the data; instead, each leadership team will develop systems based on its personnel and the specific data to be gathered. There may be a trial-and-error process as teams try out different systems and logistics before settling on clear, efficient systems.

For gathering data, the leadership team will outline procedures as it determines the process for handling minor versus major behaviors and indicate how, when, and where to document occurrences of those behaviors. The staff will need to know what forms to use to gather referral data and then how and where to enter that data, but if other data are to be gathered, such as attendance or suspension data, then the team needs to outline procedures for gathering that data. Schools may opt to use technology, such as tablets, to allow staff to enter data in a paperless format, therein making the process more efficient. They may also designate times for the staff to enter or provide the data. For example, a principal can designate times twice per week for two staff members to gather and enter minor referral data and for administrative staff to enter major referral data.

Once systems are in place for data collection, the leadership team provides procedures to ensure that data use and analysis can occur quickly and efficiently (George et al., 2009; Horner et al., 2010). Specifically, the school staff need protected, regular times and areas to analyze and review data. Typically, schools identify a time period for school teams to get together and examine the necessary data, such as an early release day twice a month. During this time, grade-level or department-level teams can problem solve issues related to classrooms or students, review screening data, and identify students who may need additional support. During this same time, the leadership team can also meet and review data pertinent to implementation of Tier One and its impact. If early release is not possible, teachers' schedules can be coordinated so that every teacher in a grade level or department has a common planning time, thereby freeing up each teacher to meet as a team. One elementary school that we worked with did not have early release available to use for its staff. Instead, it coordinated every grade's specials times (physical education, art, and music) to occur during the same time, thereby freeing up each classroom teacher for forty-five minutes. The teachers were then able to meet during that time to analyze data.

In addition to time to analyze the data, schools need data systems that allow for efficient analysis and summaries of the data, such as the School-Wide Information System (SWIS; see http://pbisapps.org). The data system should be easily accessible, user friendly, and capable of disaggregating the data, such as summarizing discipline data by referrals per day per month or separating suspensions by subgroups. For leading a meeting and navigating the use of data, the staff should understand which data to use at each step of the PSM (for instance, screening data for problem identification or diagnostic data for problem analysis).

Data

Within the Outcomes section earlier in this chapter, we discussed various outcomes that school teams may examine as part of Tier One. To answer those questions and ensure that the desired outcomes are achieved, leadership teams will obviously need to examine certain data. Within this section, we describe the common types of data that teams will examine for Tier One: screening data, diagnostic data, progress-monitoring data, and fidelity data. We provide details on how to use such data within the PSM in the last section of this chapter.

Screening Data

When implementing the SWPBIS system, schools use certain data to screen the system to determine the overall health of Tier One. Additionally, schools can also use these data as part of the screening process to identify students who may need additional support. We discuss a few sources of data within this section for examining Tier One. We discuss data tools for identifying students who need additional support more in chapter 3 (page 88) and chapter 4 (page 127).

Within the context of screening data, we will also discuss office discipline referrals, suspension and expulsion data, and attendance and grades.

Office Discipline Referrals

Office discipline referrals are perhaps the most common measure of a school's behavioral functioning because they provide a general indicator of school safety (Irvin et al., 2004; McIntosh et al., 2011). To efficiently gather data related to ODRs, schools create forms that the staff use to document occurrences of major and minor behaviors. The forms can vary in appearance and format (paper or electronic), but each form has minimal requirements to ensure that the data can be entered into databases efficiently and to ensure that the data can be used for problem solving. The ODR form should include:

- ▲ Who was involved, including the student, referring staff member, and any other parties
- ▲ What the behavior is, including major versus minor
- ▲ Where the behavior occurred
- ▲ When the behavior occurred, including the time and date
- ▲ Why it occurred (for example, best estimation of the function of the behavior)
- ▲ The action taken by the person managing the behavior

See figure 2.6 for an example of a minor ODR form.

Student: _____	Teacher: _____	M/F Grade: _____
Reported by: _____	Date: _____ Time: _____	Ref ID #: _____

Location		Problem Behavior
☐ Classroom	☐ Commons	☐ Disrespect
☐ Hallway	☐ Library	☐ Defiance or noncompliance
☐ Playground	☐ Music Room	☐ Disruption
☐ Cafeteria	☐ Off campus	☐ Physical contact or physical aggression
☐ Gym	☐ Bus loading zone	☐ Inappropriate language
☐ Office	☐ Parking lot	☐ Other: _____
☐ Restroom	☐ Other: _____	

Motivation		Others Involved
☐ Obtain peer attention	☐ Avoid adult	☐ Substitute
☐ Avoid tasks/activities	☐ Avoid peers	☐ None
☐ Obtain items/activities	☐ Unknown motivation	☐ Peers
☐ Obtain adult attention		☐ Teacher
		☐ Staff
		☐ Unknown
		☐ Other: _____

Action Taken	
☐ Time-out or detention	☐ Individualized instruction
☐ Conference with student	☐ Parent contact
☐ Privilege revocation	☐ Other: _____

Source: Springfield Public Schools, n.d.; Todd & Horner, 2006.

Note: Information on how often a behavior occurs is gathered by examining instances of behavior over time. Ref ID # refers to the reference number generated by the data warehouse software system.

Figure 2.6: Minor ODR form.
*Visit **MarzanoResearch.com/reproducibles** to download a free reproducible version of this figure.*

Some schools or districts will create a separate form for major versus minor behaviors, whereas others will have one sheet. Having separate forms ensures a simpler process for entering, reviewing, and making decisions with the data. We also want to point out that a referral form is a source of data, not a punishment. The referral provides documentation of when, where, who, what, and why the behavior is occurring; the response of the staff is the punishment designed to prevent future occurrences of that behavior. As an analogy, consider a speeding ticket. The ticket itself provides information on when the speeding violation occurred, where it occurred, who was driving, and how fast the person was driving. The punishment, or the action designed to stop someone from speeding again, is the fine or other consequence. The ticket is an important data-collection tool, but the ticket in and of itself is not a punishment. This may require a bit of a mindset shift for teachers who have traditionally viewed referrals as a consequence. For example, at a school we worked with, the primary-grade teachers did not want to write even minor referrals for behaviors that clearly met the definition of minor behavior because teachers viewed these behaviors as developmentally appropriate with new teaching. However, the team worked to assure those teachers that documentation of the behavior incidents helped the SWPBIS team better support teachers in modifying the school environment to set students up for success. Documenting these incidents of behavior did not necessitate a harsh punitive consequence, but the actual referral was important information for the SWPBIS team to have a complete picture of behavior happening in the school.

Suspension and Expulsion Data

Leadership teams can use suspension and expulsion data to gauge the impact of their SWPBIS model, as an excessive number of suspensions and expulsions is likely indicative of an unhealthy Tier One. School teams can compare their rates of suspensions and expulsions to district or state norms to determine if their use of such practices is excessive. The leadership team will also want to examine the frequency counts of suspensions and expulsions disaggregated by race and ethnicity, gender, and disability status to be able to examine any inequity issues. Each subgroup should have similar rates of such discipline practices, so any differences could be indicative of misuse or inequity of the practice.

Attendance and Grades

Other sources of the health of Tier One can be attendance, grades, and grade point average (GPA). Schools with low attendance or an overall low GPA among students may be indicators of an unhealthy Tier One. To assess a critical level for these data, school teams can compare their attendance rate to standards within the literature such as 90 percent (Balfanz & Byrnes, 2012) or 95 percent (Bruner, Discher, & Chang, 2011). They can also examine attendance rates among subgroups, so the school team will want to be able to disaggregate these data.

The school team can also use GPAs and grades as another marker of a healthy system. School teams can examine the frequency of different letter grades or GPAs among students and subgroups. As schools implement SWPBIS well, their behavior and attendance should improve, thereby leading to more instructional time for students and higher academic achievement that can be reflected in grades or GPAs (Bradshaw et al., 2010; Horner et al., 2009; Muscott et al., 2008). A relatively low average GPA compared to district or state averages can indicate signs of behavior concerns and issues with the overall system, but low grades or GPAs may be related to academic factors as well.

Diagnostic Data

At Tier One, school teams use diagnostic data to understand systemic or systems issues. School teams will use ODR data to analyze problems of impact and fidelity data to analyze problems of implementation. When analyzing impact problems, such as, Why are students receiving more referrals in the hallways over the past month?, school teams can analyze data gathered with ODRs. They can examine data on the five Ws and an H (*what* the problem is, *when* it is occurring, *where* it is occurring, *who* is engaged in the behavior, *why* it is occurring, and *how* often it is occurring) to precisely define the cause of the problem. For problems related to implementation, school teams can analyze subscales and items related to fidelity measures. Teams are also able to conduct interviews, administer surveys, or examine trends of data when analyzing a problem. We discuss use of diagnostic data further in the problem-solving section later in this chapter (page 55).

Progress-Monitoring Data

The school team uses progress-monitoring data to monitor the health of Tier One. In fact, the same data a school used to assess its Tier One health can also progress monitor the health of the system throughout the school year (for example, ODRs can indicate the overall functioning of the system and provide a quick check of the system at different points in the year). Consequently, we don't discuss such data again. Instead, schools will examine data at regularly scheduled intervals to check the health of Tier One.

Fidelity Data

Throughout implementation of SWPBIS, leadership teams will routinely examine the extent to which they are implementing SWPBIS as it's intended to be implemented (which is referred to as *fidelity of implementation*). Each tier has four critical elements that can take several months to design and implement (recall that those elements are the [1] outcomes, [2] practices, [3] systems, and [4] data). Consequently, school teams will need to routinely gather fidelity data on each tier to ensure that they are actually implementing the elements of each tier well.

To check fidelity of Tier One, school teams need to ask themselves about all aspects of Tier One, including if they are

- ▲ Implementing the necessary practices—for instance, Have we identified and taught the schoolwide expectations?
- ▲ Developing the systems—for instance, Do we have a leadership team that meets regularly?
- ▲ Gathering the needed data—for instance, Do we have an ODR form and process to gather the data?

Instead of having to create their own assessments to answer those questions, teams can use existing validated fidelity tools to measure the key elements of Tier One. These tools are self-report questionnaires or observation tools that measure the critical elements or specific markers of Tier One. There are several free tools available that vary in their specific focus, duration to complete, and frequency of administration (see table 2.12, page 56). School teams administer these tools to measure their own progress toward full implementation of

Table 2.12: Tools Used for Assessing Fidelity of Tier One

Measure	Frequency of Administration	Format	How Used
Benchmarks of Quality (BoQ; Kincaid, Childs, & George, 2010)	Annually	Survey	Determine which components are in place Assist with action planning
PBIS Self-Assessment Survey (SAS; Sugai, Horner, & Todd, 2009)	Annually	Staff survey	Assess staff perceptions of implementation and priorities
PBS Implementation Checklist (PIC; Childs, Kincaid, & George, 2009)	Twice annually	Survey	Determine progress of implementation Provide midyear correction or adjustments
Schoolwide Evaluation Tool (SET; Horner, Lewis-Palmer, et al., 2005)	Annually	Survey and observation	Determine which components are in place Assist with action planning
Team Implementation Checklist (TIC; Sugai, Horner, Lewis-Palmer, & Dickey, 2014)	Three or four times annually	Survey	Determine progress of implementation Provide midyear correction or adjustments
Tiered Fidelity Inventory (TFI; Algozzine et al., 2017)	Two or three times a year (during implementation), annually thereafter	Survey, artifact review, and optional walkthrough observation	Determine which components are in place across all three tiers of SWPBIS Assist with action planning
Tier One PBS Walkthrough (White, George, Childs, & Martinez, 2009)	Multiple times a year	Observation and survey	Brief indicator of Tier One functioning

Tier One. They use the results of the tool to acknowledge where the model is strong and to develop an action plan to improve the areas of relative weakness.

When first beginning to implement SWPBIS, teams will complete a summative fidelity measure that measures Tier One (for example, the BoQ, TFI, SET, or SAS) at the beginning of the year to provide a baseline measure of implementation. Throughout the year, the team will implement Tier One, but it's not uncommon to encounter barriers to implementation. Consequently, teams will want to check their progress with implementation by administering midyear fidelity tools (for example, PIC, TIC, or Tier One PBS Walkthrough). The results can be used in a formative manner to correct any deviations from implementation. At the end of the year, the team administers a summative measure again to check their level of implementation and use the results to also inform action planning for the next school year. Leadership teams will examine implementation frequently during the initial stages of implementing Tier One as they'll want to make sure they're on track to achieving fidelity. As fidelity improves and Tier One becomes more engrained and sustained, the frequency of administering fidelity measure may change (for instance, only an annual assessment instead of twice a year).

We provided a brief description of the tools in this section, but we discuss how to use these tools in the Problem-Solving Model section when we discuss implementation.

Problem-Solving Model at Tier One

Having discussed the four elements, we turn our attention to using the PSM at Tier One. The four key elements are the *what* of Tier One and specify all the moving parts teams will need to ensure that the model is implemented well and that it's sustainable. After leadership teams have outlined the outcomes they wish to achieve, the practices they'll use to reach those outcomes, and the systems they'll put into place to enable use of those practices and to gather the data they need to inform their outcomes, they then examine all this information by using the PSM. The PSM drives Tier One; that is, the leadership team will meet regularly to check implementation and impact of Tier One. The leadership team poses specific questions between implementation and impact, and it uses the PSM as an organizing framework to answer those questions (which consider the four key elements). In this section, we discuss each question in table 2.13 and then provide a concrete example of using the PSM to address that question.

Table 2.13: Problem-Solving Questions for Tier One

	Implementation	Impact	
	Fidelity	Systems	Students
Questions	Is Tier One being implemented with fidelity?	Do we have a healthy model at Tier One?	Are there groups of students displaying undesired behavior?
Example Outcomes	Scores on fidelity measures indicate high implementation (for instance, 70 percent or more on the TFI)	Eighty percent or more of students need only Tier One supports (as indicated by at least 80 percent of students having zero to one referral, no more than 15 percent having two to five referrals, and no more than 5 percent having six or more). Rates of referrals are similar to national mean. There are decreases in truancy and absenteeism. There are decreases in suspension and expulsions. There are improvements in grades.	Rates of referrals are not excessive relative to other areas within the school. Rates of referrals are not excessive for particular groups of students. Rates of referrals for one behavior are not excessive relative to those for other behaviors. There is equity in the use of suspensions and expulsions among student subgroups.

Implementation

When implementing SWPBIS, leadership teams need to assess the fidelity of their SWPBIS model for each tier. That is, they need to measure fidelity of Tier One against a documented measure (presented in table 2.14) to ensure the key elements of Tier One are in place. It's not uncommon for schools to experience fluctuations in implementation (Fixsen, Naoom, Blase, Friedman, & Wallace, 2005; McIntosh et al., 2009; McIntosh, Filter, et al., 2010), so school teams will need to keep an eye on how things are progressing with building and implementing the framework in their schools. For example, schools may implement Tier One, have defined expectations, and have staff handing out high-frequency acknowledgements; however, they may not have a clearly defined evaluation plan. Or schools may experience turnover in staff from year to year, so they may see a drop in certain aspects of SWPBIS. By measuring fidelity of Tier One, the results tell the school team which critical components of SWPBIS are in place and which components are missing, thus allowing them to create an action plan to improve implementation throughout the school year.

When using the PSM to examine implementation of Tier One, at step 1 of the PSM, Problem Identification, school teams examine their fidelity data. If overall fidelity scores are below the criterion set by the leadership team or by a specific measurement tool, the team identifies that a problem exists and then proceeds to analyze the problem in the next step. At step 2 of the PSM, Problem Analysis, the leadership team investigates the identified area or areas of weakness, defines the problem in detail, and determines the causes of the low fidelity. Determination of causes might be done through analysis of the results of a fidelity tool, observations, surveys, or interviews with staff. For step 3 of the PSM, Plan Identification and Implementation, the team identifies a goal, determines how to monitor progress toward that goal, and then creates and implements a solution to solve the problem. The final step, Plan Evaluation, involves checking that the steps of the solution have been carried out and gathering new fidelity data to gauge the success of the solution.

Illustration of Tier One Implementation Problem Solving

To illustrate how a school team can check fidelity, imagine a leadership team that administered the Benchmarks of Quality (Kincaid et al., 2010) at the beginning of the school year to assess its Tier One implementation. (Recall that the BoQ is a fidelity measure of Tier One implementation.) For step 1 of the PSM (Problem Identification), it examined its overall score on the BoQ, which provides a general indicator of implementation fidelity. The overall score of 61 percent was below the 70 percent criterion for the BoQ, which indicates an issue with implementation. This triggered the need for step 2 (Problem Analysis), during which the team analyzed the problem in detail. In this example, the team examined the problem in more detail by reviewing the individual subscales of the BoQ to identify why they were scoring low with implementation.

The BoQ provides scores on ten key elements of SWPBIS (Kincaid et al., 2010), and as seen in figure 2.7 for this example, the data indicate that the leadership team rated itself *below* 70 percent in faculty commitment, reward system, lesson plan, implementation plan, classroom systems, and evaluation, and *above* 70 percent in team, dealing with discipline, data entry and analysis plan, and expectations. After this analysis, the team had a good understanding of its strengths and weaknesses with implementation. The leadership team then examined the individual items on the BoQ for their lowest-scoring elements. The

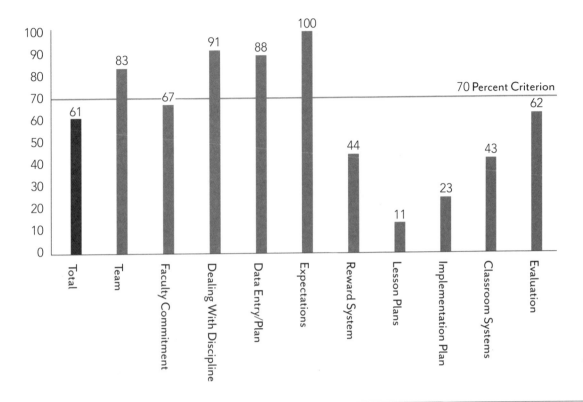

Figure 2.7. Example of implementation data with benchmarks of quality.

items were similar, as many of them focused on teaching schoolwide expectations and reinforcement, which gave them ideas for ways to improve fidelity. The team also interviewed
staff members to ascertain their perceptions of why fidelity of Tier One is low; common
themes from the interviews were that the staff did not have clear lesson plans for teaching
the expectations, and they did not consistently use a reward system.

During step 3 of the PSM, Plan Identification and Implementation, the school team
developed a plan to address its areas of weakness with fidelity. Members elected to focus
on their reward system and lesson plans. By improving the reward system, they felt they
could improve several areas among the four elements that they scored lowest within. They
developed an action that included these four steps.

1. Create a reward system for the entire school to consistently use.
2. Create forms of high-frequency acknowledgment and other reward components.
3. Gather feedback from the staff regarding the acceptability and efficiency of the
   reward system, as well as additional ideas for rewards.
4. Develop lesson plans and reteach lessons within classrooms.

The team identified a goal of increasing the four lowest elements to the 70 percent criterion, and decided it would monitor its goal by administering specific questions from the
BoQ after two months to determine if there was improvement in its scores. It also decided
to monitor implementation of the plan by assigning team members tasks to complete and
by checking in with them at their monthly meetings.

During step 4, Plan Evaluation, the team evaluated and monitored its plan. The team
administered questions from the BoQ at the two-month mark, and team members reported

that they were completing the action plan's steps. They found evidence that they were implementing their plan as intended and that it was working well, so they continued with it.

Impact

Leadership teams will also need to check the impact of their Tier One. To evaluate Tier One and determine whether it's effective, the leadership team examines the extent to which its SWPBIS framework is healthy. Leadership teams will need to examine systems-level and student-level issues to check that Tier One is healthy. We discuss each next.

Systems-Level Problem Solving

Systems-level problem solving at Tier One entails evaluating the overall impact for Tier One and concerns the foundational health of the SWPBIS model. There are several sources of data that leadership teams can examine to evaluate the health of Tier One. Questions to ask include the following.

1. What do our patterns of major and minor referrals look like over the course of the school year?
2. Do at least 80 percent of our students have zero to one major ODRs? No more than 15 percent with two to five major ODRs? No more than 5 percent with six or more major ODRs?
3. How do we compare to the national median rates for major and minor ODRs?

To examine patterns of referrals over the course of a school year and answer question 1, school teams will need to graph their average rate of referrals per day per month so they can analyze trends throughout the school year. Teams will typically analyze majors and minors separately, but they may want to examine major and minor ODRs together, especially if the number of referrals is relatively small.

Leadership teams can compare the percentage of students with certain numbers of major referrals to the parameters for a healthy model to address question 2. In a healthy SWPBIS system, at least 80 percent of students have zero or one major referral, no more than 15 percent of students have between two and five major referrals, and no more than 5 percent of students should have six or more major referrals. Rates outside of these ranges usually indicate a problem. We also caution that even though a school may have 80 percent of students with zero or one major referrals, this does not indicate that the rest of the system is healthy. For example, a school may have 80 percent of its students with one referral (or none), but it may simultaneously have 10 percent of students with six or more referrals. School teams will want to examine the health across the entire system as part of Tier One problem solving to ensure a healthy SWPBIS model.

For question 3, leadership teams can also examine how the school's rate of referrals compares to the national median for both major and minor ODRs. The *median* (as opposed to the average) is the preferred method of comparison because it accounts for skewed data or outliers that may influence the data (Thorndike & Thorndike-Christ, 2010). Leadership teams can use the national database SWIS provides (see http://pbisapps.org) to determine if they have a higher rate of behavior issues compared to the rest of the United States. SWIS data also allow comparison to schools of similar size and geographic location (whether they are rural, urban, or suburban). If a school's referral rates are significantly higher than national rates or those of similar schools, there may be a problem.

To compare the school's current rate to the national median, leadership teams can follow these five steps (University of Oregon, 2011).

1. Divide the school's total enrollment by one hundred.
2. Using that number, multiply it by the *median ODRs per one hundred per school day* for the school type similar to one's school in order to get the value per one hundred students (in table 2.15). This number represents the 50th percentile for schools similar to yours.
3. Draw a line on a graph that depicts the *average referrals per day per month* for major ODRs for a school year and then examine if the referral rate is high or low compared to the line.
4. Optionally, teams can calculate the 25th and 75th percentiles using the numbers in the last two columns in table 2.14 and using steps 1 to 3.
5. Following examination of major ODRs, teams can also compare their rate to national rates on minor ODRs (see table 2.15). To compare to national rates, teams will want to generate separate graphs for major and minor ODRs, respectively, but teams may examine their ODRs collectively to consider their patterns of behavior or the total percentage of students with referrals.

Table 2.14: SWIS Summary Data for Major ODRs, 2015–2016

Grade Range	Number of Schools	Mean Enrollment per School	Mean ODRs per 100 Students per School Day	Median ODRs per 100 Students per School Day	25th Percentile ODR per 100 students per School Day	75th Percentile ODR per 100 per School Day
K–6	3,405	456	0.32 (0.46)	0.20	0.09	0.39
6–9	979	624	0.48 (0.59)	0.31	0.16	0.60
9–12	488	879	0.52 (0.78)	0.33	0.17	0.62
PreK–8	347	425	0.45 (0.69)	0.28	0.12	0.51
PreK–12	86	307	0.60 (1.25)	0.29	0.15	0.50

Source: Adapted from PBISApps, 2016.

Table 2.15: SWIS Summary Data for Minor ODRs, 2015–2016

Grade Range	Number of Schools	Mean Enrollment per School	Mean ODRs per 100 Students per School Day	Median ODRs per 100 Students per School Day	25th Percentile ODR per 100 Students per School Day	75th Percentile ODR per 100 Students per School Day
K–6	2,788	448	0.46 (0.63)	0.26	0.10	0.57
6–9	773	597	0.57 (0.68)	0.36	0.14	0.73
9–12	375	834	0.50 (0.93)	0.22	0.06	0.50
PreK–8	294	436	0.70 (1.71)	0.27	0.08	0.67
PreK–12	83	302	0.74 (0.96)	0.42	0.20	0.88

Source: Adapted from PBISApps, 2016.

If any of the data discussed previously indicates a problem (for example, patterns of referrals, percentages relative to tiers, or comparison to national rates), school teams then proceed to step 2 of the PSM (Problem Analysis). Here, the leadership team examines other information to develop a precise problem statement and understand why the problem is occurring. The team can explore existing ODR data, and it may also gather additional information through interviews, observations, surveys, or permanent products.

Following development of the precise problem statement, leadership teams create a plan during step 3 of the PSM (Plan Identification and Implementation) to solve the issue. The plan should include the six aspects mentioned in chapter 1: (1) prevention, (2) teaching, (3) reinforcement, (4) extinction, (5) consequences, (6a) monitoring implementation, and (6b) monitoring impact (Newton, Horner, et al., 2009; Newton, Todd, et al, 2009; University of Oregon, 2011).

During step 4 of the PSM (Plan Evaluation), leadership teams will examine the agreed-upon solution and determine if the problem was resolved. This evaluation includes making sure all parts of the plan were carried out and gathering data to see if the solution was successful.

Illustration of Tier One Systems-Level Problem Solving

As an example of Tier One systems-level problem solving, consider a leadership team at one middle school that compared its major ODR rates to the national median during step 1 of the PSM (Problem Identification). Enrollment is 790 students, so the comparison was calculated to the national database: 790 students divided by 100 = 7.9.

Looking at the chart in table 2.14 for major ODRs, it would locate the median for grades 6–9 schools and multiply 7.9 × 0.31 = 2.45.

A line is drawn on its average-referrals-per-day-per-month graph to represent the median. The bold line on figure 2.8 illustrates the median (50th percentile) for their school. Additional information can be calculated to represent the 25th (7.9 × 0.16 = 1.26) and 75th (7.9 × 0.60 = 4.74) percentiles. The dotted lines indicate the 25th and 75th percentiles.

As seen in the figure, the team's average rate of major ODRs per day per month is higher than the median scores for seven of the eleven months. It also has four months above the 75th percentile. Keep in mind that schools do not need a year's worth of data to compare their rates to national rates; with only data from August and September, this school would still score higher compared to the national median.

Having compared their major referral rates to the national median, the leadership team considered that having seven of eleven months above the 50th percentile was a large enough magnitude to conclude that a problem existed. The team then proceeded to step 2 of the PSM, Problem Analysis, to investigate why the problem was occurring. The team looked at additional ODR data in graphic form disaggregated by type of problem behavior, location, time of day, grade level, and function of behavior. It identified that the majority of referrals were for acts of defiance and inappropriate language, happened in the classroom, were for acts committed by eighth graders, occurred during the hours of 12 and 12:30 (the class period after lunch), and functioned to avoid a task. Further, the leadership team examined students who received referrals and found that only four students had more than one referral, and only two students had more than six; therein, it concluded that there weren't a handful of students generating the majority of referrals, and instead, there was a more widespread, systemic issue.

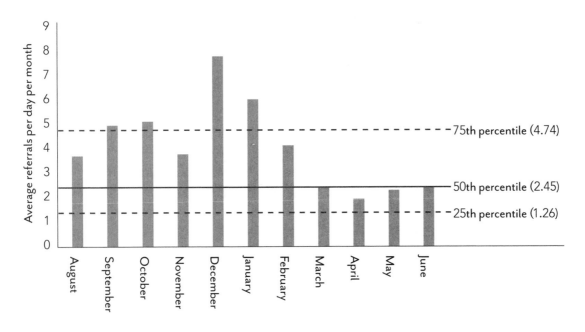

Figure 2.8: Schoolwide referral data with 25th, 50th, and 75th percentiles of national data.

The leadership team developed a summary statement: *"Eighth-grade students are receiving referrals within the classroom after lunch during language arts for defiance and inappropriate language. This behavior appears to be maintained by avoidance of tasks."* The team also explored the ODRs by day of the week and found that Tuesday was the day when most referrals were written. The team identified that the first class after lunch on Tuesday was language arts. At this point, the team hypothesized that eighth-grade students were refusing to follow directions and using inappropriate language in order to avoid work related to language arts. Therefore, the solution needed to only focus on eighth-grade students receiving language arts on Tuesdays. With a clear sense of the problem, the team could then develop a solution for it in step 3 of the PSM.

For step 3 of the PSM, Plan Identification and Implementation, the team decided that it wanted to decrease the number of referrals by eighth graders to a level similar to the sixth- and seventh-grade students. Members agreed to examine the rate of referrals in one month to compare them. They then outlined a plan that centered on reminding students of expectations and using antecedent strategies to offset the problem behavior. The plan is listed in figure 2.9.

Component	Description
Prevent	Establish a "Two for Tuesday" in which one PBIS ticket is worth two tickets on Tuesdays for all students. Remind eighth-grade students with an announcement at the end of lunch about schoolwide expectations. Notify parents of eighth-grade students with letters of the renewed focus on being compliant and using appropriate language.
Teach	Reteach and practice the expectations related to respect and following directions on Monday.
Reinforce	Provide two tickets for students who are compliant and using appropriate language.

Figure 2.9: Intervention plan.

continued ➡

Component	Description
Extinguish	Send work home with students or have them complete it during lunch (as noted in the letter home to parents).
Monitor implementation	Develop a checklist of the plan and track each step.
Monitor impact	Track ODRs students receive and monitor progress toward the goal of reducing ODRs for eighth graders.

Note: Summary statement—Eighth-grade students are receiving referrals within the classroom after lunch during language arts for defiance and inappropriate language. This behavior appears to be maintained by avoidance of tasks.

At step 4 of the PSM, Plan Evaluation, the leadership team met a few weeks after the plan was implemented and examined data on both the implementation and impact. Data from the implementation checklists indicated a score of 95 percent, which is good fidelity. Next, the team analyzed the updated ODR data and found that there weren't any new referrals from eighth graders since the start of the plan, so the team continued with its use. After one month, the team members had still met their goal, so they faded out the plan by gradually removing aspects of the plan (for instance, they reduced the "Two for Tuesday," checked that the students' behavior was still maintained after two weeks, and then removed the announcement at the end of lunch).

Student-Level Problem Solving

Having discussed a systems-level problem-solving example, we now discuss student-level problem solving at Tier One. School teams may find that they have a healthy Tier One, but they'll still want to examine potential issues with groups of students that the systems-level problem solving may miss. (Note that we discuss problem solving for individual students as part of Tiers Two and Three in chapters 3 and 4.)

Student-level problem solving at Tier One focuses on groups of students to determine if there are any areas in the school with excessive referrals or if there are particular behaviors that students are displaying at higher rates relative to others. To address such questions, teams will need to disaggregate their ODR data by where behavior occurs (location), when it occurs (time of day), what the behavior is (category of problem behavior), who conducted the behavior (student's name), and why it occurred (the function of the behavior). Doing so will allow them to look for specific trends such as:

▲ **Time-based trends**—Increases or decreases in misbehavior at a certain time of day or month of the year

▲ **Location-based trends**—Areas of the school that have higher or lower incidences of misbehavior (general guidelines for referral rates by location are in table 2.16)

▲ **Trends among student subgroups**—Differences in the rates of referrals between different gender, age, or racial and ethnic groups

Table 2.16: Criterion Level for Expected Referrals for Classrooms and Common Settings

Location	Elementary	Middle	High
Classroom	42 percent	60 percent	60+ percent
Common Settings	20 percent	20 percent	20 percent

Note: Rates higher than those specified in the table may indicate possible problems. These are general guidelines and not definitive rules.

Source: University of Oregon, 2011.

School teams will also want to examine their suspension and discipline data across groups of students to determine if there are any inequitable practices occurring. Leadership teams can calculate the percentage of students with suspensions, detentions, or expulsions by gender, race, grade level, and students with disabilities to examine any differences. Teams will ideally have similar rates of use of those practices across all subgroups.

Illustration of Tier One Student-Level Problem Solving

Here we provide an illustration of using the PSM to address a student-level issue. Imagine one leadership team at an elementary school for grades 4 through 6. At step 1 of the PSM, Problem Identification, this team examined its schoolwide referrals and identified that over 80 percent of students had zero to one major referral. Although this school had a healthy system, the team further examined referrals between subgroups and identified an increase in referrals for sixth-grade students relative to the other grade levels in the school. Over the past two weeks, sixth-grade students had received fifteen minor referrals compared to less than three for fourth and fifth graders. This difference in referrals indicated that a problem existed and prompted the team to examine in step 2 why the problem was occurring.

During step 2 of the PSM, Problem Analysis, the team disaggregated the recent referrals by time and location, and it discovered that students were receiving referrals for being disruptive during physical education class for access to gym equipment. The team hypothesized that students were not aware of the rules for physical education to access the equipment and that all sixth graders would benefit if teachers retaught expectations for physical education. The summary statement was, "Sixth-grade students are displaying disruptive behavior to gain access to items during physical education class."

For step 3, Plan Identification and Implementation, the team set a goal to have zero referrals for the next three weeks from sixth-grade students in physical education. The team elected to have the physical education (PE), teacher reteach expectations to students related to accessing equipment (being respectful, being safe, and being responsible) at their next physical education class. After reteaching expectations to sixth graders, regular education teachers would precorrect students prior to class and ask that the PE teacher provide praise and high-frequency acknowledgments (tickets) for students who displayed the behavior. If students displayed disruptive behavior, they would be provided an error correction procedure (for example, model appropriate behavior and have the student perform that behavior). When students were able to display zero rates of disruptive behavior, the physical education teacher provided eight minutes of free play at the end of each class during which they could access any of the available gym equipment. Implementation was measured by a short observation done by the sixth-grade teachers as they each agreed to conduct a ten-minute observation of their class once a week. The team examined ODR data to monitor the impact of the plan.

At step 4 of the PSM, Plan Evaluation, the team examined the implementation and impact data after two weeks. The implementation of the solution was 100 percent, and there were no minor referrals. The team continued the intervention and checked progress again at the three-week mark to determine if its original goal was met.

Within this section, we discussed how leadership teams could use PSM to identify and solve problems for Tier One for implementation and for impact at a systems level and student level. The steps of the PSM can appear complex, but in practice, it is using screening or initial data to identify that a problem exists, examining additional data to determine why the problem exists, identifying a solution, and evaluating the extent to which the solution solved the problem. As mentioned earlier, the PSM is the engine that drives the four key elements of Tier One. In fact, the PSM requires consideration of all four key elements: data are needed to identify and analyze a problem, an outcome is identified at step 3 of the PSM, and when discussing possible solutions, the practices and systems of Tier One are examined to develop a specific solution. We summarize the questions and steps of the PSM across implementation and impact for Tier One in table 2.17.

Summary

Within this chapter, we described the four key elements across Tier One and how the PSM can be used to resolve issues related to implementation of Tier One and to the impact of Tier One. Tier One is the foundational component of SWPBIS and is provided to all students with the goal of meeting the needs of at least 80 percent of the student population. A leadership team will determine the exact outcomes that they will want to achieve by using SWPBIS, but often they include improvements in school climate, discipline, and academic achievement. To achieve those outcomes, leadership teams implement Tier One practices of SWPBIS, which include identifying and teaching three to five schoolwide expectations to students. After students are taught the expectations, staff regularly acknowledge the students who meet the school expectations with high-frequency acknowledgments, long-term acknowledgments, group recognition, and noncontingent acknowledgment. The Tier One practices also include those to reduce unwanted behavior, which includes defining problem behavior and clarifying which behaviors the staff manage and which behaviors the office manages. The leadership team ensures that Tier One systems are in place. This includes developing the leadership team to lead implementation, securing resources and funding, providing training, coaching, and processes to gather the necessary data to inform outcomes. The data often used within Tier One practices are office discipline referrals, suspension and expulsion data, attendance, and grades. Across those four elements, the leadership team uses the PSM to examine both fidelity of implementation and the impact of Tier One at both a systems level (the overall health of Tier One) and a student level (collective needs of groups of students). One can see how the four key elements overlap with others and how the PSM is used to consider all those elements when examining Tier One issues.

Table 2.18: Use of the Problem-Solving Model at Tier One

	Implementation	Impact	
	Fidelity	Systems	Students
Problem-Solving Step	Is Tier One being implemented with fidelity?	Do we have a healthy model at Tier One?	Are there groups of students displaying undesired behavior?
Step 1: Problem Identification	Administer and examine overall score on a given fidelity measure (for instance, TFI).	Examine indicators of health, such as 80 percent or more of students have zero to one major ODRs; patterns of referrals; comparison to national rates; problem areas; and fair use of discipline.	Review and compare referral data and discipline data by location, time, and subgroups.
Step 2: Problem Analysis	If less than criterion specified by measure (for instance, 80 percent on TFI), then examine subcomponents.	Explore identified problems further using information on when, where, who, why, and what graphs. Other data include disaggregation of ODRs and other data.	Explore identified problems further using information on when, where, who, why, and what graphs. Other data include disaggregation of ODRs and other data.
Step 3: Plan Identification and Implementation	Develop action plan to improve implementation of SWPBIS and method to measure implementation of action plan. Identify way to measure impact of action plan.	Create and implement a comprehensive plan that includes prevent, teach, reinforce, extinguish, and monitor implementation and impact.	Create and implement a comprehensive plan that includes prevent, teach, reinforce, extinguish, and monitor implementation and impact.
Step 4: Plan Evaluation	Evaluate action plan and impact of the action plan.	Evaluate plan using identified fidelity measures and progress-monitoring data sources.	Evaluate plan using identified fidelity measures and progress-monitoring data sources.

Tier Two

Tier Two interventions (also referred to as *supports* in this book) are designed to meet the needs of 10–15 percent of the student population and are intended for students with mild behavior problems or who are at risk for developing more severe or chronic behavior problems (students with chronic, serious, or violent behavior problems, or who need individualized support are provided Tier Three support, discussed in chapter 4, page 105). Tier Two interventions increase the structure around students by providing more prompting on expected behaviors and additional feedback on these behaviors at regular intervals, such as designated times throughout the day or at certain points during the week. Essentially, Tier Two supports provide extra time for students to learn and practice the schoolwide expectations (Cheney et al., 2009), via additional prompting, practice, feedback, and reinforcement to students for displaying those expectations (Anderson & Borgmeier, 2010; Hawken et al., 2009). However, additional discrete skills related to daily organization, social interaction, and academic success can be taught as part of the support even if they are not a part of the expectations (Hawken et al., 2009). Tier Two supports may also incorporate a school-home communication and collaboration to extend and strengthen the schoolwide expectations (Horner et al., 2010). The key features of Tier Two are displayed in table 3.1.

Table 3.1: Tier Two Summary

Tier Two Is . . .	Tier Two Is Not . . .
For students with mild behavior problems	For students with severe behavior problems
For students at risk to develop chronic behavior problems	For students with chronic behavior problems
For students whose behavior is not dangerous to self or others	For students with behaviors that are dangerous to self or others
Efficient because of standard procedures and it is provided within a week of identification	For students who need weeks of additional assessment
Effective because of its use of evidence-based practices	Based on anecdotes or what we think will work
Early because it is provided at the first indication of a problem	Delayed for weeks until there are two or three indications of a problem
Supported by all staff	Handled by only a few staff
Coordinated and communicated with parents/guardians	Done in isolation from home

Three features highlight Tier Two: (1) efficient, (2) effective, and (3) early (Missouri Schoolwide Positive Behavior Support, n.d.a). First, Tier Two is designed to be an *efficient* process in three ways. One, students are provided support within a few days to a week after identification, thereby creating a quick and efficient process for students to access support (Anderson & Borgmeier, 2010). Two, Tier Two uses standard procedures to identify and provide support to students (Hawken et al., 2009). Lengthy meetings are not required, and extensive assessment is not needed at this stage; that is reserved for Tier Three. Three, all staff are trained on how to refer or identify students for Tier Two, and they are also trained in implementing and supporting students on Tier Two interventions. Instead of a specialist (such as a school psychologist or counselor) coming into the classroom and working with the student, Tier Two relies on the entire staff implementing the supports, thereby avoiding lengthy time spent waiting for a specialist or outside professional to support teachers (Anderson & Borgmeier, 2010; Hawken et al., 2009). However, although all staff are involved and trained in Tier Two, the effort to implement is kept relatively low and minimal (for instance, twenty to thirty minutes per week for a staff member; Anderson & Borgmeier, 2010; Missouri Schoolwide Positive Behavior Support, n.d.a.). Keep in mind that Tier Two is intended for students who need *just* a little more attention and instruction; therefore, the response of the staff is *just* a little more compared to Tier One.

Second, Tier Two is designed to be *effective*; therefore, it involves interventions that have evidence documenting their effectiveness (Anderson & Borgmeier, 2010; Hawken et al., 2009; Smith, Bicard, Bicard, & Casey, 2012). As such, Tier Two supports target the function of a problem behavior, thereby providing the student with a more suitable alternative behavior to use. Generally speaking, behavior is functional and serves to either *get something*, such as an item or someone's attention, or *get away from something*, such as homework or interaction with someone (Alberto & Troutman, 2013; Crone & Horner, 2003). Schools create a list of Tier Two supports that allows them to match the intervention to the student's needs. This allows schools to quickly pick an effective intervention for students. School teams will also regularly gather and review data to determine if the support is effective with a particular student or group of students, and adjustments are made quickly if the support is not working (Hawken et al., 2009).

Third, the school provides Tier Two *early* to students. Early is defined in two ways. One, the school provides the supports at the first sign of a behavior issue to prevent problem behavior from becoming engrained. The earlier the students get support, the less likely the problem behaviors will continue and become a chronic issue. Two, students are screened early on during the school year. Schools screen students for behavioral problems shortly after the school year begins and monitor office referral data or other sources of information over the school year to provide supports quickly if a student indicates a need for additional supports.

Building on Tier One, it's important that prior to implementing Tier Two (or Tier Three supports), leadership teams should ensure that Tier One is being implemented with fidelity (Hawken et al., 2009). This is because a well-established foundation of SWPBIS is essential to the success of any additional support (Mitchell, Stormont, & Gage, 2011; Yong & Cheney, 2013). Just as a house needs a strong foundation, so does SWPBIS if Tier Two and Three supports are to be effective (Hawken et al., 2009). An effective Tier One reduces the number of students who need additional supports (Harlacher, Potter, & Weber, 2015), thereby freeing up valuable resources for students who are more in need. Moreover, Tier

Two interventions can reduce the need for further support by between 60 and 75 percent of students (Cheney et al., 2009; Hawken, O'Neill, & MacLeod, 2011), including reducing the need for a special education referral (Yong & Cheney, 2013). The upper tiers of SWPBIS build on the foundation of Tier One, so lacking the foundation will likely lead to poor results (Hawken et al., 2009; McIntosh, Frank, & Spaulding, 2010).

As mentioned in chapter 2 (see page 32), school teams can examine the quality of classroom management within their schools as a means of increasing the likelihood that additional supports will be effective (George et al., 2009; Kincaid et al., 2010). Ensuring that each teacher has strong classroom management (see page 32 in chapter 2) and uses the Tier One practices will increase the likelihood that students requiring Tier Two both actually need that support and will benefit from it. The solid classroom management foundation, with a structured emphasis on teaching and acknowledging appropriate behavior, will maximize the likelihood that more intensive interventions will be successful when compared to the same intensive intervention implemented in a chaotic environment. This is similar to ensuring that all teachers have strong academic instruction as a means of ensuring that students who need additional academic support actually get it, as opposed to a lack of appropriate instruction being the culprit. Time and resources are limited within schools, so school staff must ensure that additional resources are provided to students who require them and whose needs cannot be met with fewer resources (Algozzine et al., 2008). When students who can benefit from less support are given more support than they actually need, other students who need that support miss out (Algozzine et al., 2008; Horner et al., 2010).

As with the previous chapter, we have organized this chapter along the four key elements (outcomes, practices, systems, and data) within the context of Tier Two of SWPBIS. We describe common Tier Two outcomes, then discuss the practices, systems, and data that are a part of this tier. We end the chapter with the application of the PSM for systems and students and provide examples of each.

Outcomes

As with Tier One, leadership teams should first identify the outcomes that they wish to achieve by implementing Tier Two. These outcomes can be defined for implementation and for both systems-level impact and student-level impact.

To begin, Tier Two elements should be implemented with fidelity. School teams will examine fidelity, often with nationally published measures to assess Tier Two elements, with the goal of obtaining the stated criterion on these measures. These measures commonly recommend 70 to 80 percent as a score that indicates schools are implementing Tier Two with fidelity. Additionally, each specific intervention used at Tier Two should be implemented with fidelity across all students. Although there's not a generally agreed-on criterion for fidelity for individual interventions, we suggest fidelity scores of at least 90 percent because studies that have found positive effects with interventions have used a minimum of 90 percent fidelity scores (Greenwood et al., 2008; Jimerson, Burns, & VanDerHeyden, 2007). However, each school should determine this criterion and criteria will vary depending on the nature of the intervention.

For evaluating the impact of Tier Two, it's intuitive to immediately look at whether an intervention is beneficial for any given individual student. However, teams will also need to consider the Tier Two impact at the systems level. At the systems level, school teams examine the extent to which Tier Two is effective as a whole, such as having no more than 15 percent of students needing Tier Two supports. (Keep in mind that if a school has more than 15 percent of students needing or receiving Tier Two supports, this could be an indicator that there is an issue with Tier One to resolve.) Another marker of a healthy Tier Two is if at least 80 percent of those students receiving Tier Two benefit from the support (VanDerHeyden, Witt, & Gilbertson, 2007; Vaughn, Linan-Thompson, & Hickman, 2003). This is a reasonable goal, as at least 60–80 percent of students tend to respond favorably to Tier Two supports (Cheney et al., 2009; Filter et al., 2007; Hawken et al., 2011; Nelson et al., 2009; Vaughn et al., 2003).

Schools can also consider the time it takes for students to benefit from support. That is, when students enter into a Tier Two intervention, do they reach their goals within a reasonable amount of time? The timeline will vary depending on the intervention used, but generally speaking, students should have some reductions in problem behavior or benefit from the intervention fairly quickly (one to three weeks; Fairbanks, Sugai, Guardino, & Lathrop, 2007; Hawken, MacLeod, & Rawlings, 2007). Overall, students should reach their goal from Tier Two supports and no longer need such support after eight to twenty weeks (Fairbanks et al., 2007; Franzen & Kamps, 2008; Gregus, Craig, Rodriguez, Pastrana, & Cavell, 2015; Gresham, Van, & Cook, 2006; Hawken et al., 2007). Students should be given a Tier Two support for a reasonable time period, and then teams should make decisions about modifying, changing, fading, or discontinuing the support.

On a student level, schools using Tier Two should see improvements in each student's behavioral functioning (a decrease in referrals, attendance increases, or improvements on behavior measures), improvements in their social-emotional skills (improvements in social skills or emotion management), and even increased academic performance (improved grades). In particular, a goal of any student receiving Tier Two supports is to eventually remove that support so that the student displays the schoolwide expectations with Tier One support alone. Each student should reach the goals specified within the Tier Two support, which will vary depending on the intervention. After a student has reached his or her Tier Two goal, teachers can fade and eventually remove that support. Students who are not successful with Tier Two after a reasonable about of time (eight to twenty weeks) will need changes to the support or more intensive supports. Given these Tier Two outcomes, next we discuss Tier Two practices that teachers commonly use to ensure that they achieve these outcomes.

"The implementation of PBIS allows for educators to meaningfully partner with students and families to create a positive, predictable, safe environment resulting in optimal conditions for learning. Further, it allows our schools and district to ensure that a data-driven system is in place to meet the needs of all our students, even those who may require additional behavioral supports across tiers, until they cross the stage for graduation."

—Trish Shaffer, MTSS/SEL coordinator, Washoe County School District, Reno, Nevada
(personal communication, January 11, 2017)

Practices

To achieve their specified Tier Two outcomes, schools have a list of Tier Two practices that they can use. The practices for Tier Two are the actual interventions that support students who require additional support. To assist schools with determining if a particular support meets the criteria to be a Tier Two support, the core features of Tier Two are displayed in table 3.2, as originally outlined by Cindy Anderson and Chris Borgmeier (2010). Additionally, we caution schools to avoid selecting too many Tier Two interventions at the beginning. Instead, it is likely better to choose one or two practices that can meet a large percentage of students' needs and implement those with high fidelity over a period of time. Once these practices become engrained in the system and are effective, leadership teams can identify further Tier Two intervention practices to add. When schools attempt to implement too many new practices at once, the system is likely to experience overload, decreasing fidelity of each practice, and creating staff and student intervention fatigue.

Table 3.2: Core Tier Two Features

Feature	Description
Explicit instruction of expectations or skills	Teach the student exactly what is expected using examples and nonexamples to distinguish appropriate from inappropriate behaviors. This often involves defining behaviors, role plays, and feedback during initial intervention implementation as well as regularly throughout.
Structured prompts for appropriate behavior	This might include reminders of expected behaviors, visuals, or cues on a point card.
Opportunities to practice the skills	Skill practice should be embedded throughout the school day and across relevant environments (and not just in an isolated instructional or skills group setting).
Frequent feedback to the student	Students should receive positive and corrective feedback at regular intervals throughout the school day on the expectations or skills being targeted (usually at least once per period or subject area). Feedback should be contingent and specific and focus on positive interactions.
Mechanism to fade support	This often involves reducing the number of times the student is prompted or receives feedback about a skill. It can also involve increasing the interval between delivery of acknowledgments or rewards associated with success.
Communication with students' parents*	Efforts to include or communicate with parents might include brief notes home on a daily or weekly basis, phone calls, emails, student success postcard mailers, or other quick, culturally relevant communication forms.

* Although parent communication is ideal, not all Tier Two interventions may include this feature beyond informing parents or guardians that the student is receiving Tier Two supports. Students whose behavior indicates a need for Tier Two supports should not be excluded if parents are not active participants.

Source: Anderson & Borgmeier, 2010.

Each intervention at Tier Two will address a particular function of behavior, so as teachers identify students for support, the teachers identify the function of the problem behavior as well. Teachers thusly use the Tier Two intervention to teach a replacement behavior that serves the same function as the problem behavior (Anderson & Borgmeier, 2010). For example, if a student is disruptive in class to obtain adult attention, the team selects a Tier

Two intervention that reteaches and reinforces an appropriate behavior that he or she can use to obtain adult attention. School teams do not need to spend a lot of time or exhaustive resources on identifying the function of a student's behavior at this point in time. Instead, school teams use existing data or a brief assessment to identify a reasonable function of the behavior. For example, ODRs should have staff provide an estimated guess as to the function of the behavior. The teams can then examine these data to reasonably guess as to the function of the behavior; for example, a team examines the referrals for a student identified for Tier Two and determines the most prevalent function.

To assist schools with understanding the variety of options available, we summarize some of the evidence-based Tier Two interventions available. Table 3.3 displays a list of interventions and typical functions of behavior they target. Please note this is not an exhaustive list, and we are not endorsing any intervention over another. Also, each listed function is not the only possible function; the functions of the interventions can easily be tailored to target other functions. We discuss each intervention in depth next.

Table 3.3: Tier Two Interventions and Functions of Behaviors They Target

Intervention	Description	Target Function	Results From Research
Academic Interventions	Additional support is provided to teach the student missing academic skills (which are driving escape-maintained behavior).	Escape work or tasks	Improvements in academic achievement Reductions in disruptive behavior
Check In–Check Out	Students receive feedback on behavior or expectations at designated times throughout the day. They have a staff member they check in with in the morning and check out with at the end of the day.	Obtain adult attention	Reductions in number of ODRs and problem behaviors (noncompliance, disruption, off-task behavior, talk-outs, or inappropriate contact) Improvements in social-emotional scores High fidelity of implementation Viewed as easy to implement by staff
Check and Connect	Students are assigned a mentor from school who meets periodically with the student to provide support and guidance.	Obtain adult attention	Improvements in engagement, attendance, and academic performance Reductions in ODRs Staff view parents as more supportive of child's education

Check, Connect, and Expect	This combines elements from Check In–Check Out and Check and Connect.	Obtain adult attention	Improvements with internalizing and externalizing behaviors Reductions in ODRs, problem behavior, severity of behavior, and referrals to special education Effective for sixty to eighty or more percent of recipients
Classwide Interventions	Interventions are provided to the whole class, but are designed to target one or a few students' behavior.	Obtain attention Escape work or tasks	Improvements in appropriate behavior and on-task behavior Reductions in disruptive and off-task behaviors
Mentoring	Students are assigned a mentor who provides a positive role model and promotes attachment to school.	Obtain attention	Improvements in self-esteem Reductions in total incidents and days of suspensions Reductions in infractions on school property
Service Learning Programs	Programs combine community work and academic learning to promote positive behavior.	Obtain attention	Improvements in attitudes toward school, learning, and self Improvements in social skills and academic achievement
Setting-Based Interventions	The setting in which a student displays problem behavior is modified.	Obtain attention Obtain item, task, or activity	Improvements in social interaction and appropriate play with peers Reductions in problem behavior (inappropriate contact, misuse of equipment, disruptive behavior, foul language), and bullying behaviors Social satisfaction with intervention

continued ➜

Intervention	Description	Target Function	Results From Research
Social Skills and Social-Emotional Learning Skills Interventions	Students are provided instruction in certain social or social-emotional skills using a group setting.	Obtain attention Obtain item, task, or activity Avoid attention	Improvements in social skills, social-emotional learning skills, academic achievement, and academically engaged time Reductions in emotional distress and problem behavior (disruptive behavior, out of seat, and noncompliance)

Note: Possible functions of behavior are to either (1) obtain or get or (2) escape or avoid the following things: adult attention, peer attention, items, tasks, an activity or activities, and sensory issues or stimulation.

Sources: Adapted from Cheney et al., 2009; Cheney et al., 2010; DuBois, Holloway, Valentine, & Cooper, 2002; Fairbanks et al., 2007; Filter et al., 2007; Franzen & Kamps, 2008; Grossman & Tierney, 1998; Gregus et al., 2015; Gresham et al., 2006; Hawken et al., 2007; Hawken et al., 2011; January, Casey, & Paulson, 2011; Kraemer, Davies, Arndt, & Hunley, 2012; Lane et al., 2002; Lane et al., 2003; Lehr, Sinclair, & Christenson, 2004; Lewis, Powers, Kely, & Newcomer, 2002; Marchant et al., 2007; Maynard, Kjellstrand, & Thompson, 2014; Payton et al., 2008; Simonsen, Myers, & Briere, 2011; Wright & McCurdy, 2012.

Academic Interventions

Teachers can implement academic interventions for students who display higher rates of problem behavior to escape certain task or work demands (Lane et al., 2002). Because a student may not have the academic skills required to complete certain tasks or work, and therefore misbehaves to escape or avoid work, providing the missing academic skills can result in a decrease in problem behavior (Lane et al., 2002; McIntosh, Horner, Chard, Boland, & Good, 2006). The nature of the academic interventions can vary, but they involve providing additional minutes of instruction outside of the universal instruction time. Generally speaking, elementary schools provide Tier Two interventions for academic skills three to four times per week for approximately twenty to forty-five minutes in groups of six to eight students depending on the academic skill being taught (Abbott et al., 2008; Brown-Chidsey & Steege, 2010; Greenwood et al., 2008; Vaughn, Wanzek, Woodruff, & Linan-Thompson, 2007). Secondary schools may provide Tier Two interventions for academic skills in groups of three to six students, or up to ten to fifteen students for approximately fifty minutes per day (Pyle & Vaughn, 2012; Vaughn et al., 2010).

Whereas some academic interventions will teach specific academic skills, some schools may need academic interventions that teach students organizational skills or metacognitive skills. Secondary students in particular may need further instruction on organizing their assignments and different courses, or they may need instruction on monitoring their own learning so that they can be successful (Lenski, 2011; Shinn, 2008b). School teams can provide a homework club, which is a designated time when students can receive individual support from older students or staff on their homework. The volunteers in homework club can provide support with reading and understanding the content, helping with organizational skills and with completing and managing assignments, and provide supervision and structure for students to complete their work (Stormont, Reinke, Herman, & Lembke, 2012).

Check In–Check Out

Check In–Check Out is a structured intervention in which students receive increased feedback throughout the day on their behavior (also referred to as *Behavior Education Program*; Crone, Hawken, & Horner, 2010; Hawken et al., 2011). Students check in with a Check In–Check Out coordinator in the morning and are given a daily point card. This card lists the expectations for the school (see figure 3.1) and may also list a specific behavior under each expectation that the student is learning (under "be safe" in figure 3.1, a more detailed behavior is listed: Keep hands and feet to self). In this manner, the card is aligned to schoolwide expectations and, if a student is not responsive to standard aligned schoolwide prompts, can be individually tailored for students. The students discuss their goal for the day (for example, the number of points they want to earn on their card), review and practice appropriate behaviors, and briefly set a plan to ensure that they reach their respective goals, such as *Be sure to follow directions from the teacher* or *Make sure I bring my supplies to class*. The entire Check In should only last a few minutes, and the goal is to prepare the student to be successful that day, not to lecture or rehash previous infractions (Crone et al., 2010).

Student Name: _____					Date: _____				
	3 = zero to one reminders 2 = two reminders 1 = three or more reminders								
	Be Safe			**Be Respectful**			**Be Responsible**		
	Keep hands and feet to self			**Follow directions the first time**			**Complete work in class**			**Teacher initials**
Check In	1	2	3	1	2	3	1	2	3	
Writing	1	2	3	1	2	3	1	2	3	
Math	1	2	3	1	2	3	1	2	3	
Specials	1	2	3	1	2	3	1	2	3	
Recess	1	2	3	1	2	3	1	2	3	
Small-Group Reading	1	2	3	1	2	3	1	2	3	
Whole-Group Reading	1	2	3	1	2	3	1	2	3	
Check Out	1	2	3	1	2	3	1	2	3	
Today's Goal: _____									
Total Points: _____				Percentage of Points: _____					
Parent or Guardian Signature: _____									

Figure 3.1: Example of a daily point card.

Visit MarzanoResearch.com/reproducibles to download a free reproducible version of this figure.

The student carries the card throughout the day and receives feedback on it from his or her teachers at regular intervals during the day. The feedback is provided at natural breaks during the day, such as after each class for secondary schools or after certain subjects in elementary school settings. During this interaction, the teacher briefly reviews the student's adherence to the expectations during the timeframe on the card and provides a score. The teacher should also prompt expected behaviors for the next time period and set the student up for success. The interaction is brief and meant to provide a positive interaction and constructive feedback to prepare the student to be successful for the next time period. See figure 3.2.

> "Hello, Eli. It is great to see you today. Remember, I really want to see you be responsible by completing your work. If you need help you can be respectful by raising your hand to ask for help. And lastly, please be sure to keep your hands and feet to yourself today. That really keeps us all safe."

Figure 3.2: Script for a Check In.

At the end of the day, the student returns to the Check In–Check Out coordinator and reviews the card. The student tallies up the total points and determines if his or her goal was met. If met, the student earns a reward or earns progress toward a reward (for example, some rewards may take several days to earn; Crone et al., 2010). The Check In–Check Out coordinator signs the form, and the student takes the form home for his or her parents to sign.

Check In–Check Out is perhaps most helpful for students who seek out teacher attention, but teachers can modify Check In–Check Out to target other functions or behavior. For example, teachers modify Check In–Check Out for use with students who display problematic behavior in order to avoid academic work. Justin Boyd and Cindy Anderson (2013) describe a modified Check In–Check Out intervention in which students are allowed brief breaks upon request during certain work periods. Students have a daily point card and follow similar procedures with Check In–Check Out (for example, checking in with a mentor, checking out, earning points for following specified expectations). However, students can raise their hand for a two-minute break, during which they do a preferred activity (for example, doodle or look at a book). The student uses the break at any point during academic work time, but the teacher provides permission with a thumbs-up. As additional incentive, the student can earn a bonus point on his or her daily card for not taking a break. Jessica Turtura, Cindy Anderson, and Justin Boyd (2014) describe a Check In–Check Out intervention that included a homework prompt on the student's daily card. On the back of the daily point card was a homework tracker where the student recorded any assignments, due dates, and materials needed. Additionally, students on Check In–Check Out can earn activities with peers or earn incentives for their classrooms.

Check and Connect

Check and Connect is a program designed to increase a student's engagement with school and improve attendance (Lehr et al., 2004; Sinclair, Christenson, Lehr, & Anderson, 2003; University of Minnesota, n.d.). Students referred for Check and Connect are assigned a mentor from the school who regularly checks in with the student (for example, weekly), communicates with the student's family, and provides problem solving and skill building with the student. Check and Connect builds a positive relationship between an adult at school and the student and provides a platform for the student to develop problem-solving and prosocial skills (Lehr et al., 2004; Sinclair et al., 2003).

Check and Connect consists of two components: *check* and *connect*. The mentor regularly *checks* indicators of student engagement (for example, attendance, academic performance, behavior referrals, and tardiness) and documents these indicators on a monitoring sheet. The mentor also *connects* with the student and his or her family by introducing him- or herself to the family and providing regular communication. There are two levels of Check and Connect: basic and intensive. During the basic level, students have weekly conversations with their mentor about their progress in school and the importance of regular attendance and education, as well as brief problem-solving discussions around issues that may arise (for instance, the student is struggling with taking homework home, so the mentor works with the student to identify a solution). At the intensive level, various strategies and interventions are added to the basic level based on the student's needs and grade level, such as tutoring or a counseling session. Generally speaking, Check and Connect provides a positive adult for the student to connect with at school, which affords the student someone from whom to learn and receive support. The adult also ensures connection and communication with the family as another avenue of building support for the student.

Check, Connect, and Expect

Check, Connect, and Expect is an intervention that combines the features of both Check In–Check Out and Check and Connect (Cheney et al., 2009; Cheney et al., 2010; McDaniel, Flower, & Cheney, 2011). Check, Connect, and Expect consists of a coach for students who provides daily contact and feedback to the student on his or her social and academic progress (similar to a Check In–Check Out coordinator), as well as support and guidance to overcome any social issues that may arise and to develop new prosocial skills (similar to a Check and Connect mentor). Within Check, Connect, and Expect, the coach provides daily positive interactions among the student and his or her teachers; supervises and monitors the student's social and academic performance; provides any needed social skill instruction (which can be informal discussions or more formal lessons); provides positive reinforcement for reaching daily and weekly goals; and involves the parents or guardians through use of home notes. Check, Connect, and Expect also includes structured teacher feedback, similar to Check In–Check Out.

There are three levels of Check, Connect, and Expect. The *basic* level involves a daily check in and check out with the coach at the beginning and end of the day, respectively, during which the coach reviews the student's daily point card (which is a card akin to the Check In–Check Out card) and prompts the student to use prosocial behavior. Students who are successful with the basic level (for example, at least 75 percent of daily points on more than 80 percent of days for two weeks) are then placed in the *self-monitoring level*. At this level, students rate their own behavior and compare it to teachers' ratings. If they are within one point for two weeks, they then rate their behavior on their own for two more weeks. After meeting defined criteria during those four weeks, students graduate from the program.

Students who do not reach criteria during the basic level are placed in the *basic-plus* level. During this level, the coach reduces the daily goal by 10 percent of the student's current average and adds additional incentives for reaching the criterion. He or she provides additional interventions based on the student's needs, such as academic tutoring or social skills instruction (Cheney et al., 2009). Once the student meets the basic-plus goal, that goal is increased until the student reaches the original goal from the basic level.

Classwide Interventions

Some schools may use a classwide intervention to target the behavior of students. Classwide practices and systems are a part of Tier One, but there may be times when it's helpful to temporarily intensify certain classroom practices in order to target the behavior of some students or to target a certain schoolwide expectation. Teachers deliver these Tier Two classwide interventions to all students, even though the purpose of the intervention is for one or a few students. This is advantageous because teachers use one plan instead of several separate ones for each student who needs Tier Two supports, and other students may receive ancillary benefits from the intervention in addition to the target student (Harlacher, Roberts, & Merrell, 2006). Teachers can only use temporary classwide interventions during certain times of the day—students don't need to use them all day, every day. For example, if a small group of students need further instruction on following the schoolwide expectation of being respectful after they transition from lunch back into the classroom, a teacher can use a classwide intervention solely during that time. Because these interventions are for a few students and are temporary, we view them as Tier Two practices. Additionally, the use of Tier Two classwide interventions assumes that there are strong Tier One classroom management principles in place (see page 32 in chapter 2). As we discussed earlier, stronger classroom management can increase the likelihood that any Tier Two intervention will work. If a teacher does not have strong classroom management in place, then the students' need for Tier Two may be a systems issue and thus indicate the need for an improvement in Tier One practices prior to providing a Tier Two intervention.

The nature of the classwide interventions may vary slightly, but generally speaking, they involve identifying and reteaching behaviors of interest (for example, being respectful by working quietly and not disrupting other classmates, or being safe by keeping hands, feet, and objects to oneself) and providing additional rewards or more structured incentives for adherence to the taught behavior. For example, the Mystery Motivator provides variable rewards to students based on their improvements in disruptive behavior. The rewards are high and low interest, and students do not know ahead of time which reward they will receive (Kraemer et al., 2012; Musser, Bray, Kehle, & Jenson, 2001). The Good Behavior Game is another example in which teams form within the classroom and each of them compete to earn a group reward by not engaging in problem behavior (Barrish, Saunders, & Wolf, 1969), although it can occur without teams (for instance, class versus the teacher). Additionally, interdependent group contingencies that are variations on the good behavior game exist where students focus on working together to engage in prosocial behaviors and earn acknowledgment for success (Rodriguez & Anderson, 2014). As a third example, the Classroom Kit describes the division of younger elementary classrooms into teams and the teaching of a few target behaviors. When students display the behaviors, they are rewarded with praise and points or a smiley face on a team poster. Teams can also earn sad faces if they continue to not follow rules after being prompted to follow them. At the end of a work session (for example, thirty to forty-five minutes), teams with more praise than redirects earn a brief activity (for example, freeze dance or act like your favorite animal; Anhalt, McNeil, & Bahl, 1998).

Structured classwide interventions allow the target students more opportunities to practice the schoolwide expectations and receive more feedback and praise for use of the expectations (Bowen et al., 2004; Theodore, Bray, Kehle, & Jenson, 2001). The following six-item list outlines general steps of classwide interventions (Harlacher, 2015).

1. Identify an expectation that students need to work on, a time period in which they need the most improvement, and a criterion for a reward. For example, a teacher might decide that students need to work on raising their hands instead of calling out during teacher-led instruction, and set the criterion that students must have more than ten instances of the correct behavior to earn a reward.

2. Divide the class into teams. For example, the classroom could be divided down the center to create two teams, or, if students sit in clusters at desks or tables, each table can be a team. Students can play individually, but it is likely more effective and efficient when students are in teams because the teams create social norms and expectations (Anhalt et al., 1998; Bowen et al., 2004; Theodore et al., 2001).

3. Teach students the expectation.

4. Create a simple, visual system for each team (or individual student) to use to record the praise they earn for meeting expectations, such as tally marks or stickers on a team poster or section of the chalkboard. Each tally mark or other symbol equates to one instance of correct behavior and praise, and one point within the game.

5. Throughout the time period, recognize the desired behavior and provide behavior-specific praise to students for meeting expectations. Mark each instance of behavior on the student or team's visual tracker. In the example from step 1, for instance, the teacher would give praise and mark a tally on the appropriate team's chart each time a student raised his or her hand to contribute instead of calling out.

6. At the end of the time period, provide a group reward based on the predetermined criterion for tallies earned.

Mentoring

Mentoring is defined as a one-to-one relationship between a *mentor* (a more experienced adult or teenager) and a *mentee* (a less experienced student; DuBois et al., 2002). Within a school, mentoring begins by either connecting the student with outside organizations that have mentors (for example, Big Brothers Big Sisters) or by providing school-based mentors (for example, a counselor or a teacher within the school). The mentor serves as a positive role model, provides spontaneous support for prosocial behaviors, and provides encouragement for attending school and displaying prosocial behaviors (DuBois et al., 2002; Rollin, Kaiser-Ulrey, Potts, & Creason, 2003). For example, Lunch Buddy is a program in which a college-aged mentor has lunch with a student in the elementary school two times each week. During this time, the mentor sits at the lunch table with the mentee and other students within the cafeteria and provides positive interactions and models prosocial skills for the mentee and the other students at the table (Cavell & Henrie, 2010). The structure of the mentoring can vary, but programs that included ongoing training for mentors, structured activities for mentors and youth, expectations for frequency of contact, support for involvement of parents, and monitoring of implementation had higher positive outcomes for students. A genuine emotional contact is critical to mentoring (DuBois et al., 2002).

Service Learning Programs

Service learning programs are programs that integrate community work or service work with academic content (Celio, Durlak, & Dymnicki, 2011). Service learning programs are supports in which students participate in a community project or applied learning that is linked to the school curriculum. For example, students could build a community garden as part of a plant biology lesson or work to restore a building in the community while learning about architecture or environmental issues (Dymond, Chun, Kim, & Renzaglia, 2013). Service learning programs have five elements:

1. An authentic context (for example, meets the needs of the community and students perform service in the actual setting it is needed)
2. A link to the school's curriculum
3. Support for the program (for instance, transportation to and from the site and flexibility in scheduling projects)
4. Action, which is the actual student and teacher/adult participation within the project
5. Time for reflection (for example, students reflect on what they've learned and what they can take with them; Dymond et al., 2013)

Service learning programs are designed to teach civic responsibility, enrich learning, and build ties with the community (Dymond et al., 2013). Students provide a service to others and, as a result, build social responsibility and prosocial skills through their participation and receive indirect mentoring and support from adults (Celio et al., 2011; Durlak, Weissberg, Dymnicki, Taylor, & Schellinger, 2011; Dymond et al., 2013). Related to service learning programs could be the formation of clubs for students with similar interests. Students who have limited engagement in school may benefit from participating in a club or activity with peers with similar interests to increase certain social skills and social-emotional learning skills, as well as develop a stronger attachment to school (Durlak et al., 2011).

Setting-Based Interventions

Some teams may provide support to students in specified locations. Students who do not have issues in certain settings, such as the classroom, but display more problem behavior in less structured settings, such as the lunchroom or playground, may be good candidates for setting-based interventions. The nature of the intervention can vary. For example, students who receive this Tier Two intervention can be taught the rules of a game, as well as the skills needed to join and play certain games, after which these skills are monitored and reinforced by playground supervisors (Lewis et al., 2002). Alternatively, an assigned playground supervisor checks in with students at the start of a recess period. Once students check in, the supervisor provides a game and peers for the targeted student to play with, after which the supervisor provides feedback to the students for use of certain social skills. Either a peer or adult can provide prompting and support to students. Michelle Marchant and colleagues (2007) used peers and adults to support and mediate a playground intervention targeting students with social withdrawal. In their study, they taught the target students social skills that centered on starting conversations, asking to play with other students, and playing appropriately. They also taught the students how to self-manage and evaluate their use of the skills. After three days of small-group training on the skills, they paired the target students up with peers or adults, and they used a point system to monitor their use of the skills during recess. They used adult partners more frequently later in the study because the peer partners within the study were not having much time to play on their own with their own friends. All three students involved in the study showed improvements in their interactions with others, with the adult partner portion of the study showing more dramatic effects.

The school may also restructure the setting to facilitate use of the expectations and provide activities for students to engage in. For example, staff can split a playground into different sections where students have choices of activities or games based on the area of the playground. Orchard Middle School in Cleveland organized its playground into four sections, with each section designated for a certain activity: a discovery zone where students learned a new game, a free-play game, an organized game (for instance, flag football or basketball), and a walking track area designed to promote exercise (Ott, 2010). Students are taught the rules for each game, and a playground supervisor monitors each section. The supervisor provides feedback and reinforcement to students for displaying certain prosocial skills (Lewis et al., 2002; Ott, 2010; Peace Power Tools, n.d.). Dividing the playground into sections and providing reinforcement for certain skills during recess to all students is a Tier One intervention. However, if teachers do this temporarily and for a few students, it is similar to the use of a classwide intervention that we discussed earlier (page 80).

Social Skills and Social-Emotional Learning Skills Instruction

Another Tier Two intervention is providing social-skills or social-emotional learning skills instruction to students in small groups. Social skills groups can target general social skills (Lane et al., 2003) or target specific skills students lack, such as anger management or dealing with grief (Gresham et al., 2006; Hawken et al., 2009). Any social skills or SEL skills instruction should incorporate elements of effective teaching that include teaching the skill in a small-group setting, practice of and reinforcement of the skill in controlled and applied settings (settings in which students will not be rejected if they misuse or misapply the skill), and generalization to all settings (Gresham, 2002). In school settings, this means social skills instruction is going to be most effective as a Tier Two intervention if it has clearly defined target skills (for example, asking to join a game), opportunities to practice and receive feedback on those specific target skills in both small groups and regular school settings, and then continued monitoring of these skills over time. Just like targeted academic skill instruction, specific outcomes taught in the group should monitor progress on these skills teachers should identify to determine the effectiveness of the instruction.

We should also note that longer, more intensive social skills programs tend to have a stronger effect on students compared to shorter trainings. For example, research on students in a program that involved sixty hours of training over twenty weeks found more improvement in their social skills than studies on students in a thirty-hour, ten-week program (Gresham et al., 2006; Quinn, Kavale, Mathur, Rutherford, & Forness, 1999).

Systems

Following identification of the practices that the school will use for Tier Two, school teams will then determine the exact systems to support the use of those practices. Systems for Tier Two are ones that support the staff in implementing the practices and gathering the necessary data to inform decisions for Tier Two. The following Tier Two systems are described in the subsequent sections.

- ▲ Tier Two team
- ▲ Secured funding and resources
- ▲ Training and coaching
- ▲ Data use and procedures

Tier Two Team

As with Tier One, a key system for Tier Two is a team designed to provide and coordinate all aspects of Tier Two. The Tier Two team is responsible for two broad tasks (see table 3.4): (1) implementing the Tier Two supports and (2) evaluating the impact of those supports. These tasks include training the staff to implement the interventions, monitoring fidelity of the interventions, and assigning and monitoring students within Tier Two intervention.

Table 3.4: Tier Two Team Tasks

Implementation	Impact
Train staff on using screening data to identify students, including administration of assessments.	Assign students to interventions.
Train staff on how to use and implement Tier Two interventions.	Hold regular meetings to discuss impact for individual students.
Hold regular meetings to discuss implementation.	Hold regular meetings to discuss impact as a whole.

We discuss the roles of the Tier Two team next before discussing specifics about choosing interventions and meeting times for Tier Two.

Membership and Roles

The roles within the Tier Two team are similar to those within the leadership team: administrator, minutes recorder, data analyst, team facilitator, and timekeeper (see chapter 2, page 48). In addition, the team will need a Tier Two coordinator (Pool, Carter, & Johnson, 2013). The Tier Two coordinator is responsible for programming and scheduling the students who receive Tier Two supports. This includes assigning a student into the actual intervention, introducing the intervention to the student and training the student as needed, and contacting the teacher to inform him or her that the student will be receiving the intervention. The Tier Two coordinator can also contact parents, but some teams may wish to assign this task to another team member or to the student's teacher. As schools implement multiple Tier Two interventions, they may have different coordinators for different

Tier Two interventions, or they may have one person who coordinates all of the Tier Two interventions. For schools with multiple Tier Two coordinators, it will be important that one person is designated as the point person for receiving referrals and leading the team in determining which Tier Two intervention is the best fit for each referred student.

Selecting Interventions to Use

To implement Tier Two well, the team will need to make decisions as to which interventions the school will use for Tier Two supports, how they will train the staff to be aware of or to implement the interventions, who will gather and input the progress-monitoring data, and when they will review the data. We have included a list of questions from Anderson and Borgmeier (2010) that Tier Two teams can answer to ensure that all the correct systems and logistics are in place before implementing an intervention. See the following questions to consider for Tier Two interventions.

- ▲ What behavior will the intervention increase?
- ▲ What behavior will the intervention decrease?
- ▲ What are the inclusion criteria to determine if the student is a right fit for the intervention?
- ▲ What are the exclusion criteria (for instance, avoids adult attention)?
- ▲ What is the goal of the intervention (for instance, 80 percent of daily points)?
- ▲ What defines lack of progress (for instance, ten consecutive days of less than 70 percent of daily points)?
- ▲ What is a successful outcome for fading the intervention?
- ▲ What data will be gathered, by whom, and how frequently?
- ▲ Who will enter and graph the data?
- ▲ How often will progress monitoring occur and who is responsible?
- ▲ How will implementation/fidelity be assessed and by whom?

Regular Meeting Times

A critical piece of the Tier Two team is that it meets regularly to oversee the coordination of the Tier Two supports. The team will establish regular meeting times to handle the logistics related to providing Tier Two interventions, as well as times to discuss students receiving Tier Two interventions. Tier Two teams will likely need to review data every other week, as Tier Two social behavior interventions require more frequent monitoring than Tier One supports.

The schedule will vary depending on the size of the school and other contextual factors (for example, other existing teams or integration with other systems of support for academics), but the team will meet more frequently than the leadership team. Deborah Carter and colleagues (2012) described a team process in which the Tier Two team met every other week to discuss students. During those meetings, members discussed monitoring of students within Tier Two supports and made decisions about students who had been identified for support (which intervention to provide, whether to refer to Tier Three, and so on). This team also managed the implementation of the Tier Two systems as the team held meetings to train the staff on the interventions, provide refresher trainings, and evaluate fidelity of implementation (Carter et al., 2012).

Secured Funding and Resources

Similar to Tier One, the Tier Two team will need some secured funding and resources to provide the interventions. For example, funding may be needed for substitutes to provide training to the staff on the interventions or funding to purchase intervention and training materials (for example, a book on a given intervention, printing needs, and so on). Managing and coordinating Tier Two is not a small feat, so asking a staff member to add that task to his or her current role without allocating time does not set that person up to be successful and is not sustainable. Leadership will want to consider assigning up to a full-time equivalent for the role of a Tier Two coordinator (Horner et al., 2010).

Training and Coaching

Another system related to Tier Two is appropriate training and coaching of the staff to understand and use the Tier Two supports. All staff should understand what Tier Two is, how to access that support for their students, and their exact involvement with the interventions. A *sit and get* training is not sufficient; instead, staff will need ongoing coaching to understand how to access and use the Tier Two interventions. For example, Check In–Check Out involves teachers providing feedback to students in a very specific manner, so the Tier Two team will need to observe and coach staff members on providing such feedback.

Data Use and Procedures

The Tier Two team will clarify the process for providing Tier Two supports quickly to the students. Specifically, there is a four-part process: (1) select students for Tier Two supports, (2) match the students' needs to an intervention, (3) begin implementation of the intervention, and (4) monitor the students' progress.

Select Students

Following the collection of screening data or a teacher request for assistance, the Tier Two team will need to determine which students should actually receive Tier Two supports. The team will examine the data to verify the students' risk status and to make sure that Tier Two supports can address the behavior. We do not advocate providing supports to students on the basis of one score (Good et al., 2002), so teams will want to consider other data to ensure that a student's risk status is accurate. For example, a student may have three major ODRs, which suggests Tier Two placement, but the team will want to examine other indicators of risk (for instance, grades, attendance, or location of ODRs) to make sure the student actually needs Tier Two. Following that, the team should consider the student's actual behavior. Students with aggressive or violent behavior would be better suited to Tier Three supports than Tier Two (Crone et al., 2010; Hawken et al., 2009).

Match Students' Needs to an Intervention

Once a student is identified for Tier Two supports, the team then selects an appropriate support based on the presumed function of the behavior. For example, a school can provide a homework intervention or tutoring sessions for students with escape-maintained behavior, and it can use Check and Connect for adult-attention-maintained behavior. We discuss identifying the function of a behavior extensively within the Data section (page 88), but, as an example, teams can examine ODRs to determine the students' likely function of problem behavior. The team should have a list of different Tier Two interventions that can target different functions, thereby letting the team match each student's function of behavior to an appropriate intervention.

Begin the Intervention

Following identification and determination of which intervention to provide, the school needs procedures to ensure that the team can provide the support quickly. Keeping in line with a team-based approach, they divide up the tasks needed to begin an intervention, which include contacting the parties involved (parents, student, and teachers), training the student, and providing refresher training to the teacher. For parents, some schools may send home a standard letter at the beginning of the year that introduces SWPBIS to parents. If a parent's child is placed into Tier Two supports, they can send a more specific letter home, providing parents an opportunity to passively consent to their student's participation. Alternatively, a member of the Tier Two team can contact parents to discuss the intervention teachers will provide and obtain verbal consent.

Carter and colleagues (2012) described a Tier Two process in which the Tier Two team met twice a month to identify students who might need Tier Two. The team would review the screening data or teacher requests and ensure that the students needed Tier Two by ensuring that Tier Two could address the behaviors. The intervention coordinator would then contact the student and train him or her on the intervention. The coordinator would also contact the teacher, discuss the details of the intervention, and provide refresher trainings to the teacher. Another member of the Tier Two team contacted parents to discuss the intervention. Notice that no one person had too many tasks to do. In particular, the teacher of the student was not burdened with a list of things to do prior to implementing the intervention. Instead, a few members of the team had a small part to play to provide support to the student. From the teacher's perspective, she either gathered screening data or completed a request for assistance, after which she would receive word on the intervention the student was to be provided and any refresher trainings on the intervention the team had chosen for the student. One can see the difference between this approach and a historical, student-study team. In the historical model, a teacher would come to a meeting, receive suggestions about other things to try with the student, and then be told, "Try this and come back." All of the responsibility lies with the teacher. With SWPBIS, the responsibility is the team's responsibility, and each member plays a part, including progress monitoring, which is discussed next (George, 2009; Horner et al., 2010).

Monitor Student Progress

The Tier Two team will also outline procedures to gather and analyze the data for progress monitoring. Such procedures will vary between schools and interventions, but there should be a division of labor for gathering and entering the data. There should also be attempts made to blend data collection with the actual intervention. For example, the team records daily points for Check In–Check Out on a card, which the team can use as progress-monitoring data. For a social skills intervention, students or teachers can rate their use of the skills being taught each week during their sessions, which the team can then enter into a data system and used as progress-monitoring data. In these instances, there is not an additional, separate, or cumbersome method of data collection. Using a data warehouse system to quickly access and summarize data in a graph is related to progress monitoring. There are available systems (for example, SWIS), but teams may elect to create their own using computer-based programs or district-level personnel.

Thus far, we have outlined the practices of Tier Two, which are the actual interventions provided to students, and the systems that are needed to support the use of those Tier Two practices. Now we discuss the types of data used for Tier Two that allow teams to make decisions about the implementation and impact of Tier Two.

Data

As briefly mentioned in the Systems section, Tier Two teams need data within Tier Two for a few reasons, the first of which is to identify students for supports. The teams use screening data to initially identify students, after which students' need for Tier Two support is verified with additional data. They examine brief diagnostic data to determine the function of problem behaviors, and they need progress-monitoring data to examine students' growth. Teams will also examine data to determine the implementation of Tier Two as a whole and for specific Tier Two interventions. We discuss each of those data sources—screening, diagnostic, progress monitoring, and fidelity—next.

Screening Data

To identify students who need additional support, schools use universal screening. Universal screening is the process of examining data to determine which students meet criteria for the risk status that is associated with Tier Two supports (Hosp, 2008). Schools have three sources of possible data: (1) pre-existing data, (2) screening instruments, or (3) teacher nomination.

Pre-Existing Data

The main sources of pre-existing data for identifying students who may be at risk for social-emotional issues are office discipline referrals (ODRs). As part of Tier One, schools complete ODRs to track the frequency and nature of behavior issues within the school. Teachers can use these data to identify students who may need Tier Two supports (Tobin & Sugai, 1999; Tobin et al., 1996). School teams identify a threshold of the number of referrals that trigger consideration of a Tier Two intervention (for example, two to five minor ODRs within a four-week period). Generally speaking, rates of minor referral data are good indicators for students who may need Tier Two supports (because they highlight students who engage in frequent, low-level misbehavior), whereas rates of major referral data are good indicators for students who may need Tier Three (because they often indicate higher-intensity problem behaviors). Kent McIntosh, Jennifer Frank, and Scott Spaulding (2010) found that half of students who received six or more total ODRs during the school year had two or more by the end of October, and approximately 79 percent of these students had two or more ODRs by the end of December. Therefore, it is often helpful for schools to review their data at the end of October and the end of December to identify students who may benefit from Tier Two supports and provide them quickly at this point.

Other sources of data are useful for screening. For instance, attendance, grades, previous state testing scores, and previous suspensions and expulsions received are indicative of school dropout risk (Centers for Disease Control and Prevention, 2009). Schools can examine such data, determine an appropriate threshold for referral, and use these data to also identify students for Tier Two consideration. Many teams start with draft decision rules and then adjust them over time as they monitor the implementation of their SWPBIS systems and determine which cut points appear to be most representative of students' needs. We provide an example of how one school district could organize their data criteria for both elementary and secondary schools in figure 3.3. *Low risk* indicates students who likely don't need any additional supports, *some risk* indicates students who may need Tier Two supports, and *at risk* refers to students who may need Tier Three supports.

Measure	Low Risk	Some Risk	At Risk
Major ODRs	zero to one	two to five	six or more
Minor ODRs	two to four	five to twelve	thirteen or more
Absences	five per semester	six to nine per semester	ten or more per semester
Tardies	three per semester	four to nine per semester	ten or more per semester
Suspensions	zero	one	two
Course Grades	2.5 or higher	D or F in one course	Ds or Fs in two or more courses

Figure 3.3: Example of a district's risk criteria.

Source: Adapted from Missouri Schoolwide Positive Behavior Support, n.d.b.

Screening Instruments

As another source of data, school teams can administer screening instruments to identify students for Tier Two consideration. Whereas ODRs and other pre-existing data do well to identify students with externalizing concerns (disruption or aggression), students with internalizing behaviors (depression, anxiety, or withdrawal) may be missed with such methods, thus requiring use of screening instruments (Hawken et al., 2009). Schools can administer one instrument that measures various behaviors, and students that meet risk status on the administered tool are considered for Tier Two. The Strengths and Difficulties Questionnaire (Goodman, 1997), the Student Risk Screening Scale (Drummond, 1994), the Student Internalizing Behavior Screener (Cook et al., 2011), and the Social Skills Improvement System (Gresham & Elliott, 2008) are a few examples of screening instruments. Schools can also use software systems, such as AIMSweb Behavior, which combines frequency of ODRs and teacher-reported data to identify students (AIMSweb, 2010). Within AIMSweb Behavior, the teacher completes a form in which all students are ranked on certain behaviors. Another strategy for screening is the use of sociometrics; for example, students rate their top three friends and three least liked peers (George, 2009). Caution is necessary when using sociometrics, as students' answers should be anonymous when possible, and students should be instructed to keep their answers confidential and to not discuss their responses openly.

It will depend on the district's discretion whether individual schools select the screener or whether the district dictates the tools schools should use. Schools may opt to use a gating process instead of administering just one instrument. Although this process requires certain resources and a few steps, it can save teachers time because it filters out students who do not need more extensive assessment. The gating process refers to a series of steps in which teams use different tools (AIMSweb, 2010; Walker, Small, Severson, Seeley, & Feil, 2014); students who pass all of the gates receive consideration for Tier Two.

Note that gating includes methods to identify students with internalizing behaviors and students with externalizing behaviors. Gating can consist of two gates. During the first gate, teachers complete shorter assessments, such a brief questionnaire or rank order of students on the presence of internalizing and externalizing behaviors (see figure 3.4 for an example of a form). At the second gate, a teacher will complete a screening measure on the top three students identified.

Please identify three students from your class who display inappropriate externalizing behavior. Externalizing behaviors are those behaviors the student outwardly displays toward an external social environment, such as aggression, hyperactivity, noncompliance, arguing, or not following directions.

Student Name: Externalizing Behaviors	Academic Concerns?	Retaught Expectations?	Increased High-Frequency Acknowledgments?
1.			
2.			
3.			

Please identify three students from your class who display inappropriate internalizing behavior. Internalizing behaviors are those inwardly displayed behaviors, such as sadness, depression, anxiety, fearfulness, shyness, or withdrawnness.

Student Name: Internalizing Behaviors	Academic Concerns?	Retaught Expectations?	Increased High-Frequency Acknowledgments?
1.			
2.			
3.			

Source: George, 2009.

Figure 3.4: Teacher nomination form.

Alternatively, a teacher can rate students on certain dimensions (gate 1), and then the grade-level team (or department-level team) can pool its ratings and identify students for more extensive assessment (gate 2). Some gating procedures include a more extensive gate 3 in which the team conducts observations and uses more extensive rating scales (Severson, Walker, Hope-Doolittle, Kratochwill, & Gresham, 2007; Walker et al., 2014). We believe this third step is most reasonable when considering students for Tier Three.

Teacher Nomination

Schools can also have teachers identify single students for consideration for Tier Two through a *request-for-assistance* form (see figure 3.5). Teachers complete a request-for-assistance form when they have a need for support regarding one student. Such a process is beneficial because it allows identification of students throughout the year, as opposed to only the times when behavioral screening occurs. The nomination procedures can vary between schools, but individual teachers can identify a student at any point for referral for Tier Two, or the grade-level or department-level team may identify students together who need referrals for Tier Two (George, 2009).

Student's Name: _____ Date: _____

Teacher: _____ Grade: _____

Please describe the student's strengths:

Please fully describe the behaviors of concern:

1. What does the problem behavior look like? Please describe.

2. How often does the problem behavior occur?

3. How long does the problem behavior last when it does occur?

4. What is the intensity or level of danger of the problem behavior?

5. What do you think reinforces the behavior?

6. In what settings or situations is the behavior most likely to occur?

Please describe any previous strategies or interventions you used to address the behavior. How successful were they? _____

_____

_____

_____

How do you want the team to support you? _____

_____

_____

_____

Figure 3.5: Request-for-assistance form.

*Visit **MarzanoResearch.com/reproducibles** to download a free blank reproducible version of this figure.*

Diagnostic Data

At Tier Two, analyze certain data to determine the function of a student's problem behavior, but the key goal is to conduct brief analyses. (Recall that in order to create an efficient schoolwide system, Tier Two assessment is designed to be efficient, and more detailed assessment is reserved for Tier Three.) One common method is to analyze the student's ODR data to identify the student's function of the problem behavior. School teams can identify the student's most frequent function across all of the student's referrals or for particular behaviors and select an intervention that matches the function. For example, a student who has received five referrals, four of which are related to adult attention, would likely benefit from an intervention focused on providing adult attention, such as Check In–Check Out or mentoring. On the other hand, a student who has received several referrals for escaping adult attention would likely not be a good match for Check In–Check Out or mentoring.

Another avenue for school teams is to conduct a brief functional behavioral assessment (FBA; Steege & Watson, 2009). A brief FBA is a process in which team members interview staff members and observe the student's behavior to identify the function of that behavior. However, a brief FBA does not require extensive observation and interviews that are typical of a full FBA. Within appendix B (page 193), we have provided an example of an interview that staff can use to begin a brief FBA.

Progress-Monitoring Data

Once students are placed into Tier Two, the Tier Two team and those involved in providing the intervention will gather data to determine the extent to which the intervention is working. Use of progress monitoring ensures that the intervention is effective (Hosp, 2008; Shinn, 2008a) and allows schools to make decisions regarding adjustments. Whereas teachers monitor academic interventions using general outcome measures (Shinn, 2008a), there is no similar general outcome measure for social-emotional behavior (Cummings, Kaminski, & Merrell, 2008; Hawken et al., 2009). As a result, data collection will vary considerably across interventions.

The general approach is to ensure that the data-collection method is efficient (to facilitate ease of collection) and woven into the intervention itself. For example, if students are rated on their behavior at regular intervals each day, such as with Check In–Check Out, then those data are used as the data to monitor progress. Another point is to use a sensitive measure that taps into the desired outcome. For example, teachers of students receiving a classwide intervention or social skills or SEL instruction can provide a rating for each day or each week of a student's performance on the schoolwide expectations (see figure 3.6) or on specific social skills. Teachers then use those data to determine the impact of the Tier Two supports. Staff may also complete more extensive measures of behavior, such as a rating scale or brief questionnaire. Staff can administer such measures weekly or twice a month and use them for monitoring.

0 = Did not display expectation, even with prompting		1 = Displayed expectation with individual prompt		2 = Displayed expectation with classwide prompt or no prompting	
	Monday	**Tuesday**	**Wednesday**	**Thursday**	**Friday**
Be Safe	0 1 2	0 1 2	0 1 2	0 1 2	0 1 2
Be Respectful	0 1 2	0 1 2	0 1 2	0 1 2	0 1 2
Be Responsible	0 1 2	0 1 2	0 1 2	0 1 2	0 1 2

Figure 3.6: Example for monitoring expectations.

Schools can also structure brief observations and monitor students' use of certain behaviors. This approach requires more resources to implement, but it has the advantage of examining actual performance of a behavior instead of relying on perceptions of use of a behavior. A staff member may observe a student for ten minutes and tally the number of times the student displays a behavior. Observation data can be used when observing high-frequency behavior, such as on- or off-task behavior, or when the intervention is tied to one setting (for instance, a playground intervention). The staff member can measure behavior that occurs at a lower frequency, such as acts of aggression, by documenting each incidence on a tally sheet or observation sheet where he or she documents the antecedent, behavior, and consequences (Alberto & Troutman, 2013).

Fidelity Data

Throughout implementation of Tier Two, the team will routinely examine the extent to which they are implementing Tier Two with fidelity. There are specific elements of Tier Two that need to be implemented (which are the practices, systems, and data discussed in this chapter), and as we discussed with Tier One, it's easy to lose sight of those elements or to get derailed. To ensure that the Tier Two team is implementing the elements of Tier Two with fidelity, they will regularly measure and examine implementation, often by using existing measures (see table 3.5). The Tier Two team will administer one of the measures, examine the score, identify areas of strong implementation and not-so-strong implementation, and then create and execute an action plan to improve implementation.

Table 3.5: SWPBIS Fidelity Measures for Tier Two

Measure	Frequency of Administration	Format	Use
Benchmarks of Advanced Tiers (BAT) (Anderson et al., 2012)	Annually; can be more often if team wishes to assess progress	Team completes self-assessment	Assess whether foundational support systems for Tier Two and Tier Three are in place and use for action planning
Tiered Fidelity Inventory (TFI) (Algozzine et al., 2017)	Annually; can be more often if team wishes to assess progress	Team and coach complete self-assessment questionnaire by coming to consensus on each item; walkthrough tool available	Assess implementation of key features of SWPBIS across all three tiers; team uses for assessing what is currently in place as well as action planning next steps or changes related to implementation

Additionally, school staff gather data to ascertain how well they are implementing each Tier Two intervention for a given student. Staff can measure fidelity *directly* by observing implementation of the supports (Harlacher et al., 2014; Kovaleski et al., n.d.). With direct measures of fidelity, an observer identifies the series of critical steps for an intervention, observes the implementation of the intervention, and then records the number of steps implemented. The fidelity score is the total percentage of parts implemented. An example of observation fidelity sheet for Check In–Check Out is displayed in figure 3.7.

Time or Location	Item	
Morning Check In	Student checked in with adult Staff member provided daily point card Staff member provided a prompt for the student to be successful that day Student turned in home report	Yes No Did not observe Yes No Did not observe Yes No Did not observe Yes No Did not observe
Classroom	Student approached teacher to receive feedback Teacher assigned points to student Teacher provided verbal feedback regarding the student's behavior	Yes No Did not observe Yes No Did not observe Yes No Did not observe
Afternoon Check Out	Student checked out with adult Student presented complete card to adult Staff member added up and recorded total points Staff member provided verbal feedback regarding the student's behavior Staff member completed the parent report and handed to student	Yes No Did not observe Yes No Did not observe Yes No Did not observe Yes No Did not observe Yes No Did not observe

Source: Campbell, Rodriguez, Anderson, & Barnes, 2013.

Figure 3.7: Example of observation fidelity sheet for Check In–Check Out.

Observation can provide accurate data on implementation, but it can be time consuming and requires a great deal of resources (Alberto & Troutman, 2013; Kovaleski et al., n.d.). As a more efficient means of measuring fidelity, schools can use *indirect* methods. Indirect measurement of fidelity involves methods where the actual implementation of the intervention isn't observed; instead, the results or impacts of the intervention are observed, such as examining products of the intervention or having the staff report on implementation of the intervention (Kovaleski et al., n.d.).

For example, a teacher could report on the steps of Check In–Check Out that were followed when implementing the intervention. In fact, the same observation sheet could be used for the teacher to self-report the steps followed. Schools can also measure fidelity indirectly by examining lesson plans that teachers produced for social skills instruction or examining permanent products that the intervention produced (a completed daily report card, worksheets, or products from groups). Attendance is another indirect measure that is easily gathered (Kovaleski et al., n.d.). See table 3.6 for pros and cons of measuring fidelity with different methods.

Table 3.6: Pros and Cons for Types of Fidelity Tools

Measure of Fidelity	Pros	Cons	Example
Direct Measures			
Observations	Direct measure of behavior or skill	Time-intensive, requires specific expertise Some behaviors hard to efficiently observe	A co-teacher observes a lesson plan and marks off the components of the plan that he or she observed.
Indirect Measures			
Attendance	Data are easily gathered	Does not speak to quality of intervention	A teacher calculates the student's attendance rate for an intervention.
Lesson Plans	Quick, efficient, illustrates that the lesson or intervention was planned	Does not indicate that the intervention took place or who received the intervention	A teacher analyzes lesson plans to determine that the intervention targets the needed skills for the student.
Permanent Products	Illustrates that the intervention occurred	May not indicate how interactions are between student and others	A Tier Two team member analyzes a mentor's notes to determine how often the mentor is meeting with the mentee.
Self-Report of Occurrence	Quick, doesn't require much use of paper or recording	Can result in misinformation, as people can misreport	A staff member verbally reports at a Tier Two meeting that he or she provided social-skills lessons.
Self-Report Using a Checklist	Quick, efficient	Based on perceptions, people may misreport	A teacher uses a checklist of all the components of an intervention and marks off those that the intervention met.

If fidelity of an intervention is poor (less than 90 percent), then teams will want to problem solve why that is and make amends to improve fidelity. Table 3.7 illustrates some common reasons why a fidelity score may be low and possible ways to solve those issues.

Table 3.7: Fidelity Solutions

Problem	Possible Solution
Staff do not understand how to implement the intervention well	Staff need reteaching or systems need redesign to ensure that interventions can be implemented
Student or staff are not trained on the intervention or need additional skill instruction	Staff and student need reteaching of the intervention, such as teaching the student how to respond appropriately to feedback and teaching staff to give feedback that is timely and meaningful
Staff or student have not bought into the intervention (functional or theoretical mismatch)	Reconsider use of the intervention or create buy-in with student or staff member
Poor fidelity measure or misuse of the tool	Staff may need reteaching of how to administer and use the fidelity measure

Problem-Solving Model at Tier Two

Having discussed the four elements for Tier Two, we turn our attention to using the PSM at Tier Two. As with Tier One, the four key elements are the *what* of Tier Two and specify all the moving parts needed to ensure that the model is implemented well and with sustainability. The PSM can be considered the engine that drives all these parts together. At Tier Two, problem solving focuses on fidelity of implementation of Tier Two elements, the impact of Tier Two as a whole, and the identification of Tier Two for individual students (which includes examining the impact of the interventions for students and the fidelity of those interventions). Table 3.8 lists problem-solving questions about fidelity, systems, and students, as well as example outcomes.

Table 3.8: Problem-Solving Questions for Tier Two

	Implementation	Impact	
	Fidelity	Systems	Students
Questions	Is Tier Two being implemented with fidelity?	Do we have a healthy model at Tier Two?	Which students require Tier Two supports?
Example Outcomes	Scores on fidelity measures are indicative of strong implementation (for example, scores above 70 percent on the BAT).	No more than 15 percent of students need Tier Two supports. Tier Two is effective for at least 80 percent of students receiving Tier Two supports. Fidelity across all interventions is at least 90 percent.	Students receive Tier Two supports within 5 school days. Most students are achieving their respective goals within 8 to 20 weeks. Fidelity of an intervention for a given student is at least 90 percent.

Implementation

The process for examining implementation of Tier Two is the same process outlined for examining implementation of Tier One. School teams will follow the PSM and examine scores on a Tier Two fidelity measure (for instance, the BAT or TFI) to determine if there is a problem with implementation. We forgo explaining the steps again here because we have explained them in chapter 2 (page 57), but we include an example on Tier Two.

Consider a Tier Two team that administered the tiered fidelity inventory (TFI). At step 1 of the PSM (Problem Identification), they examined the overall score for Tier Two to determine if they were at the desired criterion of 70 percent. They scored a total scale score for Tier Two of 45 percent, which was well under the 70 percent criterion and signified that there was a problem with fidelity. This triggered step 2.

During step 2 of the PSM (Problem Analysis), the team answered the question, Why is fidelity low? To do so, they examined the subscales of the TFI to better understand the low score. The TFI consists of three subscale scores (teams, interventions, evaluation), and the team identified that they were below the 70 percent criterion on the interventions and the evaluation subscales. The team also examined the individual items on the TFI related to the interventions and evaluation subscales. They identified that they had scored low on the items related to matching interventions to student needs. (This school had only one Tier Two intervention, which was provided to any student needing Tier Two.) The team also scored zero on all the evaluation items, indicating that the team did not have a structured process for tracking student progress, fidelity, or evaluation of their Tier Two practices. Understanding that they were missing a variety of interventions and lacking any process for monitoring the impact of the interventions, the team was ready to move to the next step of the PSM.

In step 3 of the PSM (Plan Identification and Implementation), the Tier Two team, in conjunction with the leadership team, created a solution that included adopting a second Tier Two intervention. The team made sure that the function of the newly adopted Tier Two intervention was different from the currently used one, which would allow the team to better match students to an intervention based on the function of the student's behavior. Also, given the score on the evaluation component, the team wanted to create systems around data collection and progress monitoring. This included developing processes for gathering student performance data and fidelity data on each intervention being used. The team created an action plan and outlined the steps needed to implement their solution. The team set goals for the next six months and decided to use the TFI to monitor their progress with the solution as well as hold monthly meetings to check on the completion of the action steps. During step 4 of the PSM (Plan Evaluation), the team met, reported out on the completed action steps, and administered the TFI after six months to check impact. The team saw improvements in its TFI score, indicating that the plan was working.

Impact

The Tier Two team will also want to examine the impact of their Tier Two, which includes examining the impact of Tier Two as a whole and for individual students. At a systems level, school teams will examine data to determine the extent to which Tier Two is healthy, such as examining if no more than 15 percent of the student population needs Tier Two or that at least 80 percent of students receiving Tier Two are successful. On a student level, teams will determine which students need Tier Two and the extent to which a given student is being successful with an intervention.

Systems-Level Problem Solving

For this systems-level question, the school team determines if Tier Two is healthy. Specifically, school teams examine if no more than 15 percent of students need Tier Two supports and if at least 80 percent of students receiving Tier Two are successful.

At step 1 of the PSM (Problem Identification), the Tier Two team can determine the percentage of the student population that needs Tier Two by examining the percentage of students who are at some risk on screening measures or other indicators of risk. The team could also look at the exact percentage of students currently receiving Tier Two interventions. If any of those numbers are greater than 15 percent, they would proceed to step 2 of the PSM. Also, the team can determine if at least 80 percent of students are reaching their respective goals by calculating the percentage of students who are meeting their goal with each Tier Two intervention (for example, are 80 percent of students in Check In–Check Out reaching their goal at least four out of five days each week?). If less than 80 percent of students are successful with a given Tier Two intervention, then the team concludes there is a problem and proceeds to step 2.

During step 2 (Problem Analysis), the Tier Two team will examine possible reasons for the problem by gathering and examining data that can inform the context of the problem. If more than 15 percent of students need Tier Two, this likely indicates an issue with Tier One. Tier Two can't accommodate more than 15 percent of the student population, so the team will need to reduce the number of students needing additional support by strengthening Tier One supports.

When examining why less than 80 percent of students are successful with Tier Two, teams will want to be sure to examine the fidelity of the Tier Two interventions as part of this analysis. As mentioned previously in the Outcomes section, we recommend that fidelity of an intervention be at least 90 percent (Greenwood et al., 2008; Jimerson et al., 2007; Sailor et al., 2009). If fidelity is low (less than 90 percent), teams will want to improve fidelity and then re-evaluate the intervention's effectiveness. If fidelity is high (above 90 percent), teams can examine the key elements (practices, systems, and data) to find out why the intervention is not producing effective outcomes. Schools can examine a variety of data to determine why students are not successful with an intervention, including referrals, interviews with teachers, and fidelity data, to understand the factors contributing to the problem. Once the school team has a good understanding of why the problem is occurring, they proceed to step 3.

At step 3 of the PSM (Plan Identification and Implementation), the team identifies a goal and develops an action plan to reach that goal. The action plan details a list of steps that designated people will take to achieve the goal. The team also considers how to monitor implementation of the action plan. At step 4 of the PSM (Plan Evaluation), the team examines the implementation and impact of the action plan.

Illustration of Tier Two Systems-Level Problem Solving

To illustrate this process of evaluating Tier Two as a whole, we present an example here. Imagine a school that has no more than 15 percent of students receiving Tier Two. As part of step 1, Problem Identification, the team examined the extent to which ten students who are receiving Check In–Check Out were successful or not. A quick glance at figure 3.8 reveals that five of the ten students are successful with this Tier Two intervention. Therefore, this school only has 50 percent of students successful with Check In–Check Out. Because this is well below the ideal 80 percent criterion (indicated by the horizontal bar in figure 3.8), the team considered this a problem and proceeded to step 2.

At step 2 of the PSM (Problem Analysis), the team analyzed why 50 percent of students are successful with Check In–Check Out. This begins by examining Check In–Check Out fidelity data. The team used two sources of information for fidelity: (1) a self-report checklist from the Check In–Check Out coordinator that measured the extent to which the coordinator followed the right steps when checking students in and out, and (2) the daily point cards to determine if teachers were assigning students points at their respective

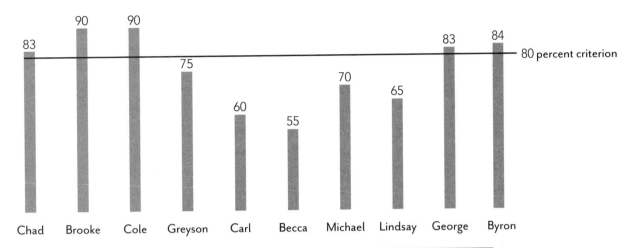

Figure 3.8: Students receiving Tier Two supports and percentage of daily points earned on Check In–Check Out.

designated intervals. The team discovered that fidelity for the checking in and out portion of the intervention was 96 percent, but that students were missing an average of 35 percent of their daily possible points, indicating that students weren't receiving their feedback at specified times. To explore why, the team divided up the task of interviewing teachers who had students on Check In–Check Out to explore why there may be missing data. The team spent a week gathering the information and identified two themes: (1) teachers felt that students should prompt teachers to receive their points and believed teachers should not initiate the conversation with the students to assign points, and (2) some teachers reported that assigning points was tough because of the specified times on the card (for instance, they were in the middle of tasks when the student's time period indicated that the teacher needed to assign points).

With that information, the team entered step 3 of the PSM (Plan Identification and Implementation). It set a goal to reduce the missing data (that is, missing points from students' daily point cards) to no more than 5 percent. It developed a plan that included several components:

▲ Two members of the Tier Two team retrained all of the staff in Check In–Check Out. They elected to use fifteen minutes at the next staff meeting, during which they reviewed the fidelity data the team used with the staff. The two members then focused on the importance of providing points each time and indicated that although students should initiate the conversation for points, these students may need prompts and scaffolding at first to ensure they ask for points.

▲ The Tier Two leadership team also adjusted the point card for Check In–Check Out by removing the times on the card and instead listed the subjects each student had during the day. In this way, teachers would provide points at the end of each subject covered instead of at a specified time.

▲ The Check In–Check Out coordinator had conversations with students in Check In–Check Out about initiating the conversation with their teachers about feedback and the responsibility of getting the daily point card completed each time.

▲ Implementation of the plan was documented with self-report information, as all team members reported that the retraining occurred at the next Tier Two meeting. The team monitored impact by analyzing the percentage of missing data on students' daily point cards.

At step 4 (Plan Evaluation), the team analyzed the fidelity data two weeks later. The percentage of missing data had declined to just 3 percent, and the fidelity of the checking in and out of students had stayed above 95 percent. The team concluded the plan was successful because it had reached its goal of no more than 5 percent of missing data on students' daily point cards. This example illustrates how the Tier Two team took a systemic view of its Tier Two and used the PSM to solve an identified issue. This is in contrast to problem solving for an individual student, as in this example, the team viewed all ten of the students as the whole. We next discuss using the PSM to problem solve for individual students.

For Tier Two student-level problem solving, teams begin by asking which students need Tier Two supports. By walking through the PSM with this question, Tier Two teams will identify and provide students with Tier Two supports and determine the effectiveness of that intervention.

At step 1 (Problem Identification), students are initially identified for Tier Two using screening data (as discussed in the Data section earlier). Part of this step includes examining other sources of information to ensure that the students actually are at some level of risk and require Tier Two. If a student has one red flag, the school team examines other data sources to determine if the new source is accurate and indicates the need for Tier Two, such as attendance, visits to health aid or the nurse's office, school records, grades, teacher nomination data, or other screeners. Once the student's risk status is verified, the school team analyzes information to determine what level of support is most appropriate during step 2.

In step 2 of the PSM (Problem Analysis), school teams gather or examine additional data to determine why the problem is occurring or why the student is at risk. This involves identifying the problem behavior's function, which can be as simple as looking at the functions of behavior marked on the student's ODRs. If they gather additional data to determine the behavior's function or to understand its context, they do it with efficiency and ease, such as administering a brief questionnaire that a teacher completes, conducting a brief FBA, or reviewing records and pre-existing data. In-depth assessment during this step is reserved for students who need Tier Three.

In step 3 (Plan Identification and Implementation), the team uses information from step 2 to design or select an intervention that matches the function of the student's problem behavior. For example, students whose behavior functions to obtain adult attention may be assigned to Check In–Check Out or mentoring (Hawken et al., 2011; McIntosh et al., 2009), whereas students escaping from work may be assigned an academic intervention (Lane et al., 2002). School teams have a menu of Tier Two interventions matched to functions of behavior, so during step 3, they select the most appropriate one for the student.

In step 4 of the PSM (Plan Evaluation), school teams examine the impact of the support for each student by examining a student's growth and making decisions as to whether the student will reach his or her goal. Additionally, the team also analyzes the implementation of the specific intervention the student is receiving. Whereas the intervention may be implemented well overall, teams will want to examine fidelity data for that particular student.

If the fidelity is poor, then the student has not received the desired intervention. In such instances, the school team will improve fidelity and continue the intervention (essentially, the intervention is a redo since the student hasn't received it yet). If fidelity is strong and the student is successful with the intervention, the team can discuss fading out and discontinuing the intervention. If fidelity is strong and the student is not successful, then the team can focus on information as to why that is the case. The team can examine the match between function of the student's problem behavior and the focus of the intervention, adjust the intervention, provide a different intervention, or refer the student for more intensive services.

An additional consideration is the context of the intervention and the rest of the students receiving that intervention. It's tempting to change an intervention for a single student who is not making growth; however, the team should examine if the other students in the group are making growth. If multiple students are doing poorly or encountering the same or a similar problem in an intervention, the team is dealing with a systemic issue. For example, a team may review student-level data and identify that a student is not regularly checking out at the end of the day. If this problem then arises for another student or two, it may indicate a need to adjust the check-out system for all students or a subgroup of students (for instance, fourth graders have physical education at the end of the day and don't want to miss it) rather than try to make three or four individual changes for each student with the end-of-day check-out challenge. On the other hand, if the rest of the group is making growth, then decisions can be made for that student. (Incidentally, the school can also be fairly confident that this intervention is effective, but not for that one particular student.)

Illustration of Tier Two Student-Level Problem Solving

To illustrate the process for identifying and providing support for students at Tier Two, we share an example of a student-level Tier Two process. Consider one student in the sixth grade. This student had received three referrals within one week while on the playground for saying inappropriate things to his peers, which led to a total of five referrals over the past quarter (he had three previous referrals for repeated disruptive behavior in the classroom). Step 1 was triggered when the student's sixth-grade teacher completed a request-for-assistance form for the Tier Two school-level team. The Tier Two team determined that the student needed additional support because of his repeated past behavior and the current number of major referrals. The referrals and the request-for-assistance form were considered two points of data to indicate that a problem existed and a solution was needed.

At step 2 (Problem Analysis), the Tier Two team examined why the problem was occurring by estimating the function of the student's behavior. It examined the student's referrals and found that "seeking peer attention" was the estimated function of his undesired behavior. The team surmised that the behavior was maintained by peer attention. You'll note how brief this stage was for a student for Tier Two. The team quickly pulled up the student's referrals and produced a frequency count for the functions of behavior for the student's referral because they had an efficient, easy-to-use system supporting them.

During step 3 of the PSM (Plan Identification and Implementation), the team decided on a goal and an intervention that matched the hypothesized function of the behavior (peer attention). It decided that the student needed more instruction on interacting appropriately with students during recess, so the team assigned the student to a social skills intervention. The team also felt that the intervention only needed to focus on the student's use of certain skills on the playground, as that's where the problem behavior occurred. The social skills coordinator, who was the school psychologist, contacted the student and his parents to discuss the purpose of the intervention. The Tier Two team lead contacted the student's teacher to inform the teacher of the intervention.

For this intervention, the student was taught more appropriate skills to use when interacting with classmates by the school psychologist over the course of three sessions in two weeks. Following those three sessions, the student checked in with the dean at the start of recess. The dean then monitored the student's behavior at recess by providing proximity supervision and reinforcement for use of appropriate social skills (the dean also provided reinforcement to other students for use of the schoolwide expectations, but she paid particular attention to this student). The dean was chosen to monitor the student's use of skills because she was already acting as the playground supervisor and could easily supervise the student. The team set a goal to have zero major referrals for four weeks (which was the end of the quarter and a natural break in the school year). The team agreed to use major ODRs as the measurement of impact and to gather fidelity data by having the school psychologist and dean self-report on the extent to which they provided the intervention. Note that fidelity was verbal data provided to the Tier Two team, making it easy data to gather.

During step 4 (Plan Evaluation), the team met after one week and examined the plan. The school psychologist and the dean reported that they had provided the intervention to 100 percent fidelity; the school psychologist provided three sessions and the dean monitored the student for five out of five days. These data were recorded on the minutes sheet and kept in the records for the Tier Two log. The team noted that there were zero referrals for the student since the start of the intervention (the dean also noted that the student was using the skills and she was seeing appropriate interactions with the student and others). As a result of the data, the team decided to continue the intervention and check on the student's progress in two weeks. The student continued to have zero referrals and display appropriate behavior, so the team pulled back the supervision of the dean and instead had the student report to the dean after each recess how his behavior was for the next two weeks. The team met again right before the end of the quarter, and the data showed that the student had zero referrals. The team decided to fade back the Tier Two intervention at that time, as the student had met his goal of zero referrals in four weeks.

Within this section, we discussed how we can use the PSM to identify and solve problems for Tier Two for implementation and for impact at a systems level and student level. We summarize the questions and steps of the PSM across implementation and impact for Tier Two in table 3.9.

Table 3.9: Use of the Problem-Solving Model at Tier Two

| | Implementation | Impact | |
	Fidelity	Systems	Students
Problem-Solving Step	Is Tier Two being implemented with fidelity?	Do we have a healthy model at Tier Two?	Which students require Tier Two supports?
Step 1: Problem Identification	Administer and examine the overall score on a given fidelity measure (for example, BAT or TFI).	Identify an overall measure of impact, such as no more than 15 percent of students need Tier Two supports or that 80 percent of students reach their Tier Two goal.	Identify students by using screening measures, pre-existing data, and teacher nomination. Validate the need for support.
Step 2: Problem Analysis	If the outcome is less than the criterion specified by measure, then examine the subcomponents.	Gather and analyze data as to why the problem is occurring, including fidelity information.	Examine ODRs or other information to identify a function of behavior.
Step 3: Plan Identification and Implementation	Develop an action plan to improve implementation of Tier Two and a method to measure implementation of the action plan. Identify a way to measure the impact of that action plan.	Develop an action plan to improve the effectiveness of Tier Two.	Provide supports for individual students.
Step 4: Plan Evaluation	Evaluate the implementation and impact of the action plan.	Evaluate the implementation and impact of the action plan.	Monitor supports using fidelity measures and progress monitoring as determined by the team and the intervention. If the student is not showing growth, consider the fidelity of the intervention and the intensity of supports, and match of function of behavior to make decisions regarding the intensity of the plan. If the student is making progress, consider reducing or fading services.

Summary

Within this chapter, we described the four key elements for Tier Two and how the PSM can be used to resolve issues related to implementation and impact of Tier Two. Tier Two is designed to meet the needs of 10–15 percent of the student population who need a little bit more support to learn and meet the schoolwide expectations and is intended for students with behavioral challenges (but not for those with dangerous or unsafe behavior problems).

Tier Two teams will determine exact Tier Two outcomes, but these outcomes typically include that no more than 15 percent of students in the school need Tier Two, that at least

80 percent of students receiving Tier Two interventions are successful, and that individual students see improvements in their behavioral functioning. The practices of Tier Two are the specific interventions that will be used in the school to reach those outcomes. To support the staff's use of those practices, schools put systems into place for Tier Two, which begins with the creation of a Tier Two team. This team oversees all of the Tier Two processes and procedures, including securing funding and resources, providing training and coaching to staff members, and overseeing procedures to select, provide, and progress monitor interventions for students. Overall, the systems should allow students to receive support quickly matched to the function of their problem behaviors. Data for Tier Two includes screening data to identify students, brief diagnostic data to identify why students need support or why a problem is occurring, progress-monitoring data to evaluate impact of their interventions, and fidelity data to ensure interventions are implemented as intended. Across those four elements, the leadership team uses the PSM to examine fidelity of implementation and the impact of Tier Two at both a systems level (Tier Two's overall health) and a student level (which students need support). The four key elements overlap, and the PSM provides a framework that entails knowledge and consideration of those elements.

Tier Three

Once schools have implemented Tier One and Tier Two with fidelity, they can turn their attention to implementing Tier Three. Tier Three interventions are designed for 3–5 percent of the student population whose behavioral needs warrant individualized and comprehensive supports (Scott et al., 2009). Such supports are provided to students who have not been successful with less intensive supports (that is, Tiers One and Two) and for students who demonstrate behavior that is chronic, severe, intense, or dangerous enough to warrant immediate Tier Three supports (Anderson & Scott, 2009; Horner et al., 2010). Like Tier Two interventions, Tier Three interventions incorporate reteaching expectations, increasing the explicitness of expectations, and providing additional structure for prompts, practice, feedback, and acknowledgment for engaging in appropriate behaviors. In fact, Tier Three interventions may utilize modified or intensified Tier Two interventions (Greenwood et al., 2008; Sailor et al., 2009). However, teachers may deliver Tier Three interventions for a longer time compared to Tier Two supports and Tier Three supports are more individualized. Teachers provide Tier Three supports in addition to Tier One supports after students have received high-quality Tier Two supports (although some students' behaviors may warrant Tier Three without going through Tier Two first), and teachers plan them so that there is an opportunity to fade back to Tier Two or Tier One supports over time, if possible (Anderson & Scott, 2009; Scott et al., 2009). Some students may need individualized, comprehensive behavioral supports throughout their educational careers (Walker, Ramsey, & Gresham, 2004). A summary of the features of Tier Three is in table 4.1 (page 106).

Tier Three supports have three distinguishing characteristics: (1) intensive, (2) individualized, and (3) comprehensive. Tier Three is *intensive*, as students receiving Tier Three supports receive the school's strongest and most thorough supports (Chard et al., 2008; Horner, Sugai, et al., 2005). The school does this to match the severity of the behavior concerns students have at Tier Three (Anderson, Horner, Rodriguez, & Stiller, 2013). Because schools devote a lot of resources to students at this level, it's important that those students considered for Tier Three have the most severe needs and that those needs cannot be met with Tier One or Tier Two supports.

Tier Three supports are also *individualized* (Scott et al., 2009). School teams need more time to develop and provide Tier Three supports compared to Tier Two supports, but the

Table 4.1: Tier Three Summary

Tier Three Is . . .	Tier Three Is Not . . .
For students with severe, dangerous, violent, or chronic behavior problems	For students with mild or acute behavior problems that can be addressed with Tier Two or Tier One supports
For students who need individualized assessment to design a unique comprehensive behavior plan	A canned approach to dealing with behavior
Provided by staff with behavioral expertise	Provided by staff without the necessary skills or training to provide it
Provided efficiently, even though several weeks may be needed for assessment	Delayed for months
Coordinated with parents or guardians and sometimes also with community or outside agencies	Done in isolation from home

result is a more comprehensive and individualized intervention (Greenwood et al., 2008). At Tier Two, the school provides supports to students based on group needs with efficient assessment and intervention delivery. For Tier Three, the school team carefully examines the unique needs of each individual student identified for supports. School teams conduct in-depth assessments and use the information they gather to design an individualized plan for each student receiving Tier Three supports (Harlacher, Sanford, & Walker, n.d.).

Lastly, Tier Three is *comprehensive* (Chard et al., 2008; Crone & Horner, 2003; Scott et al., 2009). It is comprehensive because the supports it provides address the antecedents that trigger the problem behaviors, the consequences that maintain the behaviors, and any setting events that may influence them. The supports also include teaching relevant skills to increase short- and long-term success. They ideally have a strong school-home component to the supports and some connection of the parents or guardians and the student with community supports (Scott et al., 2009). On a final note, because the supports necessary to implement individualized plans are complex and student success is context-dependent (each individual teacher defines acceptable behavior for the individual classroom or setting, and different settings may have slightly unique environmental features and criteria for success), it is ideal to implement individualized behavior supports in school environments that proactively set clear expectations and maximize student success (for example, the school is implementing Tier One supports well or has classrooms with high levels of student engagement).

"The training I've received in PBIS has given me the skills to work with students at every tier. It is empowering to know that I can assist my teams to help increase student success using positive approaches and that these ideas can be applied to all levels of need and ability. As a practitioner, PBIS is truly applied to all aspects of my job, every day, with everyone."

—Candice Orr, licensed educational psychologist, Glendora Unified School District, Glendora, California
(personal communication, April 13, 2016)

As with the previous chapters, we organized this chapter along the four key elements (outcomes, practices, systems, and data) within the context of Tier Three of SWPBIS. We describe common outcomes of Tier Three and then discuss the practices, systems, and data that are a part of this tier. We end with the application of the PSM for systems and students and provide examples of each.

Outcomes

As with Tiers One and Two, the leadership team should identify the outcomes they wish to achieve with Tier Three. These outcomes can be defined for implementation and impact at both the systems level and the individual student level.

First, the Tier Three elements should be implemented with fidelity. As with Tiers One and Two, there are critical elements necessary to have an effective Tier Three system within the SWPBIS model, so schools will use fidelity measures to ensure that they have all the necessary components of Tier Three in place. School teams should also see Tier Three specific interventions implemented with fidelity, which means that they generally provide interventions with scores of at least 80 to 90 percent on fidelity measures. We discussed a rationale for 90 percent fidelity for interventions in chapter 3, but for Tier Three, fidelity is dependent on the intensity of the intervention, the number of components, and which components are function based. Teams will need to define an acceptable level for each intervention dependent on the unique situations encountered, but we offer 80 percent as a suggested fidelity starting point criterion for Tier Three interventions.

At the systems level, the goal of Tier Three supports is to reduce the frequency, intensity, and severity of behaviors of concern among the student population (that is, only 3 to 5 percent of students need and receive Tier Three supports) and ensure all students who need this level of support have access to it. Additionally, although the individualized nature of Tier Three supports makes it difficult to compare students to each other and to set group-level outcomes, schools should nevertheless evaluate their Tier Three supports overall. The school can assess if their Tier Three services are reaching all students who need them and determine whether they are effective for most students. To do this, teams will likely use the 80 percent criterion discussed for Tier Two (that is, at least 80 percent of students are progressing toward individualized goals with Tier Three supports). Schools may consider other outcomes, such as what amount of time it takes for students to progress toward goals and if the processes related to Tier Three are well received and working for the students, school staff, and parents. The Tier Three team can also look at the big picture and determine if the time between identification of Tier Three supports and the implementation of Tier Three supports is reasonable. It's not uncommon that schools identify students who need support, but logistics or other barriers delay or prevent provision of that support. As such, schools can also examine if all students who need Tier Three are receiving such supports.

Students should see increases in their prosocial skills and reductions in the frequency, intensity, and severity of their problematic behaviors. Other goals may include improvement in social-emotional skills and increases in academic performance. For those students who are not progressing after a reasonable amount of time, an individual outcome may be a change in their current supports to better accommodate their needs (for instance, referral for a special education evaluation or further intensifying the intervention).

Schools will outline the outcomes they wish to achieve as a system, such as implementing Tier Three elements with fidelity and ensuring that most students are successful with Tier Three supports. They will also identify individual outcomes for students who are receiving

Tier Three interventions. Having discussed examples of outcomes for Tier Three, we next discuss the practices we use for Tier Three to achieve those outcomes.

Practices

Tier Three practices are those strategies and methods that support student behavior to achieve the defined outcomes. Instead of selecting an intervention from a menu for a student (as in Tier Two), schools conduct a more extensive process that includes conducting an individualized assessment and using the results to identify the exact interventions and strategies they will use for each student who receives Tier Three supports. Within this practices section, we describe this individualized assessment process, called a *functional behavior assessment* (FBA; Crone & Horner, 2003), and we discuss the corresponding individualized interventions and strategies, which comprise the behavior support plan (BSP; also referred to as a *behavior intervention plan*; Scott et al., 2009). An FBA is an assessment process where data are gathered to determine student strengths as well as the conditions under which the behavior of concern occurs. This includes identifying the setting events, antecedents, and consequences associated with the behaviors. The result of the FBA is a summary statement indicating a clear definition of the behaviors of concern, the conditions under which the behavior occurs, the most common outcome of the behavior, and a hypothesis as to why the behavior is occurring (that is, the function of the behavior). The results of the FBA are used to inform the creation of a BSP (Carr et al., 2002; Crone & Horner, 2003; O'Neill et al., 1997). A BSP is an intensive, individualized plan that is function based and addresses the behavioral needs of the student. A BSP is not just one practice; instead, it is a collection of various practices, strategies, and interventions that are designed to teach, prompt, and encourage the student to engage in appropriate replacement behaviors and to mitigate the need for use of the problem behavior (Bambara & Kern, 2005; Crone & Horner, 2003; Loman, Rodriguez, & Borgmeier, 2014; O'Neill et al., 1997). As such, the specific strategies within a BSP should vary between students receiving Tier Three interventions. We first discuss what an FBA entails, followed by what a BSP entails.

Functional Behavior Assessment

As mentioned, an FBA is an intensive and iterative assessment process designed to help teams understand the function of a student's behavior (Crone & Horner, 2003). The ultimate goals of the FBA are to explicitly define the behaviors of concern for the student and to identify the environmental conditions that appear to trigger and maintain the student's behaviors (Scott et al., 2009). Each FBA should result in a summary statement, which describes a prediction of the problem behavior and a detailed summary of when and where it occurs. By gathering information on the student's behavior, the team creates a hypothesis as to why it is occurring. From this hypothesis, the team can create a BSP. A complete FBA includes the following five outcomes. We discuss each of these in depth next.

1. A clear description of the problem behavior
2. Identification of the antecedents that predict the behavior
3. Identification of the consequences that serve to maintain the behavior
4. Summary statements that describe specific behaviors and situations that trigger and maintain the behaviors
5. Data to indicate accuracy of summary statements (O'Neill et al., 1997).

A Clear Description of the Problem Behavior

The FBA process begins with a clear description of the problem behavior. A problem behavior is one that is undesired or one that educators or families want students to stop using. The team first operationally defines the behavior, meaning that it describes the behavior in concrete and observable terms so that two or more people who are otherwise unfamiliar with the behavior can consistently identify and measure it. The operational definition of behavior should clearly describe what the behavior looks like, including the frequency, intensity, or duration (O'Neill et al., 1997). In fact, the description should be so clear that a stranger could read it and identify the behavior if he or she observed it. For example, a problem behavior of "not doing work" should be defined in observable and measurable terms (for example, the student completes, on average, 50 percent of her independent work). One way to further clarify the definition of problem behavior is to use examples and nonexamples of behavior to illustrate the definition. For example, the behavior of bullying can be defined as "making inappropriate comments or actions toward a peer." The definition can be further refined to indicate that a nonexample of bullying is "playful teasing among friends where both are laughing and enjoying the interaction." In addition to ensuring that the team defines target behaviors so they are concrete and measurable, it is also import to consider and ensure that changing the target behavior will result in meaningful changes for the student (for example, the target behavior is not just annoying to others but interferes with a meaningful life activity for the student such as learning or safety).

Table 4.2 shows sample behavioral descriptors that are broad and not measurable as well as examples (not all-inclusive definitions) of ways to make these terms more observable and measurable.

Table 4.2: Problem Behaviors That Are Operationally Defined

Nonobservable and Immeasurable Description	More Observable and Measurable Description
Disruption	Talks when teacher is lecturing; calls out in a loud voice; sings or makes noises that the teacher or other students can hear during instruction
Off-task	Draws pictures on paper rather than completing assignment; completes less than 50 percent of assigned independent work
Inattention	Taps or drums on the desk; looks around the classroom; starts but does not finish tasks
Noncompliance	Passively (for example, without verbally refusing) does not follow direction within one minute of providing direction
Defiance	Verbally refuses when given a direction (such as yelling, "No" or stating, "You can't make me")
Academic engagement	Student is looking at the board, overhead, teacher, or seatwork, contributing to or writing or reading the assigned task, and is quiet when the expectation is to work independently

As part of operationally defining a problem behavior, it is critical to assess whether there are skills deficits (that is, the student has not acquired the appropriate behavior and must be taught), fluency issues (that is, the student knows how to do the appropriate behavior but has difficulty doing it well), or performance issues (that is, the student knows how to do the behavior and has practiced it but is not engaging in the desired behaviors in the desired environmental context; Gresham et al., 2006). It is also important to assess whether problem behavior may be competing with (or more effective for the student in getting his or her needs met) an appropriate behavior. This helps us understand how problem behaviors are working for a given student, and this information allows us to build interventions accordingly. Research suggests that many students who need support engaging in appropriate social behaviors do not have a skill deficit but rather have a fluency or performance deficit (Gresham et al., 2006). This helps us understand why many students with intensive needs require more than just reteaching expectations. We must develop interventions that help minimize the payoff for the competing problem behavior while simultaneously motivating and shaping the student's skill set to engage in increasingly appropriate or desired behaviors.

Identification of the Antecedents That Predict the Behavior

Once the team has operationally defined the target behaviors, it then gathers data and information regarding the *antecedents* of the behavior, which are the conditions, routines, and situations that trigger the behavior. Essentially, the antecedents are the "go" buttons for the behavior: What are the conditions that predict the behavior will occur? Antecedents can be various things, such as asking the student to read aloud, presenting the student with a worksheet, completing independent seatwork, or a peer saying something mean to the student. The more precisely defined the antecedents are for the behavior, the more likely the team can develop effective interventions. For example, if a student is disruptive within reading group, this is helpful but incomplete data. However, if the team also discovers that the disruptive behavior occurs during reading group *and* when the student is asked to read out loud, a more complete picture of the student's antecedents emerges. In determining the antecedents, the focus is on precision and finely defining the exact conditions that trigger the behavior so that the team can put a very specific, feasible, and efficient strategy into place (discussed later in the BSP section).

School teams may also identify setting events as part of their FBA process. Setting events are events that are removed in time from the antecedent but ones that influence the strength of the consequence for the student, thereby altering the probability that a behavior will be reinforced (Alberto & Troutman, 2013). In many cases for students, setting events introduce fatigue or stress that change the value of doing what is asked of them. For example, if a student is very tired, getting out of the task and taking a nap may be more reinforcing than completing the task and earning a fun activity at the end. Common examples of setting events can be the presence of stressors in the home, feeling tired or hungry, and having a previous confrontation with someone. In some cases, teams may not identify a setting event, but they will always identify antecedents.

Identification of the Consequences That Serve to Maintain the Behavior

Once the Tier Three team has defined the behavior of concern and identified the antecedents, it then assesses the consequences of the behavior, which are the events that occur after the behavior. Unlike the colloquial use of the term *consequences*, which has a negative connotation, consequences in this case refer to any events following behavior. By gathering information on the consequences, or what happens after the behavior occurs, the team can then hypothesize about the function of the behavior—in other words, What is the purpose of the behavior? The functions of behavior are categorized as either to get or get away from one of three things: (1) something tangible, such as an activity, task, or object; (2) social attention, either an adult's or a peer's; or (3) something sensory or a source of stimulation (Alberto & Troutman, 2013; Baer et al., 1968; Skinner, 1953, 1976; Watson, 1913; Wolery et al., 1988). Documenting what typically happens following the behavior enables school teams to look for patterns in how the behavior is beneficial for a student in a context. This will allow the team to understand the function or purpose the behavior serves for the student. See figure 4.1.

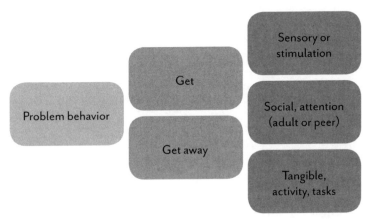

Note: Get = obtain, get something; Get away = escape, avoid something.

Figure 4.1: Common functions of behavior.

Because the same behavior can serve different functions or purposes in different contexts, it is important that teams discuss the behavioral function within the context of specific settings or routines after they have defined antecedents (see figure 4.2, page 112). For students with chronic problem behaviors across multiple settings, it will likely be necessary to build multiple hypothesis statements for each different setting. For example, a team may determine that a student engages in physical aggression during small-group instruction and during recess. During small-group instruction, the student uses physical aggression, is then removed from the group, and does not have to do the work. This results in a hypothesized function of escaping work. During recess, however, the same student uses physical aggression to obtain a ball on the playground. This leads to a hypothesized function of obtaining an item. Therefore, even though the student is engaging in the same problem behavior (physical aggression) in multiple settings, the team will need to articulate two different hypothesis statements that will lead to different interventions for each setting. Other times, the same behavior can have the same function across multiple settings, thereby leading to only one hypothesis statement. Teams will determine the number of hypotheses needed based on the results of the FBA. A hypothesis about a student's behavior is called a *summary statement*, which we discuss next. We present common examples of setting events, antecedents, and consequences in table 4.3 (page 112).

Sometimes very similar behaviors can serve very different purposes and warrant very different interventions. For example, a school team was having difficulty understanding the function of a kindergarten student's behavior. When they asked for support from the behavior specialist, they said, "This child (pseudonym Sam) just wants to be in control, but we know we need a more precise function of problem behavior. We need help. He can't be in control all the time." When the specialist went in to work with the team, she realized Sam had one primary form of communication—physical aggression. During independent work time, he hit, pushed, and tried to bite the adult working with him to avoid the work. During time to line up, he engaged in similar behaviors, but the function was to attempt to gain the first spot in line. During recess, he hit and kicked peers to interact with them (to access peer attention). Therefore, it became clear that the team needed to think about why Sam was engaging in physical aggression within each context and routine as well as identify specific triggers to his behavior to start to develop interventions that would be effective in each routine. One intervention strategy targeting physical aggression was not going to work for Sam. His behavior was serving different functions in different contexts. The team also identified that Sam needed more socially appropriate forms of communication to meet his needs, and they designed a plan that focused on teaching him simple gestural and picture communication strategies in addition to specific strategies to minimize the likelihood of problem behavior in each context based on the specific triggers and functions of behavior in each context.

Figure 4.2: Why understand behavior in the context?

Table 4.3: Examples of Setting Events, Antecedents, and Consequences

Setting Events	Antecedents	Consequences
Argues with parent at home before school	Asked to do group work	Ignored by other students
Lacks sleep	Asked to share items with peers in learning centers	Talked privately with students
Forgets to take medication	Requested by teacher to move to end of line	Completed work later
Experiences changes in routines	Asked to write five-sentence paragraph	Didn't complete work
Has previous conflicts with peer	Asked to read silently	Interacted with peer

Summary Statements

Once the team gathers information about antecedents, consequences, and setting events, it can develop a clear hypothesis about the function of the behavior. A summary statement includes information about (1) context and antecedent triggers for problem behavior (when and where); (2) an operational definition of the problem behaviors; and (3) outcomes that follow the problem behavior and appear to maintain it (that is, consequences that may be positive or negative; Crone & Horner, 2003; Loman et al., 2014; O'Neill et al., 1997). The statement also should include a hypothesis about why the student engages in the problem behavior (that is, the function of behavior) and may include information about environmental events that are more removed from the immediate triggers but appear to consistently and systematically relate to the behavior pattern (that is, setting events). The team can write out the summary statement. For instance, *During English class, when Joie is asked to write a paper more than two pages long, Joie tears up her paper and throws it on the floor, which results in her being sent to the hallway. This is more likely to happen when Joie has skipped lunch. Therefore, we hypothesize that the function of this behavior is to avoid writing papers more than two pages long.* The team can also display the summary statement in a visual format (see figure 4.3).

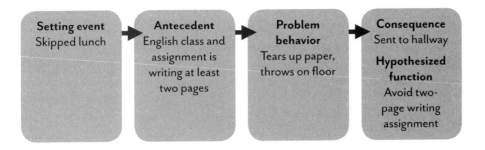

Figure 4.3: Summary statement illustration and example.

Data to Indicate Accuracy of Summary Statements

The fifth outcome of an FBA is having data to confirm the hypothesis or summary statement. It is fairly easy to interview someone and develop a summary statement about a student's behavior, but that information is meaningless if it's not accurate. Consequently, Tier Three teams will gather confirmatory data on the summary statement to ensure that their hypothesis about the student's behavior is correct. We discuss the information gathered for an FBA later in the Data section, but for now, we simply note that FBAs need data to confirm hypotheses.

Behavior Support Plan

The FBA is one key practice of Tier Three. The second is the BSP. Using the results of the FBA, the Tier Three team designs a BSP that addresses each of the components of the summary statement (setting events, antecedents, behavior, and consequences). The team puts strategies into place to do the following five things.

1. Neutralize or offset any setting events
2. Reduce or remove antecedents that trigger the behavior and prompt appropriate behaviors
3. Teach new behaviors to the student
4. Reinforce the alternative and desired behaviors and remove reinforcement for the problem behavior
5. Monitor the implementation and impact of the BSP

BSPs have three key characteristics (Crone & Horner, 2003; O'Neill et al., 1997). First, effective environments should make the problem behaviors irrelevant by removing aversive antecedent triggers or modifying the antecedent so that it does not trigger the problem behavior. Second, effective environments work to make sure problem behaviors are inefficient. Teams should teach and provide appropriate behavioral alternatives that efficiently meet a student's needs. Specifically, the student should have access to a more appropriate behavior that requires less energy and time to use than a problem behavior. For example, a student who throws tantrums to have his or her needs met can be taught to simply show a help card to have his or her needs met; here, the new behavior (the help card) is more efficient to use than the problem behavior (tantrum). Lastly, problem behaviors should be made ineffective by ensuring that they are not rewarded. The staff and environment should ensure that the appropriate behavior *is* rewarded and the problem behavior *is not* rewarded. For the student who throws tantrums, this would entail ignoring the tantrum or waiting until the student shows a help card before providing adult attention (reinforcement in this case). Those three words—(1) *irrelevant*, (2) *inefficient*, and (3) *ineffective*—are ultimately the collective goal of a BSP for creating effective environments conducive to positive behavior.

Prior to creating the BSP, the school team providing Tier Three supports completes a competing behavior pathway (see figure 4.4), which is a visual display of the summary statement from the FBA (see boxes AA, A, B, and C of figure 4.4) and includes the long-term (box E) and short-term (box D) goal behaviors for the student (Crone & Horner, 2003; O'Neill et al., 1997). This is the outcomes element of Tier Three at the student level. The team identifies the desired behavior that the student should be using (that is, the long-term goal; see box E in figure 4.4). The team also identifies the natural outcomes for this behavior (that is, what the typical student receives for performing this behavior; see box F in figure 4.4). However, it may take several days, weeks, or months for a student to fluently use a desired behavior, and the payoff for using desired behaviors is often different than the payoff (function) of problem behavior. Consequently, the student is using the problem behavior to obtain a desired payoff (box C in figure 4.4) because of its functional purpose (noted in box G in figure 4.4). To prevent this, a team can teach a temporary alternative behavior (that is, the short-term goal) to the student that serves the same function as the problem behavior but is decidedly less aversive compared to the problem behavior (see box D in figure 4.4). This alternative behavior should meet three critical criteria. It should serve the same function or purpose as the problem behavior (Carr, 1997; Sprague & Horner, 1999), be as easy or easier to do than the problem behavior (Horner & Day, 1991), and be socially acceptable (Haring, 1988).

During _____ (Routine)

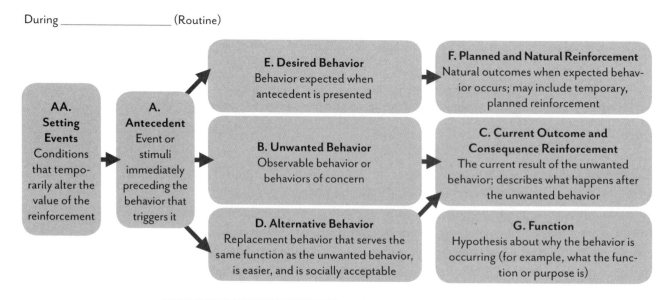

Figure 4.4: Competing behavior pathway.

Table 4.4 shows a brief description of each strategy component as part of a comprehensive BSP as well as the critical features for each component. Note that the groups of strategies (prevention, behavior, and consequence) align with the elements of the competing behavior pathway.

Table 4.4: Behavior Support Plan Strategies

	Prevention Strategies		Teaching Behavior Strategies	Consequence Strategies
	Setting Event Strategies	Antecedent Strategies		
Focus	Although not always present or identifiable, manipulate the setting event to offset its impact on the reinforcement (when possible)	Manipulate the antecedent to prevent problem behavior and promote desired behavior	Explicitly teach alternative (short term) and desired (long term) behaviors	Alter consequences to reinforce alternative and desired behaviors while also extinguishing the unwanted behavior.
Guidelines	Intervention should directly address the setting event by removing the setting event or minimizing its impact by building neutralizing strategies	Intervention should: (1) directly address the identified antecedent, (2) directly address the function of the problem behavior	Provide explicit instruction of the alternative behavior that serves the same function, is easier or as easy as the problem behavior, and is socially accepted; explicitly teach skills necessary to engage in desired behaviors or approximations thereof	Include reinforcement of alternative behavior and desired behavior, ensure that reinforcers are valued, set up reinforcement schedule based on reasonable expectations and timeframe, prompt the appropriate behavior at earliest sign of problem behavior, eliminate or limit access to reinforcement for engaging in problem behavior

Once the team identifies the long-term goal (desired behavior) and short-term goal (alternative behaviors) for the student, the team can then proceed to specifying the BSP. Comprehensive BSP strategies incorporate three main components outlined in table 4.4.

1. **Behavior teaching strategies** to teach a replacement behavior and the desired behavior
2. **Prevention strategies, which include antecedent and setting event strategies,** to prompt appropriate behavior and remove or neutralize events that precede the problem behavior
3. **Consequence strategies** to reinforce appropriate behavior (or approximations thereof) and prevent the problem behavior from benefitting the student; this may include crisis response and safety plan strategies for students whose behavior has the potential to become extremely dangerous

A BSP will also include strategies to monitor the implementation and impact of the BSP. As perhaps is clear now with SWPBIS, using any practice includes measuring the implementation and the impact of the practice. We discuss measuring implementation and impact within the Data and Problem-Solving Model sections (pages 127 and 133, respectively) within this chapter, but for now, we describe each of the three strategies of the BSP. We also present an example of student-level problem solving for Tier Three in the PSM section (page 136) later in this chapter.

Behavior Teaching Strategies

Behavior strategies are those specific interventions and strategies that teach the student the new desired behaviors as well as the temporary alternative behaviors. Although a team should identify the specific behaviors based on the student's current skills and desired level of performance, there are many common skills that students likely need to learn, depending on the hypothesized function of the student's problem behavior. The team will then determine the specific techniques to teach both the desired and alternative behaviors. We have summarized some of the common skills deficits according to function of problem behavior in table 4.5. As mentioned earlier, the team may use interventions that are a part of Tier Two, but these interventions are modified to meet the needs of the students in Tier Three. For example, teachers can teach new skills in a social skills group or as part of a classwide intervention in addition to incorporating other components for preventing and responding to behaviors in the individual's BSP. The key is to remember the behavior strategies are used to teach students the skills necessary to have their needs met.

Because chronic problem behaviors are essentially habits for the student, the short-term goal behavior serves to break the habit chain while still ensuring that the function of the problem behavior is obtainable for the student with a more socially acceptable behavior. In our experience, developing alternative behaviors that meet all three criteria is a practice that teams often overlook, and then their plans are not successful. For example, consider the student who is engaging in a tantrum and ripping up his paper to avoid a difficult task. The teacher could teach the student a replacement behavior to avoid the task by turning his paper over to signal that he needs a break. This first step will stop the habit of throwing a tantrum and make the learning environment more tolerable for all involved. Once the problem-behavior habit is adjusted to the break strategy, the teacher can teach and reinforce additional skills or expectations (for example, trying one problem, circling the ones the student can do, or asking for help rather than a break). The specifics of how one moves from replacement to desired behaviors depends on the size of the discrepancy between the problem and the student's current skill level (both behaviorally and academically); the larger the discrepancy, the longer the process.

Prevention Strategies for Antecedents and Setting Events

Once the team has identified behaviors that must be taught, the team should discuss practices that will modify the specific antecedents to the problem behavior as well as practices to prompt the appropriate behaviors. Imagine that you want to change your habit of driving straight home after work and instead remember to go to the post office. An example of an antecedent prompt might include setting a reminder alarm on your phone or placing a sticky note on your steering wheel. This is a simple change to the environment that helps you remember to engage in a different behavior (in this case, stopping at the post office) than you typically do (in this case, driving straight home). These modifications to antecedents

Table 4.5: Behavior Strategies by Function of Behavior

Function of Behavior	Teaching: Designed to teach the student skills needed to engage in replacement and desired behaviors
Attention	Teach students appropriate ways to gain adult or peer attention: • Raise your hand and wait patiently for the teacher. • Check your work with a peer. • Ask to join an activity.
Escape Difficult Task	Teach more appropriate ways to ask for help or break (for instance, raise your hand and wait patiently for the teacher to call on you; use a break card). Teach students to ask for easier problems or tasks or intersperse easier and mastered problems with new content. Provide academic instruction and support to address student skill deficits, such as additional instructional time or additional support, and practice at home. Provide more focused instruction in class. Conduct an additional assessment to identify specific skill deficits and provide corresponding instruction.
Access Preferred Activity or Item	Teach the skills needed to appropriately request or access a preferred activity or item. If students have limited verbal skills, utilize picture symbols to request a preferred activity or item. Teach students how to respectfully ask for an item or activity or more time. Teach students to raise their hands and wait. Teach the "first, then this" strategy. Provide students with opportunities to practice the new skill in various environments and situations (ensure that students experience success when learning new behaviors).

are practices that should directly relate to the antecedent (Kern, Choutka, & Sokol, 2002) and directly address the function of the misbehavior (Kern, Gallagher, Starosta, Hickman, & George, 2006). Antecedent strategies can include a variety of approaches, but the key is that they are environmental modifications to set the student up to be more successful in engaging in specified prosocial alternative and desired behaviors. We summarize a few examples in table 4.6 (page 118). As you review the examples, remember that it is important for the Tier Three team to choose strategies that directly relate to the specific competing behavior pathway for each student receiving Tier Three supports.

As one example, consider a student who exhibits *noncompliance* (operationally defined as refusal to follow directions within five seconds) and *disruption* (defined as talking out or stating things like "This is stupid") during a whole-class read aloud (the specific trigger is the student being asked by the teacher to read aloud, and the routine is reading time). When the student is noncompliant after being asked to read aloud, typically, the teacher will call on another student to read or send the student to a time-out in the hallway, suggesting that the function or purpose of the behavior may be to avoid reading aloud. We recognize the

Table 4.6: Antecedent Strategies by Function of Behavior

	Prevention
Function of Behavior	Antecedent: Designed to prevent the problem behavior or to offset the potency of the antecedent
Attention	**Adult Attention** • Give attention early for positive behaviors. • Check in with the student upon arrival. • Provide adult attention before the problem behavior occurs. • Place student at a desk where he or she is easily accessible. • Give the student leadership activities allowing for teacher interaction. • Give the student frequent intermittent attention for positive or neutral behaviors. **Peer Attention** • Allow the student to work with a peer during classroom activities. • Allow the student to check his or her work with a peer. • Provide a group activity prior to independent work. • Allow the student to work with a peer for positive behaviors. • Place the student at desk where he or she can work easily with peers. • Give the student leadership activities that allow peer interaction.
Escape Difficult Task	• Intersperse brief or easy tasks among more difficult ones. • Establish clear classroom rules and expectations. • Use effective instructions and commands. • Provide additional instruction on specific skills needed. • Provide a visual prompt to cue steps for completing tasks. • Preteach content. • Precorrect frequently and deliberately to remind students to ask for help. • Modify assignments to meet instructional or skill levels. • Adjust timelines, provide graphic organizers, break into smaller chunks, and so on. • Alter the mode of task completion. • Provide additional support focused on instructional skills. • Utilize Homework Club, study hall, and so on. • Assign the student to work with a peer. • Differentiate instruction. • Build natural breaks into the assignment (for example, complete three problems, and then tell the teacher).
Access Preferred Activity or Item	• Increase predictability in the environment. • Give cues or several warnings about upcoming transitions. • Establish a clear and predictable schedule. • Make use of visible routine schedules, activity boards, photographs, or picture schedules. • Arrange highly preferred activities before other preferred activities, avoiding high-to-low-preference transitions. • Establish clear classroom rules and expectations. • Keep the rules to a maximum of five, allow students to help formulate them, make them brief, positively state them, and post them visibly on the wall. • Provide opportunities for choice during instruction and free time. • Create an enriched environment that includes student interests and preferred activities.

problem behavior is worse when the student has not slept well the night before. As we begin to think about intervention ideas, we could consider multiple ways to modify the trigger (for example, preteach and practice reading passages ahead of time, give the student an easier passage, or have the student read with a partner rather than the whole class). However, when we think about how to modify the trigger, we should consider *why* the behavior is occurring. We know it is to escape reading aloud, but the selection of the specific intervention components should ideally involve our best hypothesis about why the student is trying to escape the task. If we know the student is a struggling reader, it is very likely that practicing ahead or modifying text difficulty might resolve the problem by minimizing the aversiveness of the read aloud. However, if the issue is that the student is very self-conscious about his stuttering (which is worse when speaking in front of large groups), this modification is not likely to be as successful as having the student partner read or silent read during this time (until we can address the stutter, which may take some time). This example illustrates the importance of understanding the specific trigger (read aloud) *and* the function of behavior (avoid public speaking versus avoid mistakes in front of peers) to identify the best way to adjust the trigger. In addition, if we teach a student to request a "pass" rather than throw a tantrum to avoid reading, we will want to prompt the student at the start of the lesson to use the pass card if needed. Lastly, if we know the student has not slept well, we might give him an opportunity to rest for a few minutes between lunch and reading, or we could reduce the demands during reading on days the student is not well rested.

As part of prompting the appropriate behavior and preventing the problem behavior, a BSP may also include setting event strategies. These strategies separate the setting event from the immediate antecedent and reduce the impact. For example, if a setting event is a stressful interaction with parents on the way to school, a brief check-in with an adult might neutralize the impact of the home stressor and set the student up to be more successful during the day. Other times, we can eliminate a setting event by meeting a biological need (for instance, providing food if hunger is a setting event) or working with families to enhance school-home communication. Setting events can be difficult to manage, as they may occur well outside school hours or occur such that the staff are unaware of them. However, we list a few common setting events and possible strategies to use in table 4.7 (page 120).

Consequence Strategies

Following identification of behavior strategies and antecedent or setting-event strategies, the team also identifies consequence strategies. These are strategies put into place to reinforce appropriate behaviors—both the alternative short-term goal behavior and the desired long-term goal behavior—and to ensure that nothing reinforces the problem behavior. Because many students may not have the skills to engage in the desired behavior initially, the team should ensure that there is a plan for reinforcing the alternative behavior (Petscher, Rey, & Bailey, 2009) that moves the student from using the alternative behavior to using the desired behavior (Wilder, Harris, Regan, & Rasey, 2007). In determining what reinforcers to use with the student, the team should select those that are valued by the student (Horner & Day, 1991) and involve reasonable timeframes and expectations (Cooper, Heron, & Heward, 2007). When selecting practices to respond to problem behavior, it is ideal if the first line of response is to prompt the alternative behavior at the earliest sign

Table 4.7: Setting Event Strategies by Function of Behavior

Example	Prevention
	Setting event: Designed to offset or reduce the impact of prior setting events that the student has experienced
Student is hungry because he or she missed breakfast	Provide breakfast or a snack, if possible. Check with home or family to ensure that a meal can be provided.
Student experienced a fight or argument prior and the conflict is unresolved	Greet the student when he or she enters the room; provide a one-to-two minute debrief or "how was your evening or day" discussion.
Student has history of academic or behavioral difficulties	Provide a pep talk; ensure that academic content has review material or mastered material interspersed into it.
Student has medical issues or concerns	Check with the student regarding whether needs have been met when he or she enters the room.
Student doesn't adjust well to unplanned change in routine	Provide a warning and discuss changes with student. Provide a pep talk so he or she can handle the change in routine.
Student doesn't adjust well to a change in teacher or staff	Introduce the student to new staff members at earliest convenience (for instance, introduce a sub or new staff the day prior).
Student is tired	Check in with the student first thing; provide encouragement and allow breaks during instruction.

of misbehavior; provide acknowledgment for engaging in the alternative short-term goal behavior; and limit or eliminate the payoff for problem behavior by identifying a response that does not inadvertently reinforce problem behavior (Kern & Clarke, 2005; Mace et al., 1988). In addition, the team will need to discuss whether a safety plan is needed and what this plan should look like if the other practices do not eliminate unsafe behavior. We have provided examples of consequence strategies in table 4.8 sorted by functions of behavior, including those to reinforce the appropriate behavior and those to remove reinforcement of the unwanted or problem behavior. Just as with the previous components, it is important that the Tier Three team consider each student's unique summary statement and competing behavior pathway when selecting strategies for the BSP.

For Tier Three, the two key practices are the FBA, an individualized assessment process, and the BSP, which includes the specific strategies and interventions used to support the student. Teams that design Tier Three supports will conduct the FBA and use its results to design a BSP. We presented strategies for antecedents, setting events, behavior, and consequence components. A BSP also needs strategies to monitor implementation and impact of the BSP. We discuss these within the Data and Problem-Solving Model sections on pages 127 and 133.

Having discussed the practices associated with Tier Three, we now discuss the systems that need to be put into place to use those practices effectively.

Table 4.8: Consequence Strategies by Behavior Function

Function of Behavior	Consequence (Reinforce Appropriate): Designed to increase reinforcement for the desired behavior	Consequence (Minimize Payoff for Problem Behavior or Extinction): Designed to remove reinforcement for the unwanted or problem behavior
Attention	Respond quickly if a student appropriately asks for attention. Give the student frequent attention for positive behavior. Allow the student to earn time for extra attention through positive behavior. Allow the student to earn time with a peer for quietly working in class. Allow the student to earn lunch with the teacher for raising her hand and waiting quietly. Use Tier Two interventions, such as Check In–Check Out.	Eliminate or minimize the amount of attention provided to a student for engaging in a problem behavior. Limit verbal interaction—create a signal to prompt the student to stop the problem behavior and redirect it to appropriate behavior. Avoid power struggles. Avoid consequences resulting in high rates of intense attention. Provide a time-out or quiet space away from teacher or peers if work avoidance is not also a concern.
Escape Difficult Task	Respond quickly if the student appropriately asks for help or for a break. Deliver a break when the student asks, and provide a larger payoff for engaging in the task (if appropriate based on student skill). Increase specific praise for appropriate behavior. Reward the student for being on task, trying hard, completing work, and asking for a break or help appropriately. Consider the student's interest. Use Tier Two interventions, such as academic interventions.	Minimize the payoff for a student engaging in problem behavior. Eliminate or minimize the amount of missed instructional time or work provided to a student for engaging in problem behavior. Hold the student accountable for work (or time) missed due to problem behavior. Make sure the student can do the work, or provide support or instruction so the student can complete the work.
Access Preferred Activity or Item	Use specific verbal praise. Provide a reward on a continual schedule of reinforcement (immediate at first) and decrease (to intermittent) after a period of successful appropriate behaviors. Use Tier Two interventions, such as a setting-based intervention (for example, access to playground equipment).	Make sure the student does not access the preferred item after engaging in problematic behavior. Prompt the student to appropriately request the activity or item if he is engaging in problematic behavior. Ensure that the student doesn't miss instructional time upon engaging in problematic behavior.

Systems

As with Tiers One and Two, schools will need to define the systems needed to ensure that their school can support use of a Tier Three process. To be able to identify students for Tier Three, complete FBAs, and design BSPs, certain systems need to be in place to support staff. Subsequent sections describe the following Tier Three systems:

1. Tier Three team
2. Secured funding and resources
3. Training and coaching
4. Data use and procedures

Tier Three Team

The Tier Three team is responsible for overseeing the process for identifying students who need Tier Three supports, completing the FBA and designing the BSP for each individual identified, as well as monitoring the outcomes for all students receiving Tier Three supports. For efficiency and effectiveness, it is likely that a unique subteam (made up of one or two key members of the Tier Three team along with all other relevant parties for each individual student) will be formed to complete each FBA and BSP; however, some schools use the whole longstanding Tier Three team to complete this. The critical members of each individual student support team should include someone with knowledge of the student, knowledge of the context in which the behavior occurs, and expertise in behavioral theory (Benazzi, Horner, & Good, 2006).

The Tier Three team is responsible for overseeing the implementation for students receiving Tier Three supports, which includes monitoring the implementation and impact of Tier Three (see table 4.9). To monitor implementation, the team will ensure that the key elements for Tier Three are in place, and it will ensure that the school staff understand the processes associated with a student receiving Tier Three supports. For monitoring impact, the various tasks it will have include overseeing or conducting the FBA for each student and designing the respective student's BSP. The team also ensures that the school puts BSP into place and monitors the student's progress, and it makes decisions about each student's the BSP and decisions about referrals for special education or other agencies when appropriate. The team should meet at least twice per month to examine student progress.

Table 4.9: Tier Three Team Tasks

Implementation	Impact
Train staff on processes for referring students for Tier Three supports	Assign students to interventions
Train and involve necessary staff for conducting individualized assessment or FBA and creating a BSP	Hold regular meetings to discuss impact for individual students
Hold regular meetings to discuss implementation	Hold regular meetings to discuss impact as a whole

The roles for the Tier Three team are like the leadership and Tier Two teams, which include a minutes recorder, data-management person, team facilitator, and administrator. However, the Tier Three team will also include personnel who have specialized training in behavior and FBAs (and this person may serve in one of the other roles). Typical members with knowledge of FBAs and BSPs include the school psychologist, school counselor, behavior specialist, and special education teachers. A Tier Three coordinator, also part of the team, is responsible for overseeing the assessment of the student's behavior and ensuring that everyone completes their part for the FBA.

Secured Funding and Resources

As with the other tiers, secured funding and resources ensure that the team can achieve its goals and function. The Tier Three team needs extensive knowledge of behavioral theory. As such, leadership teams should work to establish a foundational level of function-based thinking for Tier Three team members (counselors, learning specialists, special education teachers, general education teachers, school psychologists). This allows teams to work from a behavioral-theory perspective that has a high likelihood of generating successful, function-based interventions. Teams will also need to have access to someone with behavioral expertise who can guide the FBA and development of the BSP to ensure that the selected strategies have a high contextual fit with those who will be implementing the plan.

Training and Coaching

There are a few considerations under training and coaching capacity for a Tier Three team. One, it is important that key stakeholders (for instance, parents of the student and teachers of the student) receive information about Tier Three supports as it relates to the individual students they serve, as well as information related to how to access supports and to the overall success of Tier Three supports. (See the teacher communication form in figure 4.5.) This often means making time at staff meetings to share broad data on how students are doing and reviewing progress with grade-level teams and teachers. Communication is critical for all aspects of SWPBIS, but with Tier Three, more people are involved with the individual students' cases, so the team needs to identify clear procedures and processes for communication.

Elementary Tier Three Update

Date: _____

Hi, _____

The Tier Three team met to review your student: _____

Our data suggest the student is:
☐ Meeting or exceeding current goals ☐ Beginning to struggle ☐ Not making progress toward goals

▸ We will continue to track the student's progress
▸ We will schedule a planning meeting. We would like to have this meeting completed no later than _____.
▸ I'll come talk to you about your concerns.

If you need help sooner, please contact me.

Thanks,

_____

Comments: _____
_____
_____
_____

Figure 4.5: Tier Three team teacher communication form sample.

*Visit **MarzanoResearch.com/reproducibles** to download a free reproducible version of this figure.*

Second, the Tier Three team will want to teach staff how to access the behavioral support within the school (for example, completing a request-for-assistance form). Third, the team and staff may need reminders or training on discussing students in a professional, sensitive manner. It is easy to become overwhelmed by the intensity and logistics of assessing and providing supports to students in Tier Three, so some staff may benefit from reminders on how to approach parents when students are displaying high rates of unwanted behaviors. Finally, the Tier Three team will be stronger if members have access to district-level or additional behavioral expertise in those cases that are extremely complex.

Data Use and Procedures

At Tier Three, there also needs to be clear processes for how students are identified for supports, who will complete what pieces of the FBA, who will develop the BSP, and when and how BSP development will happen. We discuss identifying students, completing the FBA, and developing the BSP.

Identifying Students

Within the Data section (page 127), we discuss the exact data that identify students for Tier Three supports. Here, we point out that Tier Three teams need to create decision rules and guidelines for identifying students who may need additional supports. For example, students who have received a modified Check In–Check Out for at least six weeks but have not responded well to basic modifications to the intervention may be candidates for Tier Three, or a school team may determine certain data decision rules that incorporate severe or intense major referral behaviors rather than minor behaviors. In addition to creating and sharing data decision rules, teams should also consider request-for-assistance forms that teachers can complete to receive supports for students and to track interventions over time as part of moving from Tier Two to Tier Three interventions (see figure 4.6).

| Student name: _____ | | | Date: _____ |
| Teacher: _____ | | | Grade: _____ |

Student strengths:

Primary area or areas of concern:

How is this student performing compared to others in your class?				Reading benchmark or recent progress-monitoring scores Date: _____	Mathematics benchmark or recent progress-monitoring scores Date: _____
	Below	Average	Above		
Reading					
Math					
Writing					
Behavior					
Language					

Interventions tried in classroom			
Intervention	Date started	Date ended	Outcome data
1.			
2.			
3.			

If student needs are primarily academic or language and communication, stop here.
If concerns involve social behavior, please complete remainder of the form (including back).

What does the problem behavior look like?
How often does the problem behavior occur? How long does it last?
What is the intensity level or danger of the problem behavior?
Why do you think the behavior continues to occur (for example, what reinforces it)?
Where, when, and with whom problem behaviors are most likely:

Time	Activity and staff involved	Likelihood of problem behavior	Specific problem behavior	Current intervention for the problem behavior
		Low High 1 2 3 4 5 6		
		1 2 3 4 5 6		
		1 2 3 4 5 6		
		1 2 3 4 5 6		
		1 2 3 4 5 6		
		1 2 3 4 5 6		
		1 2 3 4 5 6		
		1 2 3 4 5 6		
		1 2 3 4 5 6		

Strategies attempted

☐ Ignore behavior
☐ 5 to 1 positives
☐ Preferential seating
☐ Precorrection
☐ Proximity
☐ Prompts or signals
☐ Class discussion

☐ Provide extra support: What support?
_____
☐ Modified Assignment: How?
_____
☐ Preteach expectations
☐ Clarify rules
☐ Practice expected behaviors
☐ Breaks

☐ Self-management program
☐ Behavior contract
☐ Other: _____

Figure 4.6: Request-for-assistance form for Tier Three.

continued ➔

Positive rewards	
☐ Classroom reward program: tokens and group contingencies ☐ 5 to 1 positives ☐ Clip ups ☐ Reinforce around target students	☐ "Wows!" How many? _____ ☐ Systematic feedback about behavior ☐ Other: _____

Other consequences	
☐ Reprimands ☐ Removal of privileges ☐ Time-outs ☐ Owed time ☐ Apology or self-reflection	☐ Meet individually with student ☐ Contact parent. How many calls? _____ ☐ Meet with parents. How many meetings? _____ ☐ Office referrals. How many referrals? _____ ☐ Other: _____
Do you think this student would be a good candidate for Check In–Check Out? (circle one) Yes No	How do you want the team to support you?

Specialist team response to request-for-assistance form		
Student name: _____ Date: _____ Teacher: _____ Grade: _____		
Student strengths:		
Primary areas of concern:		
Next step or follow-up	**Who's responsible**	**By what date**
Intervention response tracking	**Date started or ended**	**Outcome data**
1.		
2.		
3.		
4.		

Visit **MarzanoResearch.com/reproducibles** *to download a free reproducible version of this figure.*

Another system is the coordination of the FBA.

Completing the FBA

A team conducts the FBA, so it will have a process for dividing up the exact tasks of the FBA (who will gather the data to confirm the FBA, who will contact the parents, and so on). The exact makeup of the team members to support the FBA should be based on each student's unique needs. At minimum, the team should include someone knowledgeable about the student, someone knowledgeable about the context in which the behavior occurs, and someone with behavioral expertise (Anderson et al., 2013; Benazzi et al., 2006). For students in special education, the FBA process should also consider the rights and responsibilities of the special education team when determining who should be a part of the FBA team (for instance, the student's IEP team).

Developing the BSP

After the team has collected the FBA information, it should convene to review the information and finalize the competing behavior pathways. Once the team has agreed upon the competing behavior pathways, the team should use this information to develop the individual strategies and features of the BSP. It is important to build the BSP with a team that includes someone with behavioral expertise, someone knowledgeable about the student (a parent, guardian, or teacher), someone knowledgeable about the context where the plan will be implemented (such as the classroom teacher), and someone, such as an administrator, who can allocate necessary resources to implement the plan. The team may also include other specialists who work with the student both inside school and outside in the community, and the student, when developmentally appropriate. The development of the BSP should always be a collaborative effort with the team members who will be implementing it; otherwise, teams run the risk of never fully implementing the BSP because it does not fit the skills, interest, expertise, or context of the implementers.

For students whose behavior is extremely complex, the team may choose to pick one behavior or routine to focus on initially and then reconvene to address other areas later, or the team may choose to build multiple competing behavior pathways and design intervention components linked to each pathway. Remember, the plan is only going to be as effective as it is technically sound and implemented. Therefore, it is critical that the team members work together to build a plan that is based on the FBA results and that fits the context of the school and locations where it is to be implemented (considering the current skill level and resources available to support those implementing the plan).

Data

Having determined the outcomes, practices, and systems associated with Tier Three, schools will need to also consider the data it will want to gather to inform the other elements. The data gathered for Tier Three supports falls into three uses: (1) screening data for identifying students for Tier Three, (2) diagnostic data for developing the behavior support plan, and (3) progress-monitoring data to measure each student's growth. Teams will also gather fidelity data related to implementation of Tier Three (as a whole and for individual interventions). Within this section, we discuss the data they will use in Tier Three supports.

Screening Data

School teams will use similar data and procedures for identifying students for Tier Three supports (for example, pre-existing data, screening instruments, or teacher nomination), but they will also use progress-monitoring data from the supports students have received prior, such as previous Tier Two supports (Chard et al., 2008). When using screening data for the identification of students for Tier Three, the teams determine a criterion for screening measures. Schools do not need qualitatively different data for identifying students for Tier Three. Instead, they need levels of criteria to indicate what level of support a student has previously received, how he or she has responded to that support, and what level of support the student currently needs.

Those students who have scores within the high-risk category are those who may need Tier Three supports. This raises a common question: Do students need to go through Tier Two interventions before they receive Tier Three supports? Our recommendation is generally to provide Tier Two interventions prior to Tier Three, but we also acknowledge that some students' intense behavior needs may warrant Tier Three supports immediately.

Screening and assessment within SWPBIS aims to identify each student's risk-level status and then to provide a corresponding level of support to address those needs. If a student is scoring within a high-risk range across multiple data sources, then he or she most likely needs intensive Tier Three support. Providing Tier Two supports prior to Tier Three interventions may not meet the needs of students, particularly when all data indicate Tier Two will not be sufficient. School teams will want to carefully consider the student's situation and how well certain supports are in place.

Another source of identifying students for Tier Three is the student's response to previous interventions. Students with chronic challenging behaviors may participate in Tier Two interventions, and their lack of responsiveness to Tier Two interventions can result in a referral for more intensive interventions (Chard et al., 2008). In this case, the progress-monitoring data from Tier Two supports can also be used to determine students who may need additional intensive intervention. We want to emphasize that the decision to provide Tier Three supports following Tier Two supports should be based on the data and not solely on subjective or emotional information. A student should be placed into Tier Three supports if the student's growth is insufficient and if the fidelity of previous supports is high.

It is important that part of the referral process for determining Tier Three supports includes examining progress on Tier Two interventions and ensuring that those interventions were implemented with a high level of fidelity. This step is critical to ensure that schools are appropriately utilizing resources for those students whose needs are not met by high-quality Tier Two interventions rather than those who may respond to a Tier Two intervention but did not receive an intervention implemented as designed (Rodriguez et al., 2015). As we discussed earlier with respect to fidelity, school teams want to avoid blaming an intervention for lack of a student's growth when fidelity is the culprit. During this examination process, data review for lack of progress and implementation fidelity may illuminate ways in which the Tier Two intervention can be modified or intensified to meet unique student needs (Rodriguez et al., 2015). In this type of common situation, the first line of Tier Three supports is often an individualized Tier Two intervention where components are intensified. For example, teams might increase the number of check-ins per day, provide additional opportunities for feedback, deliver reinforcement more frequently, focus on one or two specific behaviors rather than general behaviors, and so on. In other cases, it is apparent that the intensity or severity of a student's behavior warrants interventions that are intensive or individually tailored.

Diagnostic Data

To gather diagnostic data for the BSP, school teams conduct an FBA. As discussed, the results of the FBA provide information as to the operational definition of the problem behavior, the context and situations in which the behavior occurs, and information about the consequences and function of the behavior. This information helps determine the function of the behavior and why the problem is occurring, and teams then use it to develop a BSP to solve the problem.

When collecting data for the FBA process, the team should always use multiple sources of information. RIOT (review, interview, observe, test) and ICEL (instruction, curriculum, environment, learner) are acronyms that refer to the types of assessment and domains to assess for problem solving, respectively. RIOT and ICEL provide a framework for the assessment process (Christ, 2008; Hosp, 2008; Howell & Nolet, 2000). We discuss RIOT and ICEL in depth next, before discussing progress-monitoring (impact) and fidelity (implementation) data.

Review, Interview, Observe, Test

RIOT refers to types of assessments and is an organizing framework to enhance the likelihood teams conduct comprehensive information review and to help organize information to use for problem solving individualized supports.

Review consists of examining existing and past records of the student. Examples might include school attendance records, report cards, office discipline referral data, academic assessment scores, previous interventions (and data on effectiveness), and relevant permanent products.

Interview involves, at minimum, talking to the teachers or school staff members (including paraprofessionals, administrators, or previous teachers) who know the student well and who see the student in the context where the behaviors occur. It is often also appropriate to interview parents and the student. Interviews are used to obtain information about student strengths as well as for operationally defining problem behaviors; understanding expectations; and determining possible routines, setting events, antecedents, and consequences for behaviors. Ultimately, interviews should conclude with at least one hypothesis statement about why problem behavior is occurring and the context where it occurs.

Observations can provide several important functions in the FBA process. A team often conducts observations to better understand the severity of the behavioral problems by collecting information about how the student's prosocial and problem behaviors compare to those of typical peers. Additionally, observation data can help us to understand why a behavior is happening by revealing information that identifies possible antecedents and consequences that surround problem behaviors. The team should, at a minimum, conduct observations in the routines identified as a focus during the teacher interview. Ideally, observations also occur in areas of relative strength for the student to better understand how behavior differs across contexts.

Testing typically refers to the administration of tests to directly measure the student's skills. A team may wish to administer academic tests or social-emotional measures (rating scales, checklists, and so on) to understand the student's current level of academic and behavioral functioning. Such information can inform the behavioral plan; for example, if avoidance of work is suspected as a function of the behavior, testing can confirm if the student is missing the needed skills for the setting in which the behavior occurs. For behavioral testing, this can be a structured and standardized observation of a student that provides information to help the team better understand why a student may be struggling under certain conditions (Christ, 2008). This form of testing is used less often when conducting FBAs in school settings, but there are formal types of function-based assessments called structural analyses and functional analyses that involve systematic manipulation of antecedents and/ or consequences. In these types of analyses, an examiner conducts or works with a teacher to conduct systematic assessment of how behavior changes under certain conditions.

Having described the four types of assessments, we now describe the areas that are assessed, as outlined by the ICEL acronym.

Instruction, Curriculum, Environment, Learner Practices

ICEL practices are variables that teachers can modify when attempting to understand student behavior (including social and academic learning) and design supports.

Instruction practices are important to examine because they can either help or hinder student learning and behavior. As part of the FBA process, school teams will want to determine the instructional routines in which the student does well and those routines in which the student struggles. Identifying differences in instructional practices can provide information about possible antecedents as well reveal student behaviors that would benefit from additional or different approaches to instruction.

Curriculum typically represents the full set of academic skills a student should master, but it can also refer to the behavioral curriculum that is taught to students. Within SWPBIS, the behavioral curriculum is the schoolwide expectations. For students whose problem behaviors occur primarily during instructional content areas, a formal investigation of typical curriculum may help one understand how student skills align with what is expected for the grade level. In a less traditional sense, when conducting an FBA, the team might also use curriculum to consider the formal instruction that has taken place for social behavioral expectations. When examining curriculum, school teams can assess how well the student has responded to this instruction and determine the student's current behavioral skills relative to what is expected of typical students.

Environment is an extremely important focus for the FBA. Each data source should provide information about the student as well as about how the student performs in the environment. Understanding the routines broadly where the student does well and has difficulty is only the first step. We must also look at the environment much more precisely to understand within each routine (for instance, small group reading) the specific environmental conditions (for instance, being called on to read aloud) that trigger problem behavior as well as the consequences of problem behavior (for instance, the student is sent to the back table for being disruptive) in the environment that maintain behavior. This level of analysis of patterns over time allows us to develop hypothesis statements about why student behavior is occurring under specific conditions (for instance, to escape reading aloud because the student has a fear of public speaking). These hypothesis statements are then used as a basis for developing behavior-intervention plans that include modifications to the environment to facilitate student success.

Learner is the obvious focal point of all sources of information we review, but this is not because we believe the problem lies within the student or because we intend to blame the student. Rather, the learner characteristics are those unique qualities that interact with the instruction, curriculum, and environment to develop patterns of success and challenges over time (Hosp, 2008). When considering the learner, it is often important to consider the student's history as well as specific skills and deficits. Students who have never been exposed to a skill (have a skill deficit) will need direct instruction on that skill. However, students who have been taught a skill but are not displaying it need either additional practice with the skill (opportunities to increase fluency) or additional motivation to engage in the skill (opportunities to overcome performance deficits). Knowing which skills and deficits the learner brings and how these interact with the instruction, curriculum, and environment allows us to design interventions targeted to the unique strengths and needs of the learner.

FBA Complexity

We want to point out that the use of an FBA is not a canned or scripted process. Each individualized Tier Three support plan should align with the function of student problem behavior and be developed through the process of the FBA. However, because the assessment is individualized, the school team can determine the specific information that will be most helpful for understanding the student's behavior and the environment in which it occurs. Typically speaking, the more complex the behavior in terms of inconsistencies across settings and disagreement among team members about why it is happening, the more information will need to be gathered to confidently complete the assessment (Anderson et al., 2013). Although not every FBA will incorporate all aspects of the RIOT or ICEL approach, a thorough, complex FBA will often utilize sources of information across these sources of information and domains of learning. Then, the team designs function-based supports using the FBA results to guide the intervention plans (or BSPs) that prevent problem behavior while promoting desired outcomes for students (Loman et al., 2014).

Progress-Monitoring Data

Although the data-collection method will be individualized and directly tied to the student's goals and BSP, the general approach to data collection is like Tier Two in that the behavior can be observed directly or rated by a teacher or the student. As with Tier Two, it is important that the data-collection method is feasible and sensitive to student outcomes, but because it is individualized, the team should thoughtfully tie the data-collection procedures to the student's individual goals. Some students on Tier Three interventions will have data-collection procedures that incorporate a point card or other rating of behavior. The difference between Tiers Two and Three is that the data collection is likely to be more focused, frequent, and specific for the individual student. For example, figure 4.7 (page 132) displays an example of a behavior rating card for a student receiving Tier Three supports. One can see the increased level of explicitness with more descriptions of the desired behavior (compared to figure 3.6 in chapter 3) and the shorter time periods in which the student receives feedback (here, each period is broken into a first half and second half).

Student Name: _____ Date: _____									
	3 = zero to one reminders 2 = two reminders 1 = three or more reminders								
	Be Safe			**Be Respectful**			**Be Responsible**		
A Day or B Day	Keep hands, feet, and objects to self. Use kind words.			Follow directions the first time within ten seconds.			Complete at least 75 percent of work in class.		Teacher Initials
Period 1 or 5 (1st half)	3	2	1	3	2	1	3	2	1	
Period 1 or 5 (2nd half)	3	2	1	3	2	1	3	2	1	
Period 2 or 6 (1st half)	3	2	1	3	2	1	3	2	1	
Period 2 or 6 (2nd half)	3	2	1	3	2	1	3	2	1	
Period 3 or 7 (1st half)	3	2	1	3	2	1	3	2	1	
Period 3 or 7 (2nd half)	3	2	1	3	2	1	3	2	1	
Period 4 or 8 (1st half)	3	2	1	3	2	1	3	2	1	
Period 4 or 8 (2nd half)	3	2	1	3	2	1	3	2	1	
Homeroom	3	2	1	3	2	1	3	2	1	
Today's Goal: _____									
Total Points: _____ Percent of Points: _____									
Parent or Guardian Signature: _____									

Figure 4.7: Example of a daily point card for Check In–Check Out for students receiving Tier Three supports.

Visit **MarzanoResearch.com/reproducibles** *to download a free reproducible version of this figure.*

Fidelity Data

As with Tier Two, school teams will monitor implementation of Tier Three elements as well as fidelity for individual interventions. They examine implementation of Tier Three systems with fidelity measures. Refer to the Fidelity Data section (page 93) in chapter 3 for information, as the processes are like Tier Two.

School teams will monitor the implementation of each BSP. The monitoring of the implementation of interventions can vary between direct and indirect methods. Just as with progress monitoring at Tier Three, fidelity monitoring is individualized to the unique behavior support plan for each individual student. We suggest regularly graphing fidelity (implementation) and outcome (impact) data and a weekly (or at least every other week) review of student progress and fidelity of implementation to ensure that teachers and students receive the support they need. The Tier Two chapter reviews common challenges with fidelity and ways to respond to those challenges (page 95). These challenges are likely to be consistent at Tier Three levels. However, at Tier Three, the implementer of the BSP should be a critical part of the Tier Three team for that student, and therefore, this person should have input up front to help select strategies that align with teacher skill and value sets. Once they have considered this information, the actual procedures to measure fidelity will be based on the BSP but will be like the types of procedures discussed in the Tier Two chapter. The difference is largely a matter of intensity, as more individualized and extensive monitoring and assessment is needed for students receiving Tier Three relative to students receiving Tier Two supports.

We have discussed common outcomes for Tier Three, including the specific practices, systems, and data it needs. We now discuss use of the PSM at Tier Three. We have covered the "what" of Tier Three in the previous sections; now we turn our attention to what drives these elements together by using the PSM.

Problem-Solving Model at Tier Three

There are specific questions that the Tier Three team asks between implementation and impact for Tier Three (see table 4.10, page 134). To problem solve at Tier Three, the Tier Three team answers questions that include assessing fidelity of implementation of Tier Three, the extent to which most students are successful with Tier Three, and which students require Tier Three (which includes examining the impact of the interventions for students and the fidelity of those interventions).

We have organized this section to discuss each question in table 4.10 and to then provide a concrete example of using the PSM to address that question.

Implementation

Implementation and examination of the Tier Three processes is like Tier Two. School teams will examine fidelity by administering a fidelity measure as part of step 1 of the PSM and then analyzing the results to determine if a problem exists (for example, if there is a low score with implementation). The school team may also gather additional data at step 1 of the PSM (Problem Identification), such as staff input or observational data, to determine if there are any problems with providing Tier Three supports. If a problem is found, the Tier Three team examines reasons why the problem exists in step 2 of the PSM (Problem Analysis), followed by the development of a solution in step 3 of the PSM (Plan Identification and Implementation) to solve the problem and evaluate the solution in step 4 of the PSM (Plan Evaluation). We forgo providing an example here, as the process is illustrated in chapter 3 (page 96).

Impact

Monitoring the impact of Tier Three is like doing so in Tier Two. The Tier Three team examines systems-level issues, such as the percentage of students receiving Tier Three supports or how effective Tier Three is overall (for example, Are most students [80 percent] making progress with their BSP?). Because Tier Three supports are individualized, it is more difficult to review and compare how all students are doing. However, schools should still make efforts to consider the effectiveness of their Tier Three processes as a whole. Teams will also examine student-level issues, which means determining if students are being identified for Tier Three supports and subsequently benefiting from Tier Three supports. We discuss systems-level problem solving and student-level problem solving for Tier Three next.

Table 4.10: Problem-Solving Questions for Tier Three

	Implementation	Impact	
	Fidelity	**Systems**	**Students**
Questions	Is Tier Three being implemented with fidelity?	Do we have a healthy model at Tier Three?	Which students require Tier Three supports?
Example Outcomes	Scores on fidelity measures indicate high implementation.	No more than 5 percent of students require Tier Three supports. Tier Three is effective for the majority (for instance, 80 percent) of students in that they are making progress toward individualized goals. Students identified as needing Tier Three supports receive that support in a timely manner.	The majority of students receiving support see improvements in their social, academic, or behavioral functioning. Fidelity scores for interventions show acceptable implementation (greater than 90 percent).

Systems-Level Problem Solving

During step 1 (Problem Identification), teams will examine the health of their Tier Three systems. If the team determines that there is a problem, such as if more than 5 percent of students need Tier Three or if less than 80 percent of students receiving Tier Three supports are making progress toward their goals, the team will progress to step 2 (Problem Analysis). During this step, the team analyzes information to determine why there is a problem. More than likely, a problem here indicates a systemic issue, and the school team can examine such issues in similar fashion as with Tier Two. Once it understands the problem in depth, the team can develop an action plan (solution) during step 3 (Plan Identification and Implementation). This includes identifying a goal (for example, at least 80 percent of students progressing on track toward meeting goals) and methods to monitor the implementation and impact of the plan. During step 4 (Plan Evaluation), the team meets to review the data gathered and evaluates the plan.

Illustration of Tier Three Systems-Level Problem Solving

To illustrate systems-level problem solving at Tier Three, consider a Tier Three team that reviewed their Tier Three systems. The team examined fidelity data on BSPs and the results of a staff survey to gather feedback on the referral process for Tier Three supports during step 1 (Problem Identification). When reviewing the gathered information, the team identified that despite having high fidelity for their BSPs, the staff reported dissatisfaction with the Tier Three process. Over 40 percent of the staff reported dissatisfaction, when ideally at least 80 percent would report satisfaction. This identified a problem to investigate.

At step 2 (Problem Analysis), the team gathered and examined brief interview data with teachers, after which they discovered they had an issue with the referral process. Specifically, although there were identified procedures in place to identify students for Tier Three supports, including a request-for-assistance process, many staff members were not completing the forms and providing the required information. Instead, some teachers were individually approaching the school counselor and asking for help. This resulted in some students taking many weeks to access supports and other students receiving individualized supports without first receiving Tier Two interventions.

The team determined in step 3 of the PSM (Plan Identification and Implementation) that they would reteach the request-for-assistance process (including how to access Tier Two supports prior to Tier Three and how to utilize the request-for-assistance form) to all staff. The Tier Three team created an action plan to implement these strategies. During step 4 (Plan Evaluation), they examined the extent to which they implemented their plan and how well teachers were following the referral process. To do so, they ensured that they completed their action plan items (to measure implementation), and they examined the impact of their plan by briefly surveying the staff and asking the counselor to report how many teachers were following the process versus approaching her individually.

Student-Level Problem Solving

Student-level problem solving at Tier Three is like the process at Tier Two in that students are identified to be at risk and then provided with corresponding supports. We should point out that this form of problem solving is about individual students and is perhaps what most educators think of when they think of behavioral support for a student. The discussion centers on one student and how to design a personalized BSP for him or her.

At step 1 of the PSM (Problem Identification), the team determines if a student is at risk, as students who require Tier Three supports are considered high risk for behavioral concerns (as opposed to students who receive Tier Two and are at some risk). The team evaluates students for Tier Three either by reviewing screening or other referral data or by considering the student's progress with Tier Two interventions. If consideration for Tier Three is based on screening data, then they need to verify the student's risk status (as it is with Tier Two consideration). If the referral is based on previous progress-monitoring data, the team can review the fidelity and growth of the previous interventions to decide about Tier Three. If they determine a student to be at risk, then the team proceeds to step 2.

During step 2 (Problem Analysis), the Tier Three team gathers additional data to determine why the problem exists. During this step, school teams will conduct an extensive FBA to precisely define the behaviors of concern; determine the antecedents and consequences of the student's problem behaviors; identify relevant information about the context, culture, and other important factors that contribute to the student's behavior; and determine the function of the student's problem behaviors (Scott et al., 2009).

In step 3 (Plan Implementation), the team uses results of the FBA team to develop a BSP as well as a unique goal for the student. The BSP includes the components we discuss throughout this chapter: prevention strategies to eliminate or neutralize setting events and antecedents that trigger the behavior; behavior strategies to teach the desired or replacement behavior; consequence strategies to reinforce both the alternative and desired behaviors; extinction and punishment strategies to offset reinforcement of the problem behavior; and procedures to monitor the implementation and impact of the BSP (Newton, Horner, et al., 2009; Scott et al., 2009).

In step 4 of the PSM (Plan Evaluation), the school teams examine the effectiveness of the BSP for each student. During this step, they evaluate the student's progress against his or her goals and make decisions about continuing, fading, or adjusting the student's plan. They examine the fidelity of the BSP within this step before making decisions about the BSP's impact. For students with good fidelity and little benefit from the BSP, the team can have discussions about intensifying the BSP, including referrals for additional services or special education. In cases of poor fidelity, they consider having discussions about additional supports or modifications related to the BSP strategies (for example, lack of match with teacher skills indicates a need for more training, and lack of resources indicates a need for more support).

Illustration of Tier Three Student-Level Problem Solving

As an example of student-level problem solving, imagine a Tier Two team that reviewed progress-monitoring data for students receiving Check In–Check Out at step 1 of the PSM (Problem Identification). The Tier Two team identified a student who, after several attempts to modify Check In–Check Out, was still not progressing on the intervention, signaling that a problem existed (for example, the student was earning 63 percent of his daily points over four weeks when the goal was to earn at least 80 percent of his daily points). The Tier Two team referred the student to the Tier Three team, who agreed that the student was not making adequate progress although the Tier Two team had implemented his intervention (Check In–Check Out) as intended. This triggered step 2 (Problem Analysis).

At step 2 of the PSM, the Tier Three team analyzed why the student was not achieving his goal (that is, Why is the problem occurring?). The team formed a student-focused team to conduct the FBA and build a corresponding BSP. To begin the FBA process, the counselor contacted the teacher and worked to set up a meeting with the teacher and the student's parents. During the meeting, the team shared their concerns and the information they'd gathered with the parents, and the school psychologist obtained the parents' permission to conduct the FBA. The school psychologist then spent the next two weeks gathering interview and observational data. The student-focused team met several weeks later after gathering the FBA data, and the team examined the information to create the competing behavior pathway. The team identified that the student received fewer points on his Check In–Check Out daily behavior card during academic content times (for instance, reading or writing), and that the student had received two recent referrals for unsafe behaviors (for example, throwing books and writing utensils across the room) that they hypothesized had a function of avoiding tasks. The team hypothesized that the perceived function of unsafe behaviors was to avoid academic tasks. The student's complete summary statement was: *When presented with independent reading or writing tasks lasting more than ten minutes, the student uses unsafe behavior, which results in being sent to the office and missing the tasks. We hypothesize that the function of this behavior is to avoid those tasks.* They confirmed this summary statement through additional observation data that the school psychologist collected and by asking the teacher to document the student's behavior in relation to certain assignments.

During step 3 of the PSM (Plan Identification and Implementation), the team developed the BSP to solve the identified problem. The plan involved specific features for preventing the behavior, teaching alternative skills as well as supporting academic skill development, and strategies for how to respond to both appropriate and problem behaviors according to the function of the student's behavior. The team monitored the plan by tracking specific incidents of unsafe behavior using office discipline referral data as well as having the teacher provide a period-by-period rating of engagement and safety (on a scale of one to three, with three meaning high engagement and high safety). The team set a goal for two weeks after beginning implementation of the BSP for zero referrals for unsafe behavior and a mean rating of 2.5 for the student on the teacher ratings. The team monitored implementation by asking the teacher to also record how well she implemented the components of the plan on a brief rating scale.

During step 4 (Plan Evaluation), the counselor gathered the referral data and teacher's ratings for each period and then graphed it. The Tier Three team reviewed the graph against the desired goals. The student was much more successful with the BSP, and therefore, after several weeks the school psychologist consulted with the teacher on how to increase expectations for the student and begin to move from the alternative behavior of asking for a break to the desired behavior of completing tasks independently.

Within this section, we discussed how teachers can use the PSM to identify and solve problems for Tier Three, for implementation and for impact at a systems level and student level. We summarize the questions and steps of the PSM across implementation and impact for Tier Three in table 4.11 (page 138).

Summary

Within this chapter, we discussed the four key elements of Tier Three and how the Tier Three team can use the PSM to resolve issues related to the implementation and impact of Tier Three. Tier Three is designed for students with chronic, severe, or dangerous problem behaviors; these students should make up no more than 3 to 5 percent of the student population. The Tier Three team (perhaps in conjunction with the leadership team) will identify outcomes that can include implementing the elements with fidelity, having no more than 5 percent of students needing Tier Three, and ensuring that at least 80 percent of students receiving Tier Three are successful with their Tier Three supports. The Tier Three team also ensures that the school is using the practices of Tier Three with fidelity. The two practices of Tier Three are the FBA and the BSP. Each student receiving Tier Three supports has a specific, individualized BSP that includes strategies to address the setting events, antecedents, behavior, and consequences associated with each student's problem behavior. As such, the interventions or strategies with Tier Three are not necessarily qualitatively different from those with Tier Two. Instead, the school provides them in a more intensive manner and individualizes them for each student by conducting an FBA. For example, a student may receive Check In–Check Out for Tier Two, whereas another student may also receive modified Check In–Check Out for Tier Three along with other strategies to address certain antecedents or consequences unique to that student.

To ensure that the school can implement the practices, it puts certain systems into place. These include processes to identify students for Tier Three, ensuring that someone with behavioral expertise is on the Tier Three team, training and coaching the staff on Tier Three procedures, and implementing effective techniques around data use and BSP development.

Table 4.11: Use of the Problem-Solving Model at Tier Three

	Implementation	Impact	
	Fidelity	Systems	Students
Problem-Solving Step	Is Tier Three being implemented with fidelity?	Do we have a healthy model at Tier Three?	Which students require Tier Three supports?
Step 1: Problem Identification	Administer and examine the overall score on a given fidelity measure (for example, BAT or TFI).	Identify an overall measure of impact, such as "no more than 5 percent of the student population needs Tier Three supports" or a designated percentage of students reach their Tier Three goal.	Use screening measures, pre-existing data, teacher nomination, or the response to Tier Two interventions. Validate the need for support.
Step 2: Problem Analysis	If the score is less than the criterion specified by measure, then examine the subcomponents.	Gather and analyze data as to why the problem is occurring, including fidelity information.	Conduct a full FBA.
Step 3: Plan Identification and Implementation	Develop an action plan to improve the implementation of Tier Three and the method to measure the implementation of the action plan. Identify the way to measure the impact of the action plan.	Develop an action plan to improve the effectiveness of Tier Three.	Provide supports for individual students.
Step 4: Plan Evaluation	Evaluate implementation and the impact of the action plan.	Evaluate the implementation and impact of the action plan.	Monitor supports using fidelity measures and progress monitoring as determined by the team and the intervention. If the student is not making progress, gather data regarding fidelity and the targeted function of the BSP. If the student is making progress, consider reducing or fading supports.

The data within Tier Three are like the data gathered for Tier Two, but they also include examining progress-monitoring data from Tier Two to inform the provision of Tier Three supports. Across those four elements, the Tier Three team uses the PSM to examine both fidelity of implementation and the impact of Tier Three at both a systems level and a student level. The four key elements overlap and the PSM provides a framework to examine issues that entails knowledge and consideration of those four key elements.

5

SWPBIS in Action

The previous four chapters covered SWPBIS and each tier in detail. Perhaps it's evident that SWPBIS is a complex model with specific elements for each tier that can take considerable time to implement. Within this chapter, we provide direction on where to start for educators interested in SWPBIS. We discuss how to plan for change and build momentum, as well as the phases schools go through as they implement SWPBIS. We also provide a timeline of implementation and discuss a general process for implementing each tier. We then discuss how to structure the various teams within SWPBIS and end the chapter with a discussion on sustaining SWPBIS.

> "When we first explored PBIS at the high school, there were a lot of questions about what it would look like and how it would differ from elementary schools. As far as the concept and the rationale behind PBIS, we had tremendous buy-in. Our teachers fully understood the need. They understand a student will be a better student if their social, emotional, and safety needs are met first. It is a long process that requires patience and persistence, and we are still building, but the gains we have already made are encouraging. It would not have been possible without the buy-in and support from administration and staff. That part is essential."
>
> —Laura Shachmut, school psychologist, Brighton High School, Boston, Massachusetts (personal communication, April 26, 2016)

Implementing SWPBIS

Building and implementing SWPBIS is a process that can take several years (Fixsen et al., 2005; McIntosh et al., 2009). There is no set timeline for implementation, as school teams need to reach fidelity with certain aspects of SWPBIS before other components of the model are implemented. A typical process for implementation would be to spend one year with each tier (implementing Tier One to fidelity in year one, implementing Tier Two to fidelity in year two, and Tier Three during year three; George et al., 2009; McIntosh et al., 2009; McIntosh, Frank, et al., 2010; McKevitt & Braaksma, 2008). However, schools should consider natural fluctuations with implementation from year to year, as factors such as irregular or ineffective meetings, significant changes in leadership, and staff turnover can slow progress. Schools progress through four developmental stages of implementation when conducting such large-scale systems change: (1) consensus building, (2) infrastructure, (3) implementation, and (4) sustainability (Fixsen et al., 2005).

1. **Consensus building:** Develop the awareness, need, and justification for SWPBIS.
2. **Infrastructure:** Design the specifics of the model and what it will look like.
3. **Implementation:** Implement the model and work to achieve fidelity with its components.
4. **Sustainability:** Ensure that the model is achieving valued outcomes and focus on embedding the model into the fabric of the school.

During consensus building, schools establish awareness of the need for SWPBIS, as well as buy-in and support for SWPBIS. We discuss this in depth later in the chapter, but all staff within the school need to understand what SWPBIS is, why their school is using it, and what the goals of its use are, and then agree to implement it. This is perhaps the most important step, as the staff need to understand both *what* SWPBIS is and *why* the school is using it. A clear foundation as to why the school is using the model increases its chances of successful implementation and impact (Feuerborn et al., 2013; Tilly, 2008). In addition to building staff consensus, this step also often involves receiving input from families, the community, and students on what is important to these stakeholders related to school culture and climate.

Once a school agrees to implement SWPBIS, the next step is infrastructure. During this stage, the school designs what the model will look like for its site. The leadership team, with staff, family, community, and (often) student input, designs the specifics of the model, as well as teaching the staff the skills needed to implement and use SWPBIS.

During the implementation stage, the school staff implement the model, with a focus on fidelity and getting everyone used to the procedures and processes associated with the model. This stage can take several years, as the school may discover that they need to adjust certain systems or processes as they work through a bit of a trial and error over time (McIntosh et al., 2009; McIntosh, Frank, et al., 2010). Teachers can also consider stakeholder input to refine and tweak the model by surveying parents and students to determine strengths and challenges related to implementation.

Once the school team implements the model as it was designed (that is, with fidelity), the school enters the sustainability stage. Here, the school focuses on determining if they are achieving the desired outcomes and ensuring that the model is a normal, embedded part of the school's culture and fabric. If the school is achieving its outcomes, discussions focus on continuing implementation and developing ways to extend and innovate the model for the school. If the school is not achieving its desired outcomes, then discussion focuses on problem solving and determining where they need to adjust to achieve the desired outcomes. Just like with previous stages, it will be important to continue obtaining input from all relevant stakeholders to maximize sustained outcomes over time.

Teams will likely fluctuate between the implementation stages as they scale up SWPBIS (Fixsen et al., 2005; McIntosh et al., 2009). In fact, schools may move forward with implementation only to find they need to revisit previous stages or refocus on tiers that they have already developed and implemented. In our experience, teams often need to revisit consensus building as they move through consensus too quickly, experience turnover in staff, or have new staff who need refreshers on the reason why the school is using SWPBIS. Because SWPBIS takes several years to implement and because it's such a complex model, it's not unusual to lose perspective of why it is needed. Consequently, schools may find that discussions on consensus and buy-in are an ongoing aspect of implementation.

On a related note, because of the tiered nature of the model, teams may be in different stages of implementation for different tiers. For example, a team may be in the second year of SWPBIS, during which it is implementing Tier One to fidelity and ironing out small issues with that (that is, implementation stage), while at the same time developing their Tier Two procedures (that is, infrastructure stage). This raises the question as to how to handle problematic behaviors while the school is still implementing the model—What do you do during year one if students need additional support? Schools can't provide Tier Two supports, for example, until Tier One is firmly in place; yet students can't wait a year or more for Tier One to get into place. Instead, school teams and personnel must continue with business as usual until components of the model are ready. This leaves the school in the precarious situation of driving the car while it's being built. Whereas certain aspects of the model may not be implemented yet, such as Tier Two or Tier Three, students still need support and shouldn't be denied additional attention and support. The school makes efforts to provide the best support it can while also keeping an eye on the overall goal of SWPBIS. There is a general transition stage between old models for discipline and SWPBIS, so schools will have pieces of both models occurring simultaneously at some point. Unfortunately, schools must be okay with a bit of chaos and uncertainty. This ties back to leadership being critical. Schools will experience frustrations and obstacles as they implement SWPBIS, and leaders will improve the ability to navigate these obstacles if they have the big picture in mind and the staff have bought into the model. In our experience, it takes consistent, regular communication and meetings driven by the PSM to provide students support while also providing attention to the model so it can be further developed.

Having discussed a bird's-eye view of implementation, we want to now make the conversation more explicit. Where should a school start with implementation? We outline four steps next.

Planning for Change

To begin the process of using SWPBIS, schools can consider four steps. In terms of the four key elements, these are systems because they support the staff in implementing aspects of SWPBIS.

These four steps are:

1. Establishing the need for SWPBIS
2. Obtaining leadership support
3. Obtaining staff buy-in and agreement to participate
4. Establishing a team

"As a new principal, a priority of mine was to bring our students, staff, and community together in a positive way where we were all working together towards a common goal. By using PBIS and involving all stakeholders, we were able to deliver a program that our school community felt confident in. We had buy-in from all parties, which opened up communication and gave our school a positive atmosphere, where students were able to live up to their potential. Students were quickly able to recite the school rules and tell us they were excited by the incentives we put in place. Staff members reported their students were beginning to work harder on their behavior and their motivation in the classroom had increased. Our parents told us their students were having more fun at school and the school felt more welcoming. Together we built a better more positive school climate for our staff, students, and parents."

—Lacey Macdonald, principal, Walterville Elementary, Springfield Public Schools, Springfield, Oregon
(personal communication, June 9, 2016)

Establishing the Need for SWPBIS

Start by asking about the extent to which your school *needs* SWPBIS. Are there problems with behavior and discipline within your school that SWPBIS could improve? Is there concern about the school climate or culture? There are many ways to determine the need for SWPBIS, which can include examining referral data and seeing a need for improvement, realizing that students are bullying each other and being disrespectful, or acknowledging an issue with school climate. Schools will establish a need for SWPBIS, which intuitively leads to discussions about outcomes. If they find a need for better school climate and reduced bullying, then natural outcomes from that would be to improve school climate and reduce rates of bullying, for example. Schools first establish the need for change and then determine that SWPBIS can provide a solution to the issues they've identified. The identification of a need for SWPBIS can be identified by one person or by a group of people. In our experiences, sometimes a single staff member learns about SWPBIS at a workshop or conference and brings the idea back to his or her school, whereas other schools learned of SWPBIS as part of a district mandate to implement. Regardless, schools will want to identify their own need for implementation and identify their own outcomes. Schools need to identify their own purpose and reason for SWPBIS.

Obtaining Leadership Support

After identifying a need for SWPBIS, leadership needs to be on board. Without leadership supporting the charge, SWPBIS can't be successful (George et al., 2009; McKevitt & Braaksma, 2008). School staff will likely not buy in to an initiative that the administration is not supporting, and school teams that implement SWPBIS without support can accomplish relatively little before needing leadership. School teams can create foundational ideas for SWPBIS such as expectations or reinforcements, but they need leadership to bring everything together. For example, they need leadership to change schedules to allow teams to meet, to allocate funding to the team, or to invest in necessary changes in data systems to track behavior referrals (George et al., 2009; Sugai & Horner, 2006). If leadership is not in agreement, time is spent on the previous task of examining the need for SWPBIS within the school.

Obtaining Staff Buy-In and Agreement to Participate

Following backing by leadership, the school will garner support for SWPBIS and establish buy-in for the model. Schools that have spent time building the need for change and ensuring that the staff support SWPBIS are more likely to have success with implementation and outcomes (Feuerborn et al., 2013; McIntosh et al., 2009). In fact, each staff member will need to be asked if they will personally implement SWPBIS, because buy-in from at least 80 percent of staff is needed for schools to successfully implement SWPBIS (George, 2009; Kincaid et al., 2010). If less than 80 percent want to implement SWPBIS, then the school team should focus on understanding why the staff do not want to implement SWPBIS and then work to resolve those reasons (Feuerborn et al., 2013). School staff should understand the need for change within the school and what it takes to implement the model, and should identify what skills and resources they need.

One way to envision support for buy-in is to clarify to the staff that they can either be on the SWPBIS bus, or they can stand on the side of the road and wave as the bus passes by. However, they're not allowed to lay across the road and stop the bus from moving (or let the air out of the tires, for that matter).

As Feuerborn and colleagues (2013) recommend, a good place to start for gathering support for SWPBIS is to survey the staff on their perception of the current state of affairs with discipline in the school. The team can administer a brief survey to the staff, possibly also supplementing it with short interviews and conversations. The survey can reveal discrepancies between the staff's beliefs and the practices used in school, then the team can use the responses to move the staff toward realizing the need for change. For example, the survey can ask the staff the following questions.

- ▲ Who should take responsibility for schoolwide discipline?
- ▲ How effective do you feel the consequences for breaking rules are in reducing misbehavior?
- ▲ Do our school's expectations and rules make sense to you?

If the staff agree that schoolwide discipline is the responsibility of everyone, yet they also state that the rules don't make sense, then there is impetus for change. Staff members can also ask students and families similar sorts of questions to get a sense for how they perceive these practices to operate in the school, and with older students (particularly in middle and high school), student focus groups may provide insight into areas of strength and improvement related to school climate, which could ultimately improve staff buy-in. For example, a middle school might have teachers who do not believe eighth graders will want to work for positive incentives. However, asking eighth graders what they like might help staff members see the value of the positives from the student perspective. Alternatively, staff can be asked how satisfied they are with the current way discipline is handled in the school and the extent to which they see a need for change. Such discussions can reveal how motivated staff are to change the current conditions and possible barriers the school team may encounter with staff. Overall, the school team will want to assess the staff's views on the need for a change in current practices, their perceptions of using SWPBIS, and their understanding of SWPBIS (Feuerborn et al., 2013).

There are numerous ways to build awareness of and support for SWPBIS. Here we provide nine ways to build buy-in among staff.

1. **Discuss the benefits of SWPBIS nationally and locally:** School teams can share information on how effective SWPBIS can be in terms of improving student behavior and increasing instructional time. School teams can also share information from other schools within the district or state that are using SWPBIS. Sometimes, school staff need to see the effects of SWPBIS in places like their own school, so displaying data from schools nearby or similar populations may serve to build buy-in (Greenwood et al., 2008). Show the staff data on how many schools are implementing it and that it's been in use for over twenty years in education (for example, Horner et al., 2014).

2. **Explain that it's a long-term commitment and is likely a process that moves slowly:** It's reasonable that school staff may be wary of new initiatives and models, as education has a history of trying new programs or plans frequently (Tilly, 2008). Implementing SWPBIS takes several years to reach sustainability (McIntosh et al., 2009; McIntosh, Frank, et al., 2010), so spend time discussing the slow change that may occur. The process and time that implementation can take should be communicated to staff. This is a good point to make, given that the benefits of SWPBIS may take time to see.

3. **Show the benefit of the data:** As part of implementation, the school will ask staff to record and track data for behaviors and fidelity. Showing the staff that the data are important can help build buy-in because the staff can see that the data actively inform decision making (Feuerborn et al., 2013; George, 2009). The quicker the school can enter and use data, the quicker the staff will support the process and understand that collecting data is not just a box to check off on a list. Instead, it is a critical piece of resolving issues within the school. Additionally, using and showing data will help the staff see any inconsistencies in how behavioral infractions are documented and intervened upon and will provide opportunities for growth and refinement of this process.

4. **Gather data beyond behavior:** Research has correlated implementation of SWPBIS to fidelity with significantly lower levels of staff burnout and higher levels of efficacy (Ross et al., 2012) and with the organizational health of the school (Bradshaw et al., 2008). To illustrate that SWPBIS is about more than just behavior, gather data on the staff's morale, their sense of belonging to the school, the positivity in the work environment, or the overall organizational health of the school (Feuerborn et al., 2013). These data build buy-in and demonstrate that SWPBIS can make the school environment a more positive and healthy place.

5. **Show the impact on instruction:** The leadership team can determine how much time is spent on referrals and discipline and illustrate how that takes away from instruction. This will show the importance of the data that are being gathered. For example, if a school has ten referrals each day, and each referral costs teachers five minutes of instruction, that is fifty minutes each day of lost

instructional time. Reducing referral rates can translate into increased instructional time (Scott & Barrett, 2004).

6. **Discuss the unintended consequences of uncommitted staff:** School teams may also want to spend time illustrating the dangers of staff not being fully committed. Imagine a situation in which one teacher reminds students to put their cell phones away in class only to have students argue and say, "Mrs. Elizabeth doesn't care if we use our phones! Why do you?!" When one teacher ensures that students follow the expectations and another does not, this can lead to unnecessary conflicts and confusion about what is okay and not okay in the school.

7. **Build knowledge and skills:** A good way to build understanding of SWPBIS is to have the staff engage in activities to do just that. Have a book or article study in which staff read about SWPBIS and discuss their takeaways from the content. Have the staff visit other schools that are implementing SWPBIS so they can see and understand what SWPBIS looks like in action. The leadership team can also build buy-in by providing purposeful training and coaching to the staff. This provides certain staff the skills and confidence they need that may be preventing their implementation efforts (Chard & Harn, 2008; Greenwood et al., 2008).

8. **Assess what is in place:** Teams can conduct a self-assessment to determine which components of the model are currently in place, and they can use these strengths to build an action plan (Horner et al., 2014). This can make the daunting task of implementing seem less arduous if the staff see that they have many things already in place. The leadership team can celebrate what is already in place, use this information to help staff see which components of SWPBIS are already happening, and then prioritize further implementation efforts. Additionally, teams can prioritize based on the self-assessment where to focus resources (for example, team work time, funding) for beginning their work on implementation of SWPBIS.

9. **Discuss the *why*:** Simon Sinek (2009) discussed the *golden circle*, which encompasses the why, how, and what of a business. The *what* is what a person does, such as teaching reading or providing services to students in special education. The *how* is how you accomplish the *what*, such as using direct instruction or using a cognitive-behavioral model. The *why* is the purpose and reason for a person or institution. As Sinek asks, "Why do you get out of bed in the morning, and why should anyone care?" Sinek argues that starting with your *why* provides a driving force and vision for your institution. However, he points out that most people start with their *what* first. Starting with *why* is more inspiring and can unify your school around a common purpose. With SWPBIS, we argue that schools should start with the *why* behind their school and then determine if SWPBIS aligns with that *why*. If schools want to use SWPBIS, then they should discuss *why* they're doing it before they get to the *how* or *what*.

"People don't buy what you do, they buy why you do it."

—Simon Sinek, ethnographer and author of *Start With Why: How Great Leaders Inspire Everyone to Take Action*

One final note is that consensus is more than just having all staff on board with implementation. It includes providing a foundation of communication, collaboration, and operations (Feuerborn et al., 2013). As schools implement SWPBIS, they will encounter obstacles, some of which only the staff can see. To ensure that the barriers are addressed, the staff must be able to communicate their concerns to the leadership team (Chard & Harn, 2008).

Establishing a Team

Next, the school establishes a leadership team. While there may be some members who are on the leadership team prior to this point, the school officially forms the team after establishing support. This is because staff members may want to be a part of the leadership team after the entire staff learns of SWPBIS. By waiting to establish the leadership team, there will be a more collaborative approach, and the staff will feel that they are a part of SWPBIS instead of it being dictated to them (which ties back to building sufficient buy-in for the model).

This team will create the model and coordinate all aspects of its implementation. As such, it needs personnel who understand the scope of work and are willing to stick through it all. The team members should understand the multiyear commitment it takes to implement SWPBIS and that it requires personal investment in learning more about SWPBIS and behavioral theory (Feuerborn et al., 2013; Greenwood et al., 2008; Tilly, 2008). Once team members agree to this, their first task is to develop a mission statement (as discussed in chapter 2).

To provide a clearer description of implementation, we have included an example of a timeline of implementation for a school we have worked with in the past. See figure 5.1.

Date	Activities	Personnel Involved
School Year 1 Fall	▸ The school psychologist attends a national conference and learns about SWPBIS.	School psychologist
School Year 1 Winter	▸ The school psychologist shares information about SWPBIS with the principal. ▸ The school psychologist and principal review the data on problem behavior (ODRs, suspensions, and so on) and conclude that the school needs SWPBIS.	School psychologist Principal
School Year 1 Spring	▸ Staff are provided a one-hour presentation on SWPBIS. They have a chance to ask questions and discuss the need for SWPBIS within their school. ▸ The principal surveys the staff anonymously on their willingness to implement SWPBIS.	All staff
	▸ The school site learns that the district is providing SWPBIS training in the summer. ▸ The principal and school psychologist form a leadership team to attend. The principal gathers volunteers and asks specific teachers. ▸ The school team conducts a self-assessment or baseline fidelity measure (Benchmarks of Quality; BoQ) to determine features of SWPBIS already in place.	Leadership team All staff

Date	Activities	Personnel Involved
School Year 2 Summer	▸ The school team attends a district-led training on SWPBIS. ▸ The school team uses BoQ data to create an action plan. ▸ The school team develops Tier One components including expectations, lesson plans, and referral processes. ▸ The school team identifies systems and procedures for ensuring data collection related to ODRs.	Leadership team
School Year 2 Fall	▸ The leadership team introduces the Tier One components to the staff during in-service prior to school starting. The team solicits feedback and makes necessary revisions.	Leadership team
	▸ The leadership team meets monthly and revises the Tier One components based on feedback. ▸ The leadership team finalizes the office discipline referral form.	Leadership team
	▸ School staff receive training on the data-management system designed for use with SWPBIS.	All staff
School Year 2 Winter	▸ The leadership team rolls out SWPBIS. A schoolwide assembly occurs during which school leaders introduce SWPBIS to students, followed by instruction in various locations around the school.	Leadership team All staff
	▸ The leadership team holds monthly meetings during which members examine referral data to determine impact of SWPBIS. ▸ The leadership team also examines fidelity data by using the PBIS Implementation Checklist (PIC) and the PIC Walkthrough data.	Leadership team
School Year 2 Spring	▸ The leadership team administers the Self-Assessment Survey (SAS) to gather staff feedback on implementation.	Leadership team
	▸ The leadership team continues to hold monthly meetings to examine referral data to determine the impact of SWPBIS.	Leadership team
	▸ The leadership team completes a fidelity assessment (BoQ) in late spring to determine the Tier One fidelity score.	Leadership team
School Year 3 Summer	▸ The leadership team meets for a workday to review ODR data, fidelity data, and SAS data to update the action plan.	Leadership team
School Year 3 Fall	▸ The leadership team conducts a refresher training for staff on SWPBIS the week before school starts. ▸ The team provides training to students during the first week of school. ▸ The team measures Tier One fidelity to ensure it's at minimum criteria to implement Tier Two.	Leadership team All staff All students
Additional Years	▸ The leadership team continues to examine fidelity and roll out additional parts of the model in later years.	Leadership team All staff

Figure 5.1: Implementation timeline.

Having discussed a general timeline for implementation and building support for the model, we turn our attention to implementing each tier. Here, we discuss specifics for each tier.

Designing and Implementing Tier One

The leadership team begins implementation of Tier One by assessing the fit between SWPBIS and what is already in place at the school. For example, the school may have developed expectations already, so the school team can assess their expectations to see if they match what is required for SWPBIS expectations—for example, Are the current expectations broadly defined? Are there five or fewer? Following an assessment of what is in place that meets SWPBIS guidelines, the school team then designs the model and identifies concretely what it will look like. Teams start with designing Tier One, which generally consists of five large steps.

1. Identify schoolwide expectations.
2. Develop procedures for teaching the schoolwide expectations.
3. Develop procedures to reinforce the schoolwide expectations.
4. Develop procedures to correct and respond to unwanted behaviors.
5. Develop procedures for ongoing monitoring of implementation and impact of SWPBIS.

Identifying Schoolwide Expectations

To identify schoolwide expectations, a leadership team has a few options for developing a draft of expectations. First, leadership teams can examine their school's mission statement and identify traits of students within the mission statement to use as expectations. Second, they can think of traits that it takes for students to be successful, such as persistence and integrity, and then use them as schoolwide expectations. Third, and perhaps most ideal because it can create expectations that directly target problem behavior, they can use data to identify the expectations (George, 2009; George et al., 2009). The school can examine the number of referrals for problem behavior and identify the most common occurrences of problem behavior. They then create expectations that teach the skills students need to no longer use the most-cited problem behavior. For example, if schools see a high rate of cheating and plagiarism, they could identify one expectation of "be honest" (George et al., 2009). Teams can also survey students, parents, and staff to ask them about expectations, or they can have the staff draft expectations. For example, the team may conduct an activity in which each staff member writes a list of three to five traits that students need to succeed. Next, each staff member pools his or her list of traits with a peer and selects three traits from their combined list. Then that pair gets together with another pair and identifies three traits from their combined lists. This process continues until the staff makes a manageable list that they can vote on.

Once the team drafts a set of expectations, it's important to allow input from the rest of the staff before finalizing the expectations. The team may also wish to vet those expectations with students and families to get their input and to be culturally sensitive to community and family needs. This is especially for middle and high school teams because the older students are more likely to follow and support schoolwide expectations if they have a voice in creating them (Bohanon, Fenning, Borgmeier, Flannery, & Mallory, 2009; George, 2009). Just like getting buy-in for SWPBIS systems implementation, teams should obtain evidence that key parties value the expectations.

After finalizing the expectations, the leadership team will identify the common settings that all students have access to, such as the classroom, hallway, playground, commons or cafeteria, and library. In considering the settings, teams will want to identify what is unique and relevant for their school; for example, one school we worked with had pod areas made up of four connected classrooms. Thus, they had a pod setting on their matrix. Accordingly, the leadership team displays that list of common settings on the schoolwide matrix and then coordinates writing the rules for each setting for each expectation. They can do this in a variety of ways. The leadership team can divide up the sections in the matrix and team members can draft rules for each location. The team can also ask staff members to write rules for a location, after which the staff can review them and provide feedback. As with the expectations, it's important to allow the staff to provide input on the rules.

Developing Procedures for Teaching the Schoolwide Expectations

Once the leadership team creates the expectations, it will want to identify how best to teach those expectations. Again, this has a variety of options, but the general approach is to teach students using instructional principles such as modeling, leading, and practicing of the expectations and to teach in the actual setting. It's not enough to identify the expectations and post them in the school. Staff will want to actively teach students what the expectations look and sound like in each setting and provide students a chance to practice displaying the expectations.

As one example, a school had three expectations (Be Safe, Be Respectful, Be Responsible) and defined what those expectations looked like in common settings (classroom, hallways, gym, cafeteria, a commons area, and the bus). The school developed lessons for each setting that illustrated what the expectations looked like in that setting. School staff divided up each location and were allowed time to develop a lesson plan, after which the leadership team provided feedback and created final lessons. This resulted in a total of six lesson plans for the school (one for each setting that covered all three expectations per setting). Students were then taught the lessons using a rotating training schedule where groups of twenty-five to thirty students rotated to each location for the lesson (which lasted approximately twenty minutes). At each location, the staff modeled the expectations for students using examples and nonexamples to illustrate the expectations for that location, after which students role-played or practiced the expectations. As a side note, students should only practice the positive examples, as they often don't need practice with nonexamples, and staff want to avoid inadvertently teaching students nonexamples of the expectations. The staff should illustrate nonexamples, which also provides added engagement for students because the adults are being silly and "acting like students."

This is just one example of teaching, but other options include creating a lesson for each expectation that incorporates elements from all the settings identified within the school. Teachers can also introduce the expectations to their students in their respective classrooms, after which they teach their students in the actual settings. We mentioned in chapter 2 that there are often schoolwide assemblies to introduce students to SWPBIS, after which students are taught in the actual settings in smaller groups. Teams can also create skits or videos about their expectations. There is a plethora of resources online to support schools with developing lesson plans and procedures for teaching. We recommend that schools actively search PBIS websites (for instance, Florida's Positive Behavior Support Project: A Multi-Tiered Support System, http://flpbs.fmhi.usf.edu) or the national website for PBIS (OSEP Technical Assistance Center on Positive Behavioral Interventions and Supports, www.pbis.org) for resources and ideas on teaching expectations.

Developing Procedures to Reinforce the Schoolwide Expectations

Following identification of the expectations and rules and the development of the plan to teach those expectations, the leadership team determines how best to reinforce students for displaying the expectations. For this step, the leadership team and staff determine how they wish to reinforce and acknowledge students for displaying the expectations. As discussed in chapter 2, the team will want to identify four types of reinforcement: high-frequency acknowledgments, long-term acknowledgments, group recognition, and noncontingent acknowledgments. The general approach here is to brainstorm and identify what is reinforcing to students and determine how to organize and structure that reinforcement. This is an iterative process, as schools may find that after they implement a system, they need to adjust the methods or criteria to receive reinforcement to ensure that the rewards are obtainable and valued by students. We offer some guidelines to consider here when developing rewards for students.

▲ Survey students to find what is reinforcing to them and to brainstorm ideas. Students can identify things they would like to work for and provide an idea of how much they should "cost." This is especially helpful in middle and high schools, where student input is especially critical for buy-in. One school we worked with uses peer-to-peer tickets in which students give tickets to each other, an idea that came from the students.

▲ Ask students how often they would like acknowledgment. Do they think once a week is enough? Once a day? This can provide a baseline for staff on how often to provide praise (George, 2009).

▲ Space out rewards throughout the year to avoid satiation and running out of rewards after the start of the year (George, 2009). For example, for a school store, don't place all the highly desirable items out at once and inadvertently end up with a store with not many valued items by midyear. Also track what items are bought first to determine students' most valued items.

▲ Consider the developmental appropriateness of acknowledgments and plan a range because some students will need and benefit from regular access to small rewards and others will be more interested in working for longer periods of time for larger rewards.

▲ Consider setting students up for success and making rewards based on cumulative rather than consecutive success. For example, setting a criterion like "When the school earns one thousand all-star tickets, we will have a popcorn movie party" is more likely to be successful for students than setting a criterion like "If we have six weeks with no referrals for aggression, we will have a party." The latter option is difficult to implement because if students experience a failure early on, the motivation to continue to participate is lost, and a failure late in the process results in discounting all the appropriate behavior for a long period of time.

Developing Procedures to Correct and Respond to Unwanted Behavior

Another step for establishing Tier One elements is to develop procedures for discouraging and managing unwanted behavior. This involves three clear steps in which school staff and teams (1) develop and teach operational definitions of problem behaviors, (2) identify a range of strategies to use to respond to various behaviors, and (3) develop a response process or flowchart that organizes those responses to different types of behaviors. We discussed these processes at length in chapter 2 (page 27), so we'll briefly summarize each step here.

The first procedure is defining which behaviors are minor, which are major, and which are crisis behaviors. This can also include defining minors to include behaviors that are corrected but not recorded on an office referral form and those that are corrected and documented. Each school will decide on such definitions. We've worked with schools that have two types of minor behaviors (for example, corrected and unrecorded minor behaviors such as running in the hallway, and corrected and recorded behaviors such as cheating on an assignment) and with schools that always correct and record one type of minor behavior. To also reiterate a point from chapter 2, schools will go through an iterative process as they establish agreement on the different definitions and types of behavior.

Following the definitions, the staff can determine what responses are appropriate to use for minor versus major. For example, are staff allowed to use a *time-out from reinforcement* procedure for minor behaviors, and if so, when and how will that time-out from reinforcement procedure be structured? An example time-out from reinforcement procedure might involve having a student stand on the wall (or walk or run laps rather than participate in a structured kickball game) following a verbal outburst on the playground. The time-out from reinforcement procedure is meant to reduce the likelihood of future problem behavior by following a minor misbehavior with a consequence that does not allow access to a reinforcing activity (for example, kickball if it is a preferred activity). We've worked with several schools where they decided that for initial minor behaviors, students could not be sent out of the room, so they developed responses that incorporated in-classroom responses.

Organizing the responses to behaviors into a flowchart or process is an iterative process. The team can draft a response and allow for staff input, but as they implement the process, the team will need the ability to receive feedback and modify or refine the process. For example, we had one school that developed a procedure in which teachers would house their own minor ODRs in a binder and track when students received three for the same behavior. However, the school discovered that if teachers were housing the ODRs in a binder in their classroom, it wasn't clear when and how they would enter that data into their data-management system for the leadership team to analyze the behavior. This resulted in a refinement in which the school counselor would gather the binders once a week and enter the data so the leadership team had up-to-date data to use.

After the initial teaching of procedures and definitions, it can be helpful (and is almost always necessary) to incorporate brief review activities into staff meetings at least every other month or so to continue to hone the definitions and responses. One helpful activity can be for the leadership team to review actual major and minor referrals, take student names off, and share the referrals with staff. Staff can discuss them briefly and then come to consensus on whether the behavior should be office managed (major), teacher managed but documented (minor), or simply corrected and not documented. This is just one example of the ongoing coaching and practice that the staff itself will need with learning and using a new system.

Developing Procedures for Ongoing Implementation and Impact of SWPBIS

The final major step for implementing Tier One is developing those procedures to monitor both implementation and the impact of Tier One. The leadership teams will set up regular meeting times and designate agendas that allow time for examination of both the implementation of Tier One and times for examining the impact of the model. As discussed in previous chapters, teams can use a rotating agenda or designate certain minutes from each meeting to certain topics. The procedures will vary among schools, but teams will want clear procedures for gathering data (for instance, when and how to complete an office referral) and where to enter the data (for instance, designated times or on a rolling basis to input into the student information system), and then procedures to review the data as a team and with the whole staff.

Designing and Implementing Tiers Two and Three

Like Tier One, the design and implementation of Tiers Two and Three require some broad steps. The first step for Tier Two is to identify a list of interventions to use at Tier Two. The team should consider the needs of groups of students and analyze group-level data for Tier Two. In our experience, it is beneficial to start with Check In–Check Out as a Tier Two intervention because it is supported by a large body of research and includes all the critical features of Tier Two interventions outlined by Anderson and Borgmeier (2010) that we discussed in chapter 3. Additionally, Check In–Check Out is easily modifiable to meet a large range of student needs and can be used in a variety of contexts (see Boyd & Anderson, 2013). Next, it will be important for the team to develop a Tier Two teaming structure in relation to the other SWPBIS teams in the building. We discuss team structure next, but the exact formation of the team will depend on the size of the school. The Tier Two team should meet regularly (usually at least twice a month) to review and share Tier Two implementation and impact data. Because Tier Two interventions are not something everyone is doing all the time as with Tier One, the Tier Two team needs to provide an overview of Tier Two interventions to all staff and then make sure there is a process for keeping staff informed and bought in to what is going on so when it does become relevant for them (that is, a staff member has a student with a need for Tier Two supports), students and staff are able to quickly and efficiently access what they need.

Once the team has designed and implemented Tier Two elements well, the focus of the school shifts to its Tier Three elements. Like when Tier Two was added, the school teams should consider how to embed the Tier Three teaming structures with existing teaming structures and within practices relating to special education (since some but not all students may also receive special education supports). Just as staff at Tier Two must be trained on features of intervention implementation for Tier Two interventions, staff must develop behavioral expertise to implement individualized interventions for Tier Three supports. Like Tiers One and Two SWPBIS systems, Tier Three system implementation necessitates buy-in with staff for supporting all students in the building (for instance, students receiving Tier Three supports are not sent out of the room for someone else to manage). Once staff have a commitment and vision to supporting all learners, staff should receive training on the process for accessing individualized comprehensive supports and should receive regular communication about how students are progressing on these interventions.

We briefly outlined broad steps that schools will progress through as they develop the key elements (outcomes, practices, systems, and data) for each tier. As schools build the tiers of their model and implement them, they will add more teams to manage and oversee each tier. This raises the question as to how to organize the different teams. We discuss that next.

Structuring Teams

Schools that begin implementation of SWPBIS will start with one leadership team because they are implementing only Tier One at the beginning (George et al., 2009). As school teams implement the additional tiers over time, the school may add other teams to manage Tiers Two and Three. In doing so, schools must determine how best to organize their teams. There is no one right answer for how to structure teams. However, a school can consider the roles and tasks that a team must achieve, and then organize their teams around those tasks, whether it's one team or separate teams. Within this section, we offer examples on how schools can organize their leadership teams along with teams for Tier Two and Tier Three.

Schools may elect to have one leadership team that manages all aspects of SWPBIS; this team will design and manage all the tiers. One benefit of this approach is that all members are aware of the entire model, which leads to a lower risk of communication breakdown. For example, an elementary school had one leadership team that managed all aspects of SWPBIS and met weekly to examine impact of the model and to problem solve issues around implementation. The team used a rotating agenda each week to alternate between discussing implementation of the model, the impact of the model, implementation of interventions, and the impact of the interventions (see figure 5.2).

Week	Focus	Example Topics
1	SWPBIS implementation (systems-level problem solving)	Training on entering discipline data Determining when to give out certain rewards to students
2	SWPBIS impact (systems-level problem solving)	Examining discipline data for each grade level Reviewing screening data to analyze the health of the system
3	Intervention implementation (student-level problem solving)	Training the staff to implement certain interventions Clarifying procedures for referring students
4	Intervention impact (student-level problem solving)	Evaluating referrals for new students Discussing students' progress with respective interventions

Figure 5.2: Example of a weekly rotating agenda.

This is a thorough model to use, but the frequency of the meetings may burden teachers (in fact, this elementary school would often cancel meetings from time to time to avoid staff burnout). Additionally, for larger schools, this model does not allow for as even of a division of work (that is, there are more staff members to divide among different teams) and expertise (for example, more specialized support on Tier Two and Three teams around behavioral expertise may be more useful than on SWPBIS Tier One teams) as what may be accomplished when teams are more narrowly focused on one or two tiers.

The size of a school or the logistics may lead a school team to have one leadership team that oversees the design and implementation of Tier One and to then have other teams or workgroups manage Tier Two and Tier Three supports, respectively. For example, one middle school had a large leadership team that managed implementation of Tier One, which included designing and training the staff on the components of Tier One. They then had additional personnel serve on the Tier Two team (some of whom also served on the Tier One team). This team managed Tier Two, and the team was responsible for selecting interventions, training staff to use the interventions, identifying students who were to receive Tier Two supports, providing those supports, and then monitoring progress and making any necessary adjustments. For students unsuccessful with Tier Two supports, the Tier Two team would then refer students to the Tier Three team, which was responsible for providing support and monitoring progress of students receiving Tier Three supports. This Tier Three team had a structure that was like that of the Tier Two team.

As another example, one school had a schoolwide Tier One leadership team design all aspects of the SWPBIS model, and then a combined Tier Two and Tier Three behavior coordination team that managed the provision and monitoring of interventions provided to students. Although the behavior coordination team conducted brief problem solving and intervention tweaks, in-depth problem solving happened at individual student support meetings they scheduled as needed so that individuals knowledgeable about the individual student could attend. Therefore, this school had one leadership team, an additional behavior coordination team that monitored all Tier Two and Tier Three interventions, and as-needed individualized student support Tier Three meetings for students who needed intensive assessment and individualized support planning.

Ensuring Effective Teams

Here, we discuss considerations to ensure that the teams the school creates are productive and effective. Although other resources offer information on running effective teams, we summarize salient points for making SWPBIS teams effective.

▲ **Teams will need time set aside to complete the tasks needed for the start-up, implementation, and ongoing examination of SWPBIS:** Some of the tasks required during the earlier stages of implementation can be quite lengthy, such as designing expectations and updating or creating lessons plans. Teams will set aside time specifically for that purpose, and then have devoted, protected time during implementation. In fact, teams may set rules for the school staff to protect the meeting, such as no interruptions, turning off all cell phones, or the door staying closed during the meeting. Leadership teams should meet at least monthly when designing the model and more as needed. Tier Two and Three teams may need at least two meetings per month to monitor and evaluate interventions and additional meetings to discuss implementation issues. Setting aside time to complete the tasks is an important part of implementation. As Marcie Handler and colleagues (2007) stated:

> Our unpublished data indicate that the leadership team needs approximately 40 to 50 [hours] of planning and development time during the first year to identify the schools' needs, develop a plan, and present the plan to staff and students. Following the launch of the SWPBS plan, the leadership team members will need approximately 2 [hours] per month to discuss plan effectiveness and determine if the desired outcomes are forthcoming or if modifications to the plan are needed. (p. 30)

- ▲ **To create teams, it makes sense to ask for volunteers:** This is because assigning people to the team could lead to nonproductive or reluctant members (George, 2009). We also recommend that the team be limited to no more than eight people. With over eight people, the team may stall in making decisions because there are too many voices providing input. For the team to move forward and make decisions, we suggest four to eight people, with smaller schools having teams of four to five and larger schools with five to eight members.

- ▲ **The team members should understand what they're getting into with being on this team:** Time should be taken to discuss the nature and purpose of SWPBIS and the purpose of the team before beginning the work of the team. All members should have a clear understanding of what they're getting into (for example, how long they will serve on the team, and how often the team will meet). They should be receptive to further training on SWPBIS, should be able to stay positive, and should be able to keep their eye on the big picture. In short, the team members should understand that they are going to learn and adopt a different way of viewing behavior and discipline than they may have in the past (Handler et al., 2007; Sugai & Horner, 2009).

- ▲ **All staff members on the team should be supportive of each other and in favor of SWPBIS:** Although some school sites may feel it is ideal to have one person not sold on SWPBIS to be on a team in order to provide a critical perspective, we recommend that you simply not have them on the team (George, 2009). All members should feel supported by each other and be aligned toward one goal. Someone who is detracting from the overall mission or providing dissension will only stall the team's efforts.

- ▲ **The team should also receive training on how to run productive meetings and how to use the problem-solving model to identify and solve issues that arise:** One model designed for that purpose is team-initiated problem solving (TIPS; Newton, Todd, et al., 2009). One feature of TIPS is the use of a minutes sheet to organize topics so that the majority of time is spent reviewing data and focused on problem solving instead of wasting time on uncontrollable factors or nonessential topics.

- ▲ **Each team should identify and set group norms:** Team members should agree on norms for functioning, such as staying on-task, keeping emotions in check, and following time limits. One norm we like is that problem solving and discussion take place during the meeting—not in the hallway in between classes, not after school, and not during a lunch break. Issues are addressed in the meeting so that all members are within the loop.

▲ **Schools should not have several teams with overlapping purposes:** Teams may have a school improvement team, a discipline team, and an anti-bullying committee, for example. One of the early tasks of the leadership team or of administration is to coordinate and streamline efforts. Overlapping teams and initiatives can be examined and combined to reduce redundancy. Teams can list all their overlapping functions to identify areas to merge or eliminate teams.

Sustaining the System

The process of building and implementing the tiers of SWPBIS can take considerable time. Once a team has built consensus and implemented each tier to fidelity, they can turn their attention to ensuring that sustainability is achieved. Sustainability is "durable, long-term implementation of a practice at a level of fidelity that continues to produce valued outcomes" (McIntosh et al., 2009, p. 328). For SWPBIS, this means that the practice is being implemented with fidelity and is achieving the desired outcomes that have been defined for each tier. During this stage, the focus is on ensuring that the model is embedded within the culture of the school and that it's producing the desired results. A team achieves sustainability if the model continues within the school despite staff turnover. Here, the model is not dependent on any one person. Instead, the school team has implemented the model to fidelity, and it is part of the school's culture. This stage also includes examining the model for any needed changes to ensure that the school team achieves the outcomes. As such, the team may further refine certain processes or components of the model to reach the desired outcomes. Teams should not assume that once fidelity is achieved, it will simply remain forever. There are many factors that can positively or negatively influence fidelity (for example, turnover in team members, budget cuts, or administrator change). Therefore, teams continue to evaluate fidelity of all tiers of SWPBIS at least annually.

School teams will not achieve full implementation within a year or two; instead, implementation of SWPBIS to sustainability can take between six and ten years (McIntosh, Frank, et al., 2010). It's important that school teams keep in mind that development and implementation of SWPBIS within a school is an iterative process. There are a lot of moving parts and both large and tiny systems that need examination and alignment to support implementation. All of this takes time to examine and refine to find a supportive, effective process. In fact, it is common for schools to develop parts of SWPBIS, implement those parts, and then need to revisit and adjust certain parts as they roll out their model (Greenwood et al., 2008). We want to highlight the iterative and unfortunately slow-moving process that school teams will go through to achieve full implementation.

Dealing with Interruptions in Implementation

Finally, we want to discuss interruptions in implementation. What happens when a school team implements SWPBIS with enthusiasm, and it wanes over time? How can that school recapture that energy?

We believe schools need an honest discussion at times to ask, Where are we? and Where are we going? Using incentives and rewards can evoke different views about how students learn and develop skills. Having those discussions can help people respect others' views and remind them why SWPBIS uses rewards and behavioral principles. Additionally, Sinek (2009) discusses the golden circle, and we endorse this belief of reaching a shared understanding with everyone regarding where they are going and why (hence, the mission statement being one of the first key pieces to do). Staff members can have discussion and activities around identifying what they want out of SWPBIS and the exact purpose behind its use. From there, they can move into how they'll achieve that purpose and what they'll use to do so. It is also important to remember that as staff turnover occurs and as student culture shifts over time, this honest discussion will help teams assess whether they need to reteach or renew and revitalize the culture. For example, after ten years of implementing SWPBIS, a team may recognize that the schoolwide expectations established at the onset of implementation ten years ago need to be changed to reflect the current culture of students and staff in the building.

Schools can also assess themselves using a framework provided by Mary Lippitt (1987; see also Knoster, Villa, & Thousand, 2000). Schools are familiar with trying new initiatives and having new policies year after year. Working within such change can create a variety of achievements, but also frustrations and difficulties. When managing complex change, a school team can consider the components in table 5.1 needed to ensure that they have successful implementation. Within the table, we define each component and the corresponding result if that component is missing. School teams can discuss their model and the barriers to change and determine what is missing based on the components listed in table 5.1.

Table 5.1: Components for Managing Complex Change

Component	Definition	Result If Missing
Vision	The intended achievement	Confusion (Why are we doing this?)
Skills	The skills and knowledge needed to implement SWPBIS	Anxiety (How can we possibly do this?)
Incentives	The various rewards or bonuses associated with successful implementation, such as recognitions and celebrations, that stakeholders value	Resistance (Why do we have to do this?)
Resources	The resources needed to implement SWPBIS, including time, money, equipment, and so on	Frustration (How can we do this without . . . ?)
Action Plan	The explicit steps taken to achieve implementation	False starts (What am I supposed to be doing?)

Source: Knoster et al., 2000; Lippitt, 1987.

As an example, we worked with a school that had pieces of SWPBIS within its school for over seven years. Initially, the team implemented Tier One well and had a lot of enthusiasm with it. Over time, new administrators came and went, state teams came and offered new practices to try, and the school faced a changing student population over time. After seven years, the team had various teams in place, elements of SWPBIS, elements of another schoolwide behavioral model, a schoolwide playground intervention, and a basement full of curricula that had been used and discarded! The school team decided to have an open discussion during a staff meeting about challenges staff faced. The team documented and identified the common themes from the qualitative data, which was that there were too many initiatives and that the staff felt like they were being asked to do too much. As a result, the leadership team wanted to reduce the various initiatives, so they identified alignment between four initiatives that all aimed to improve student behavior. The team presented this information to the staff and allowed the staff to choose the initiative that made sense to use. The staff chose SWPBIS because it was comprehensive and included aspects of all the initiatives. Additionally, the staff acknowledged and openly discussed the frustrations they'd felt with all the various fragments of practices they had in place, which allowed them to renew their energy. They also developed a plan to use their data to guide their decisions, so they ensured clear procedures that made sense for collecting and using data. They also clarified communication processes, which allowed for input from staff to the leadership team about how they were using the processes.

Summary

Within this chapter, we discussed considerations of where schools can begin putting SWPBIS into practice. Schools can begin with the straightforward question of whether SWPBIS is needed within their school. From there, they need to develop a leadership team and build support for the model. Once the school establishes support, it works through identifying the outcomes, practices, systems, and data needed for each tier. We discussed examples and general approaches schools may take for designing their practices and systems for each tier. Schools have various options for structuring their teams, all of which need to consider the size and context of their site. Schools will focus on sustainability after they have implemented their model to fidelity. In the next chapter, we present two vignettes of schools that have implemented SWPBIS to further provide a detailed application of SWPBIS in practice.

6

Case Examples of Schools Using SWPBIS

One of our goals with this book is to provide concrete, clear examples of SWPBIS in action in order to make it feasible and practical for readers. To further ensure this goal, we have devoted this chapter to two different case examples. We describe the four key elements (outcomes, practices, systems, and data) for two schools: an elementary school, Meador Elementary School, and a secondary school, Kennedy Middle School. These schools are fictional, but their specific outcomes, practices, systems, and data are based on real schools. We describe Meador Elementary School's SWPBIS journey before discussing Kennedy Middle School.

Meador Elementary School

Meador Elementary School is a suburban K–5 elementary school of approximately 350 students; the majority are low income (93 percent qualify for free or reduced lunch), 21 percent are English learners, and 20 percent have special education eligibilities. The student population is primarily white (62 percent), followed by Hispanic or Latino (27 percent), and includes multiracial (9 percent) and African American (1.5 percent) students. The school first learned of SWPBIS via a district invitation to participate in a university-district partnership training that spanned four years (one year for training and implementation on each of the three SWPBIS tiers, and one year for maintenance). In exchange for participation, the university provided initial training and coaching support to the district, and the district developed a leadership team with an action plan to develop capacity to implement SWPBIS districtwide over the next five years.

Although the school had independently (outside of the district initiative) sought out some training and implemented some aspects of SWPBIS prior to the district-university partnership year, such as having a set of common expectations and teaching them, 2013–2014 was their first year of formal implementation. Once Meador Elementary School was asked to participate in formal implementation by the district, the administrator took this information to staff in the spring of 2013 and had them vote on whether they wanted to participate in the efforts and commit to implementation over the next five years. Over 80 percent of the staff voted yes, and no staff members were strongly opposed. Some were neutral.

During the fall of 2013, the school selected a leadership team with members from each grade-level team as well as a special education teacher, the administrator, and an unlicensed staff member who provided supervision during recess and lunch. The team attended a full-day training where they learned the critical features of SWPBIS along with several other schools in the district. Following this training, the school then conducted a self-assessment using the tiered fidelity inventory and developed a corresponding action plan. The team defined their target outcomes as increased consistency for students and staff regarding behavioral expectations and procedures for responding to problem behaviors, reductions in problem behavior, increases in student academic engagement, and an overall positive perception of the school culture for students, staff, and parents. To measure these outcomes, Meador Elementary School used monthly ODR data to assess reductions in problem behavior, a survey administered at the end of the 2013–2014 academic year in June to assess school culture and perceptions regarding consistency to responding to behavior, and teacher ratings to assess overall levels of student engagement before and after implementation of Tier One. The team also created an action plan for communicating with families and the community, which initially included sharing and obtaining feedback through the parent-teacher organization. The leadership team's goal was to implement Tier One to fidelity and lay a solid foundation for Tier Two implementation.

Tier One Practices for Meador Elementary School

Following the identification of the outcomes, the leadership team began regular monthly meetings that a district PBIS coach attended, where the team reviewed its action plan and progress toward implementation goals. The administrator (who sat on the leadership team) also made sure there was time on each monthly staff meeting agenda for the SWPBIS leadership team to share updates and receive staff input relative to the action plan.

Meador Elementary School had existing schoolwide expectations created several years prior, so the team only needed to review and update their expectations and previously developed matrices (see figure 6.1). Representatives on the SWPBIS leadership team provided input on the updates and then shared drafts with their respective grade or specialist teams for additional feedback and input, and the feedback enhanced the final version that was adopted in spring 2014. During spring of 2014, the school began a "soft" rollout of its plan by introducing expectations and piloting some of the positive behavior tickets and reward systems. They also began entering ODR data into the SWIS data system, and they reviewed this data monthly at leadership team meetings. At the conclusion of the school year, the leadership team developed and administered a short survey for staff to provide feedback on what was working and what needed improvement relative to school climate and SWPBIS.

	Meador Mallards' Expectations for Success!		
Location	**Be Safe**	**Be Respectful**	**Be Responsible**
All Settings	Keep hands, feet, objects to self. Use materials appropriately. Walk facing forward.	Follow directions the first time. Use kind words and actions. Remove hats and hoods.	Be ready and prepared. Do your best.. Take care of yourself and your belongings. Go directly to where you are supposed to be.

	Meador Mallards' Expectations for Success!		
Location	**Be Safe**	**Be Respectful**	**Be Responsible**
Classroom	Be in the assigned area. Keep all four chair legs on the floor.	Use appropriate voice level and kind words. Listen politely. Ask permission appropriately.	Do your work. Follow directions. Be on time and on task. Have supplies.
Playground	Wait for school staff member before entering play area. Walk in walk zones. Stay in assigned location.	Take turns. Follow game rules.	Follow directions. Use equipment properly. Ask permission to leave the playground. Freeze when whistle blows.
Arrival and Dismissal	Keep hands & feet to self. Wait in your assigned location until you are dismissed.	Follow safety patrol directions.	Stay in appropriate areas when walking (sidewalk, crosswalk). Be on time to your adult or driver. Go directly to your seat.
Lunchroom	Stay seated until dismissed. Eat your own food.	Use level 1 voice in line. Use level 2 voice at tables. Respond to adult signals and directions. Ask permission appropriately.	Keep your area clean and dispose of garbage. Get all utensils, milk, and condiments when going through the line. Report any spills.
Hallways and Stairways	Walk facing forward on the right-hand side. For stairs—keep right hand on the rail, left hand holds materials.	Use level 0 voice in line. Wait while other classes may pass.	Keep hallways, stairways, and pods clean. Stay with your class while moving. Go directly to where you need to go.
Bathrooms	Allow one person in a stall. Wash hands with soap and water.	Use level 1 voice. Give others privacy.	Be quick, clean, and quiet. Remember to flush. Keep trash and water off floor. Return promptly to class.
Special Events and Assemblies	Sit safely and correctly on chair or floor until dismissed.	Applaud appropriately. Use level 0 voice during presentation.	Keep your eyes toward the presenter. Listen to the presenter. Clap when appropriate.
Technology or Virtual Setting	Be sure it is a school- and age-appropriate site. Keep personal information private. Handle equipment with care.	Be polite and courteous when posting or responding to others. Use the THINK method. Leave equipment in the same or better condition than you found it.	Be sure your hands are clean. Stay on assigned task. Do only what your teacher has told you to do. Only use your assigned technology. Report any suspicious use or damage.

Note: Level 0 = voice is off; level 1 = whisper voice; level 2 = table talk for a few people to hear; level 3 = presenting voice (whole room can hear you); level 4 = outside voice; level 5 = emergency voice.

Figure 6.1: Matrix of Meador Elementary School's expectations and rules for common settings.

Tier One Practices for Teaching Expectations for Meador Elementary School

During the start of the 2014–2015 school year, the staff taught the schoolwide expectations from their matrix during the first week of school by holding an assembly, a rotating schedule, and classroom-based teaching. The school first held an assembly on the first day of school where staff participated in several skits demonstrating behavioral expectations and teaching about the schoolwide correction and acknowledgment systems. On the second day, the school held a *rules roundup* where it created a schedule and had relevant staff teach the expectations for common locations (bathrooms, hallways, playgrounds, cafeteria, arrival and dismissal areas, and assemblies). During the latter half of the first week, classroom teachers spent time reviewing classroom expectations for behavior. During the second month of school, classroom teachers taught the Stop-Walk-Talk strategy for dealing with bullying (Ross, Horner, & Stiller, n.d.). Following the initial training, the leadership team at the school used ODR data to identify target areas for each month to focus on reteaching and reinforcing expected behaviors (for example, the team saw a need to reteach lining up on the playground during the first review of the data). The team also planned booster sessions to reteach expectations briefly before and after natural breaks and holidays when student problem behavior typically escalates (George, 2009).

Tier One Practices for Reinforcing Expectations for Meador Elementary School

Meador Elementary School used a comprehensive reinforcement system that included daily tickets that students earned for displaying the expectations. Figure 6.2 displays the school's PBIS ticket, and table 6.1 describes their daily, long-term, group, and noncontingent acknowledgment.

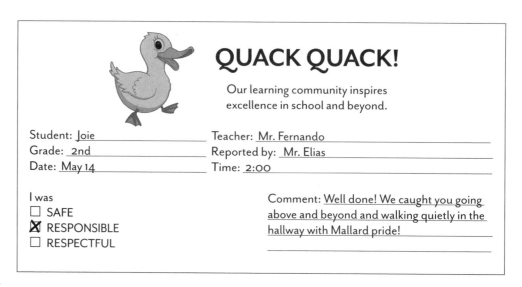

Figure 6.2: Completed example of Meador Elementary School's high-frequency acknowledgment in the form of a ticket.

*Visit **MarzanoResearch.com/reproducibles** to download a free reproducible version of this figure.*

Table 6.1 : Reinforcement Plan for Meador Elementary School

Type	Description	Criteria	Frequency
High Frequency	Students receive Quack tickets for meeting schoolwide expectations	Staff provide tickets to students they see displaying schoolwide expectations	Daily
Long Term	Ticket entry for drawing for prizes	Each Quack ticket is worth one chance to win a prize if the name is drawn	Weekly
	Positive postcard	Teachers or staff write a positive note about the student and drop in office where it is sent home to student's parents	Intermittent (usually more in spring semester)
	Self-manager	Students displaying extended period of meeting schoolwide expectations are nominated by teacher and earn additional privileges	Earned based on weekly performance
Group	Extra recess	Classrooms/grades earn extra recess or other rewards for displaying target behaviors or engaging in appropriate behaviors in target settings; the class or grade with the most tickets earns extra recess	Implemented intermittently but usually earned at the end of a targeted week
	Popcorn party	Grades can earn a gradewide popcorn party at the end of the term for receiving a limited number of major referrals	Once per term
Noncontingent	Field day	Not contingent on behavior	Yearly

Tier One Practices for Managing Misbehavior for Meador Elementary School

One challenge for Meador Elementary School during its first year and a half of Tier One implementation was agreement on how it should document problem behaviors. There was a previous conception that documentation of behavioral infractions could have severe long-term consequences for students (teachers worried, Will this follow the student in his or her cumulative file?), and the staff were leery of documenting minor ODRs because of the connotation of referral as being serious and bad. However, each time the leadership team met to review their ODR data, the team felt the data only represented the most serious problem behaviors and did not actually reflect the problems in the school. Therefore, the leadership team worked with the district coach to overcome this challenge during the 2014–2015 year (even as the focus also began shifting to Tier Two implementation). The team decided to change the referral process to include major referrals, written corrections (previously called *minor referrals*), and verbal corrections (undocumented infractions). Figure 6.3 (page 164) displays Meador Elementary School's chart and includes the behaviors that are verbal corrections (which are behaviors that do not require documentation), written (minor) corrections, and major referrals. Figure 6.4 (page 165) includes the process for responding to the behavior (teacher responses) and strategies that teachers can use for managing the behavior (possible responses). With this example, teachers have a strategy specified for how to respond to a behavior (teacher responses), but they also have additional strategies that they can use based on their personal choice and knowledge of the student (possible responses). This example provides an overall structure for handling behavior, but it also allows for teacher discretion and choice; finally, it reminds them to use the ratio of five positive comments to every reminder or redirection.

Verbal Correction (Not Documented)	Written Correction (Minor Referral)	Major Referral
A student behavior that is solved by a single adult or in-class system, often by reteaching, redirecting, or giving an in-setting consequence (for example, time-out, buddy classroom). This is a behavior that an adult witnesses or confirms through an investigation.	Correction is written after repetitions of these behavior examples within one class period or block of time with a teacher. If student engages in low-level misbehavior and responds appropriately to redirection (fixing his or her behavior), no written correction needed.	A student behavior that is solved using support from more than one adult (typically a specialist or principal). Behaviors that cause harm or are illegal. Any behavior involving more than incidental physical contact.

Figure 6.3: Meador Elementary correction types.

Tier One Systems for Meador Elementary School

The Meador Elementary School leadership team developed and updated systems to increase the likelihood that the school implemented practices and monitored outcomes. As we mentioned briefly, the school had a district coach who attended leadership team meetings and trainings with the team. The leadership team and the coach worked to create an electronic document for all the practices (for instance, expectations matrices, lesson plans for "rules roundup" and classroom teaching, procedures related to reinforcement of appropriate behavior, and how to respond to and document problem behaviors) that they had put into place. The team elected to use Google Drive, as this was part of the district-provided resources and worked well for accessing and sharing information among team members and school staff. The leadership team used the electronic document process as they added information for Tier Two and Tier Three (summaries, how to access, request-for-assistance forms, and so on). The leadership team also adopted the team-initiated problem solving process (Newton, Todd, et al., 2009) for running their meetings, and this system increased their team-meeting focus, precision, and efficiency.

The school used data to increase the likelihood that the team was implementing systems and practices and monitoring outcomes. Student data screening occurred in the fall when the leadership team reviewed ODR data as part of the "October catch" (for example, students who had received two or more office referrals by the end of October were identified as likely candidates for Tier Two supports) and monthly thereafter. Additionally, the leadership team asked teachers to complete a very brief survey where it noted the top-three students with concerns related to being safe, respectful, responsible. They cross-identified these students with ODR and previous intervention data to identify possible candidates for additional supports. Additionally, the leadership team provided an update at monthly staff meetings, which included information such as results of implementation (for example, scores on the tiered fidelity inventory), shared information related to groups of students accessing or receiving supports, and updates on action items related to staff surveys and priorities for school climate and culture. Teachers also used grade-level team meetings to review outcomes related to SWPBIS.

	Written Correction (Minor Referral)	Teacher Responses	Major Referral	Possible Responses
Disrespect	Student delivers low-intensity, socially rude or dismissive messages to adults or students. ▲ "This is stupid," "yeah whatever" (low intensity) ▲ Eye roll or other body language ▲ Heavy sighs ▲ Turning his or her back to speaker ▲ Name calling or mocking—perceived as hurtful (low intensity)	Use regular classroom systems ▲ Label the behavior ("_____ is not [safe] [respectful] [responsible].") ▲ Remind, redirect, reinforce ▲ Apply logical consequence/follow-through Student behavior is not responding to classroom management systems 1. Label the behavior 2. Remind, redirect, reinforce 3. Apply logical consequence/follow-through (for instance, in-class time-out, have student state expectation, time-out on bench) 4. Write Correction 5. Submit correction to Barb's box.	Student delivers socially rude or dismissive messages to adults or students ▲ Verbally refusing or disrespecting: "This is stupid," "You can't tell me what to do," directed at a person or repeated (high intensity) ▲ Profanity directed at a person Reminder: Racial slurs and sexual names fall under harassment	Teacher Response 1. Label the behavior 2. De-escalate student or move student to a different setting 3. Call for help from another adult 4. Document using referral form 5. Submit referral to principal (or to administrative assistant if principal is not in the building that day) Other Possible Responses 1. Principal speaks to student 2. Principal assigns consequence 3. Referral sent home 4. Parent contacted by phone or invited to face-to-face conference
Disruption	Student engages in low-intensity, but inappropriate disruption. ▲ Yelling across room ▲ Tossing things ▲ Side talking and talk-outs ▲ Dropping books with force ▲ Tapping pencil, clicking pen, excessive pencil sharpening ▲ Running or yelling in the hall disrupting classes in session ▲ Clowning around	Three written corrections for similar behavior during the last two weeks will initiate parent contact by the team. The teacher can always contact a parent when parent is involved and it seems that it would be helpful even if the student has not met the three-corrections threshold. Remember, it is important to document incidence of behavior for all students. However, student consequences may be individualized according to individual behavior support plans.	Student engages in intense behavior, causing an interruption in a class or activity, including: sustained loud talk, yelling, screaming, noise with materials, or sustained out-of-seat behavior. ▲ Yelling at teacher or classmates ▲ Throwing objects across room ▲ Slamming doors/chairs/desk ▲ Repeated, continual, ongoing side talking and talk-outs	

Figure 6.4: Process for responding to problem behaviors.

continued ➤

	Written Correction (Minor Referral)	Teacher Responses	Major Referral	Possible Responses
Defiance or Noncompliance	Student engages in brief, repeated, or low-intensity failure to follow directions or talks back ▲ Wearing a hat or hood ▲ Using phone during school hours ▲ Talking back (low intensity) ▲ Repeated refusal to follow directions		Student engages in refusal to follow directions or talks back ▲ Student refuses to leave the classroom when told for discipline issues ▲ Continued refusal to comply or modify behavior in a short period of time ▲ Outright disrespect or defiance: aggressive responses with abusive language Nonexample: Student does not have the supplies or skills to begin working or following directions	
Physical Aggression or Inappropriate Physical Contact	Student engages in minor, but inappropriate physical contact often repeated ▲ Horseplay or rough housing ▲ Unwanted physical contact ▲ Kicking feet ▲ Poking ▲ Invading personal space ▲ PDA—handholding or hugging		Student engages in actions involving serious physical contact where injury may occur (hitting, punching, hitting with an object, kicking, hair pulling, scratching, and so on) Fights: hitting, punching, kicking, hair pulling, scratching Intentional forceful contact PDA beyond handholding or hugging	
Inappropriate Language	Student engages in low-intensity, repeated instance of inappropriate language ▲ Not directed at an individual ▲ Mumbled "This is F-ing stupid" ▲ Conversationally using foul language Nonexample: Student swears impulsively out of pain or anger—not directed at anyone		Student delivers verbal messages that include swearing, name calling, or inappropriate use of words ▲ Name calling with intense or hurtful language ▲ Derogatory language ▲ Language that suggests the other person should self-harm ▲ Directed at an individual Reminder: Racial slurs and sexual names fall under harassment	

Tier Two Practices and Systems for Meador Elementary School

At Meador Elementary School, a separate team from the Tier One team managed Tier Two (and Tier Three) interventions; this team was the Meador Elementary School behavior team, and membership overlapped with the SWPBIS leadership team. The team identified two systems-level outcomes: (1) each Tier Two intervention shows that at least 80 percent of students are successful, and (2) students receive Tier Two interventions within three to five school days of identification.

The Meador Elementary School behavior team consisted of five members: counselor, general education teacher, two special education teachers (one representing primary grades and one representing intermediate), and the school psychologist. The behavior team met twice a month; however, two general education teachers rotated in their attendance (one primary, one intermediate) so that the team always had general education perspective, sometimes primary and sometimes intermediate. The district PBIS coach also participated on the team as often as possible. Because of the research on the effectiveness and ease of modifying Check In–Check Out across behavioral functions, the district implementation model focused on training the school behavior team to implement Check In–Check Out with fidelity as their first Tier Two intervention. As it implemented Check In–Check Out according to the district training model, Meador Elementary School also reviewed other possible Tier Two interventions and kept two others that seemed to fit their needs: mentoring and social skills groups (see table 6.2).

Table 6.2: Meador Elementary School Tier Two Interventions

Intervention	Description	Function or Behaviors
Check In–Check Out	The student will check in each day with an adult to review his or her goals and progress on the Check In–Check Out sheet. The adult will provide the student with positive feedback and reinforcement for progress toward meeting his or her goal and exhibiting desired behaviors. The adult will provide a copy of the Check In–Check Out sheet to the student to take home to his parent/guardian. The student can work toward a variety of rewards that range from immediate and small to larger and delayed. The rewards are identified on a menu. The rewards target a range of functions (for instance, homework passes, free choice time, lunch with a friend or preferred adult, treasure box trip).	Attention seeking and externalizing behaviors; reward menu allows school to address a variety of functions (for instance, obtain item, escape low levels of work) as part of the intervention
Mentoring	The student is assigned a mentor teacher who makes a point of having a positive connection and interaction with the student daily. It is less formal than Check In–Check Out (no card) but provides extra attention from an adult for students who need just a little boost.	Adult attention
Social Skills Group	Students meet in small groups once or twice weekly for direct skill instruction with facilitating teacher/counselor or school psychologist. Target skills are identified based on student assessments/needs identified by teacher (and sometimes students themselves if age appropriate). Specific positive behavior tickets reinforce targeted skills in group (for instance, teachers of students working on asking for help have ten tickets to give for that skill), and adults in natural environment provide specific positive feedback when students engage in the skill. Students exchange tickets in group for positive rewards. The facilitator also provides a homework/home note sheet each week.	Varies, depending on skills targeted

The Meador Elementary School behavior team managed Tier Two interventions, and the Tier Two coordinator was the counselor who tracked all students using the Check In–Check Out SWIS database system. This data system also was used to analyze fidelity and progress-monitoring data for students on Check In–Check Out. For other Tier Two interventions, the team tracked and monitored data using Excel or counselor-created data-tracking processes. The team met every other week to discuss student outcomes (group and individual) or issues with systems or processes of Tier Two and Three behavior supports. The team adopted an electronic meeting minute process (described in Tier One) and used a modified version of the TIPS process with projected minutes and agenda, a precise problem-solving process, and action planning, as well as tracking implementation and impact outcomes. It identified students for Tier Two supports in three ways: (1) as part of ODR review at SWPBIS leadership meetings, (2) via ODR data review at behavior team meetings, or (3) by a teacher completing a request-for-assistance form (see figure 4.6, page 125, for an example). At Meador Elementary School, when a student received a Tier Two intervention, the Tier Two coordinator contacted the teacher, and the classroom teacher contacted the parents to let them know additional information would arrive from the counselor (see figure 6.5).

Mallard Meet Up Initial Parent Contact Form

Student Name: _____ Date: _____

Parent Name: _____ Parent Contact Number: _____

Homeroom Teacher: _____

Made contact with parent?

Must make two attempts, and leave message letting them know we will start the program unless they let us know they do not want student to begin.

Date contacted	Name of parent contacted	Number called	Parent gave permission	Left message
1.			Yes or No	Yes or No
2.			Yes or No	Yes or No

Parent would like contact with the Tier Two coordinator? Yes or No

Notes about parent conversation

_____

_____

_____

_____

Parent Phone Call

When you call home to parents, please be sure to explain the following:

☐ Mallard Meet Up is a program that works really well for students who may need more structured feedback from supportive adults to be successful in school.

☐ The goal of Mallard Meet Up is for the student to have positive interactions with teachers, staff, and you for following school expectations so that he or she is more likely to meet expectations in the future.

☐ They will be getting regular, positive feedback throughout the day. Your student's teachers will be encouraging them to Be Safe, Respectful, and Responsible here at Meador Elementary. The student will also be able to earn additional acknowledgments for meeting daily goals.

☐ The Mallard Meet Up coordinator can call you to explain more details if interested.

Figure 6.5: Sample parent communication form for Tier Two from Meador Elementary School.

The Meador Elementary School behavior team adopted a standard Check In–Check Out point card with a consistent number of check-ins during the day to allow for a more cohesive intervention experience and efficiency for staff and students. Figure 6.6 shows the sample card, which includes the schoolwide expectations in the columns and the major subject areas for the day in the rows. In this case, not all students experienced the subject areas in the same order, but the teacher completed the row corresponding with the subject area at whatever point in the day it occurred. If students did not respond or needed modifications to the standard Check In–Check Out card, the team made that decision based on data from the first several weeks participating in Check In–Check Out. (Note that figure 6.6 was used for intermediate grade levels. The card used for primary grades had a series of neutral to smiley faces instead of "0, 1, 2" for points.)

Mallard Meet Up					
Name: _____ Date: _____					
2 = Yes! 1 = Responded to prompt 0 = No response to prompt					
Daily Schedule	**Safe**	**Responsible**	**Respectful**		**Comments**
Check In	0 1 2	0 1 2	0 1 2		
Math	0 1 2	0 1 2	0 1 2		
Whole-Group Reading	0 1 2	0 1 2	0 1 2		
Small-Group Reading 1	0 1 2	0 1 2	0 1 2		
Small-Group Reading 2	0 1 2	0 1 2	0 1 2		
Recess	0 1 2	0 1 2	0 1 2		
Specials *Music, Library, Other*	0 1 2	0 1 2	0 1 2		
Lunch	0 1 2	0 1 2	0 1 2		
Lunch Recess	0 1 2	0 1 2	0 1 2		
PE or Other	0 1 2	0 1 2	0 1 2		
Writing or Other	0 1 2	0 1 2	0 1 2		
Check Out	0 1 2	0 1 2	0 1 2		
				Total	
Safe: Walk forward; keep hands, feet, and objects to self. **Responsible:** Listen and follow directions first time; take care of self and belongings; go where you are supposed to go. **Respectful:** Do your best; appropriate voice; take care of school and personal property.				Points / Goal / Possible / Meet? Y N	

Figure 6.6: Meador Elementary School's daily point card for Check In–Check Out.

To monitor progress for students receiving interventions, the Meador Elementary School behavior team used a variety of data depending on the intervention. In table 6.3 (page 170) we indicate the interventions and data they used for progress monitoring at the school.

Table 6.3: Tier Two Interventions and Data Used for Monitoring

Intervention	Monitoring
Check In–Check Out	Check In–Check Out data are recorded daily for at least twenty school days. Individual goals may be set based on baseline for determining student rewards. However, the schoolwide Check In–Check Out goal is that student earns 80 percent of points 80 percent of time for at least twenty school days before moving to Check In–Check Out plus self-monitoring.
Mentor	Students are assigned a mentor teacher/staff member who connects with the student at least twice per week. Mentor checks in about specific behaviors the student has struggled with (for example, homework, peer relationships, attendance) and provides a positive connection with the student. Team monitors student ODR data and obtains teacher input for student success or need for more structured Tier Two intervention (for example, Check In–Check Out, social skills).
Social Skills Group	Team groups students according to target social skills. They track specific data on the targeted skill by providing teachers of students in the groups with target skill tickets (for example, if group is working on hand raising, tickets for raising hand). When student engages in target skill, teacher gives ticket. Students bring tickets back to group to exchange for acknowledgments. Teachers track how many tickets are given each week (by subtracting how many remain from how many they were provided), and they provide a quick rating on a Likert scale of student success in engaging in current target behavior as well as the previously targeted behavior and the upcoming target behavior (with the upcoming target rating serving as baseline for the yet-to-be targeted skills).

An additional focus for the Meador Elementary School behavior team for Tier Two was to adopt a process for fading and intensifying supports, and the team focused their efforts on this process for Check In–Check Out. Historically, the school had students who were successful on interventions, but teachers, parents, and sometimes even the students were not willing to stop the intervention for fear of the student reverting back to previous unsuccessful behavior patterns. Therefore, the school adopted different phases for fading their Check In–Check Out, including a self-monitoring component (see table 6.4). After four weeks of Check In–Check Out, the school placed students who had reached their goals each day on the self-monitoring Check In–Check Out. During this phase, students first focused on accurately rating their behavior by matching it with the teachers' ratings (additional rows or columns were created on the Check In–Check Out for the student to provide their ratings or students to circle and teachers to initial on the numbers for their ratings). Once the teachers confirmed accuracy, then the team systematically faded teacher checks.

Table 6.4: Check In–Check Out for Meador Elementary School

Check In–Check Out Phase	Success	Maintain	Problem Solve
Phase 1. Full Check In–Check Out	Eighty percent or more of points earned for sixteen to twenty days, move to phase 2.	Sixty to 80 percent of points earned, continue in phase 1.	Less than 60 percent of points earned, problem solve at behavior coordination team meeting.
Phase 2. Check In–Check Out–Self-Management With Full Check-Ins	Ninety percent of points earned for accuracy (for self-rating) and behavior goal met (at least 80 percent) for two weeks, move to phase 3.	Sixty to 80 percent of points earned for accuracy and/or behavior goal met less than 80 percent of time, continue in phase 2.	Less than 60 percent of points earned for behavior goal, cycle back to phase 1. Less than 60 percent of points earned for accuracy, refer to behavior coordination team for problem solving.
Phase 3. Check In–Check Out–Self-Management With Decreased Check Ins	Ninety percent of points earned for accuracy (self-rating) and met behavior goal (at least 80 percent) for two weeks, move to phase 4.	Sixty to 89 percent of points earned on accuracy, continue in phase 3. Behavior goal met (at least 80 percent) for less than 71 to 90 percent of days, continue in phase 3.	Less than 70 percent of points earned for behavior goal, cycle back to phase 2. Less than 60 percent of points earned for accuracy, refer to behavior coordination team for problem solving.
Phase 4. Full Self-Management of Check In–Check Out	Two weeks with no office referrals, teacher and student input about success, team meets to discuss exit from Check In–Check Out. Team considers whether student needs another less structured way to continue increased connection to school (for example, safety patrol, library monitor, Check In–Check Out student mentor or helper). Student chooses graduation "celebration."	Student has success (zero or one minor ODR), team may continue self-management Check In–Check Out or fade student to a different unstructured intervention or role in the school, such as safety patrol or library monitor, where student continues to receive adult attention but in a less structured way than on Check In–Check Out.	Less than 60 percent of points earned, receives two or more office referrals for behavior goal, cycle back to phase 3 and refer to behavior coordination team for problem solving.

Source: Adapted from Wesley, 2008.

Tier Three Practices and Systems for Meador Elementary School

For Tier Three, the Meador Elementary School behavior team also coordinated the Tier Three practices and systems at the school. Therefore, the school had a two-team structure for SWPBIS: a leadership team and a school behavior team (that is, the Tier Two and Three behavior team). Meador Elementary School also had a separate special education team that met weekly to review supports, evaluations, and other issues pertaining to students referred for or already receiving special education services. Additionally, a subset of the school behavior team would form to conduct the FBA and develop the BSP for each student identified for Tier Three supports. Once the BSP was complete, the school behavior team took responsibility for monitoring all students on Tier Three supports. Each student had a case manager (who could be the special education teacher or the counselor). At meetings, each team member reported on the students on their caseloads.

The outcomes that the school identified at Tier Three were like those at Tier Two in that the Meador Elementary School behavior team wanted at least 80 percent of students to be successful with their supports. The team also wanted to ensure that students who received Tier Three received high-quality, technically sound BSPs based on FBA data. To check this outcome, the team (along with the district PBIS coach) reviewed BSPs to ensure that they were based on FBA data, had team input, and had technical adequacy (that is, they had linked plans to FBA data appropriately). Additionally, the team wanted to ensure that all students receiving Tier Three supports had received previous Tier Two interventions with fidelity or had scored very high on screening assessments. The team used a combination of the Tiered Fidelity Inventory and self-rating measures to evaluate these outcomes.

One advantage of having one team coordinate both Tier Two and Tier Three supports is that the team is familiar with all the students receiving interventions and can track their success or lack thereof. The team could refer for Tier Three supports based on a student's lack of progress in Tier Two, but it also examined a student's ODR patterns or request-for-assistance forms to decide to move into Tier Three supports. If a student received Tier Three supports, the school behavior team identified unique individual student support teams made up of members familiar with the referred student to conduct the FBA and develop the BSP.

The following is an example of how Meador Elementary School used the FBA process to design a BSP. Figure 6.7 shows a competing behavior pathway example for a specific kindergarten student, Canaan. In the case of this student, the team did not find that their Tier Two interventions were a good fit for the student (that is, his behavior was too severe). Therefore, the school behavior team selected a student-focused support team to conduct the FBA. The school psychologist, who had a strong understanding of behavioral theory, led the team. The team included the parent, the classroom teacher, and the playground assistant who provided supervision for kindergarten. After interviewing and observing, the team developed the competing behavior pathway shown in figure 6.7. In the pathway, we see that when the young student, Canaan, was told to put a preferred toy ball away, he often had tantrums, and this sometimes resulted in staff letting him keep the item so that he would calm down. The staff would have liked for the student to put the item away and transition appropriately and have success with the next activity. However, the student did not have the skills to consistently do this. Therefore, the team needed to think about what to do in the short term to start to initiate a more appropriate behavior habit chain that still met the student's needs (for instance, having the student ask for more time with

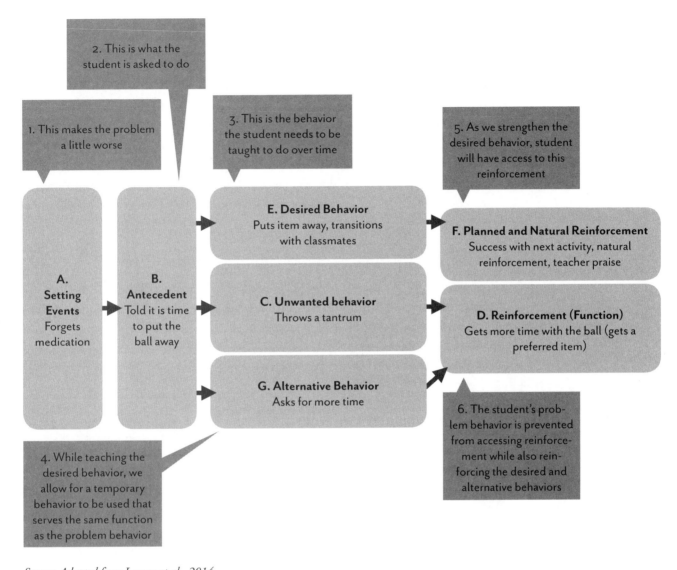

2. This is what the student is asked to do

1. This makes the problem a little worse

3. This is the behavior the student needs to be taught to do over time

5. As we strengthen the desired behavior, student will have access to this reinforcement

E. Desired Behavior
Puts item away, transitions with classmates

F. Planned and Natural Reinforcement
Success with next activity, natural reinforcement, teacher praise

A. Setting Events
Forgets medication

B. Antecedent
Told it is time to put the ball away

C. Unwanted behavior
Throws a tantrum

D. Reinforcement (Function)
Gets more time with the ball (gets a preferred item)

G. Alternative Behavior
Asks for more time

4. While teaching the desired behavior, we allow for a temporary behavior to be used that serves the same function as the problem behavior

6. The student's problem behavior is prevented from accessing reinforcement while also reinforcing the desired and alternative behaviors

Source: Adapted from Loman et al., 2014.

Figure 6.7: Competing behavior pathway elements.

the item). The team would also develop a plan for supporting the student to put the ball away and transition appropriately, and it might take several days or weeks for the student to develop the skills necessary to transition appropriately. However, in the short term, for a student who was currently engaging in problem behavior to get his needs met, they needed to consider the role of this problem behavior and teach a more appropriate way for the student to have his needs met.

Although this was the focus of the BSP, the team also identified that Canaan would benefit from antecedent and consequence modifications. For example, Canaan was only allowed to play with a highly preferred item during times of close adult supervision. Canaan also received prompts and reminders for how to ask for more time when he needed it. Canaan received more time when he asked appropriately, and he also received points toward a special activity when he transitioned appropriately. If Canaan did not ask for more time or engaged in the problem behavior, he would not have access to the item during the following recess time. The team then determined a specific goal for the student that included short- and long-term behaviors (for example, "During recess when Canaan is told it is time to put the ball away, he will ask for more time or put the ball away within thirty seconds with zero tantrums for two consecutive weeks"), and as Canaan worked toward this goal, he was also receiving instruction and reinforcement for transitions in small social skills group time several days a week; therefore, once Canaan reached this goal, the team expected that he would have additional skills, and they could adjust the expectations to limit the number of requests for additional time. The BSP also included strategies for having team members self-assess each day whether they implemented the components of the plan (0 = not well, 1 = mostly, 2 = yes) and whether the plan was having an impact (0 = no, 1 = some, 2 = positive) on the student's behavior. The Meador Elementary School behavior team reviewed Canaan's progress twice a month, and the student-focused support team for Canaan (including his teachers and parents) reconvened as necessary.

Implementation Timeline for Meador Elementary School

Having discussed each tier for Meador Elementary School, we summarize the timeline of implementation for Meador Elementary School in figure 6.8. We share this to present a chronological view of implementation, but also to point out the iterative process of implementation. For example, Meador Elementary School staff were implementing Tier Two during the 2014–2015 school year; however, they had to revisit aspects of Tier One.

Date	Implementation Focus	Tier
Prior to Fall 2013	Informal SWPBIS interest and work to set foundation, getting staff buy-in and beginning development of practices; determined three schoolwide expectations; soft rollout of teaching expectations to students; already using some schoolwide positive behavior tickets ("all stars").	Tier One
Fall 2013	Create formal Meador Elementary School SWPBIS leadership team. Conduct a Tier One Tiered Fidelity Inventory (TFI). Develop practices and systems for Tier One based on TFI, with a focus on teaching expectations in all school locations, providing positive feedback to students for meeting expectations (for example, "all-star tickets" and school store to purchase items with all stars); training on schoolwide information system and updated system for responding to problem behavior to include verbal corrections (undocumented), written corrections (minor referrals), and major referrals.	Tier One (TFI done for Tier One, Two, Three)
Spring 2014	Add quack tickets to the "all-star" reinforcement system. Quack tickets are a bigger acknowledgment with a copy the teacher sends home and another copy entered into drawing for special items each week. Assess implementation progress with TFI for Tier One and Tier Two (as baseline).	Tier One (TFI for Tier One, Two)
Fall 2014	Begin to focus on Tier Two; receive training on Check In–Check Out; use TFI results and Check In–Check Out SWIS readiness requirements to action plan Tier Two; review TFI Tier One from spring and see that office referral data are not reflective of current problems in school because written correction data are not entered anywhere; major and minor office referrals are sparse.	Tier One Tier Two (main focus)

Date	Implementation Focus	Tier
Spring 2015	Revise the Tier One system for responding to and documenting problem behavior to convert written corrections to a minor referral, eliminating the old minor referral form to have more accurate data in SWIS. Attend a full-day training including Check In–Check Out SWIS and advanced Tier Two features (for example, fading and intensifying supports, boosters). Roll out the updated Check In–Check Out to meet Check In–Check Out SWIS requirements. Conduct TFI for all three tiers.	Tier One Tier Two (main focus) (TFI done for Tier One, Two, Three)
Fall 2015	Revise the Tier One reinforcement system to do away with the school store. Use all stars in classroom systems; use quack tickets schoolwide. Make a minor tweak to the problem behavior system for kindergarten parent contact rules. Make minor revisions to the Check In–Check Out system (point card update to standardize). The behavior team attends full-day plus additional half-day training on FBA and linking it to BSP. The behavior team creates an action plan related to TFI Tier Three.	Tier One Tier Two Tier Three (main focus)
Spring 2016	The behavior team attends a half day of training on Individualized Student Information System SWIS (data system) and a half day on data collection and goal setting for BSP.	Tier Three (TFI Tier One, Two, Three)
Fall 2016	There is a lot of turnover in staff; the leadership team re-emphasizes SWPBIS; the behavior team attends a district-facilitated workday to use TFI scores from spring to help teams develop action plans for 2016–2017. The focus is on sustaining and innovating across tiers as well as training new staff on behavior team skills they need for FBA and BSP.	Tier One Tier Three

Figure 6.8: Timeline of implementation for Meador Elementary School.

Kennedy Middle School

Here we describe a middle school's use of SWPBIS. Kennedy Middle School is a sixth- to eighth-grade suburban school with over 1,200 students located in the United States. Kennedy Middle School's student population is 64 percent white, 21 percent Latino, 2 percent black, 6 percent multiracial, and 7 percent classified as other. Twenty-three percent of Kennedy Middle School students qualify for free and reduced lunch, 3 percent are English learners, and 7 percent receive special education. Kennedy Middle School's journey with SWPBIS began as a districtwide initiative to implement SWPBIS in all of its schools. Every school was given a three-year deadline to begin implementation of SWPBIS and provided district-level support in the form of annual and ongoing trainings and district-level PBIS coaches.

To implement SWPBIS, Kennedy Middle School began by spending the latter half of the 2011–2012 school year building consensus and buy-in with their staff. The administration at Kennedy Middle School introduced SWPBIS to their staff at an all-staff meeting and held conversations about their need for improved discipline and how SWPBIS might address that need. To illustrate the need for improvement with their discipline system, the administration pointed out that the school had 680 major and minor referrals during the 2010–2011 school year, which amounted to 10,200 minutes of instructional time lost by students (fifteen minutes for each referral). They also pointed out that 35 percent of the major referrals were actually for minor infractions, such as not having materials for class or being thirty seconds late to class. Teachers would send students to the office (and call it a major behavior) when it actually was a minor behavior. This illustrated an inefficient use of the administration's time (because teachers should manage minor behaviors instead of the administration) and inconsistency in discipline between different teachers' classrooms. There were conversations at additional staff meetings and during department-level meetings to gather teachers' input and allow time for consideration of change in the discipline system. At a final staff meeting for the 2011–2012 school year, the administration surveyed the staff for buy-in by asking them to anonymously rate their willingness to implement SWPBIS on a scale from 1 to 5 (1 = I don't want to implement SWPBIS, 2 = I'd like to know more about SWPBIS before I decide, 3 = I will implement but I'm not crazy about SWPBIS, 4 = I will implement but I don't want additional responsibilities, 5 = I want to implement SWPBIS and will take on additional responsibilities). Kennedy Middle School had over 80 percent of their staff respond with either a 4 or 5 on the scale, which indicated that they had enough buy-in to implement SWPBIS.

Kennedy Middle School developed a leadership team to guide the design and implementation of SWPBIS during the spring of 2012. The leadership team consisted of eight members: the principal, the assistant principal, the school psychologist, the school counselor, a special education teacher, and one regular education teacher from each grade level. The team defined their main outcomes with SWPBIS, which they identified as reductions in behavioral infractions, implementation of Tier One to fidelity within a year, and acceptance of the model by their staff and parents. The team elected to measure behavior and instructional time by using the school's ODR data, measure fidelity with the Benchmarks of Quality (Kincaid et al., 2010), and measure the staff's and parents' acceptance of the model with a survey that the leadership team created. It would analyze this information annually, plus monthly monitoring of ODR data. After identifying outcomes and the data needed, the leadership team then focused on designing the practices and systems of Tier One in the spring. We discuss each of those aspects next.

Tier One Practices for Kennedy Middle School

The leadership team developed Tier One practices and systems during the spring and summer of 2012 by using team meetings and preservice days prior to the 2012–2013 school year. The leadership team used an iterative process in which they first gathered ideas about a specific practice or system from their staff and then developed a draft of that practice or system based on the ideas they gathered. Next, they gathered feedback from the staff before finalizing their Tier One practices and systems. For example, to identify the schoolwide expectations, the leadership team asked for initial ideas on expectations from the staff, after which the leadership team developed a draft of expectations for the staff to provide further input. After getting feedback and having the staff vote on expectations, the leadership team organized the expectations using an acronym, PRIDE: productivity, respect, integrity, diligence, and empathy. The team then created a schoolwide matrix that enlisted staff input for rules. Figure 6.9 illustrates the matrix.

	P **Productivity** We are active, responsible participants in our education.	R **Respect** We respect others and accept differences.	I **Integrity** We do the right thing even when no one else is watching.	D **Diligence** We are safe members of our school community.	E **Empathy** We seek to understand the feelings of others.
Classroom	Be prompt, prepared, and ready to learn. Be an active learner. Search for answers by inquiring. Push yourself to meet and exceed expectations and overcome obstacles.	Speak and listen respectfully. Use appropriate language and accountable talk.	Do your own work. Tell the truth and accept the results. Show care for technology, equipment, and supplies.	Follow the rules within the classroom. Make safe decisions. Clean up work areas.	Work collaboratively. Respect all viewpoints and differences. Include all students in groups, activities.
Cafeteria, Hallway, Bathrooms, or Grounds	Do the right thing. Apply your knowledge to make good decisions. Seek assistance to resolve problems after you have used Stop-Walk-Talk.	Keep hands, feet, hurtful words to yourself. Treat others with kindness and respect. Accept all others. Respect the space and needs of others.	Be honest and respectful with peers or adults. Use self-manager badge with integrity. Communicate concerns to an adult.	Comply with all staff directions. Keep the school clean. Keep food in the cafeteria. Honor the dress code. Keep an orderly line and have your ID/pass at all times.	Show genuine care for others. Get to know and learn about others who are different from you.
Athletics, Assemblies, or Activities	Meet eligibility requirements to participate. Show your best effort or abilities. Encourage athletes, participants, and speakers.	Respect and welcome visitors. Show good sportsmanship, accepting all ability levels. Listen to new things.	Remain seated and respectful for the entire event. Play fair, cheer fair.	Follow the rules for the event. Be aware of responsibilities and behavior expectations for all activities. Be a positive participant or spectator.	Appreciate and recognize the efforts of all participants. Win with class or lose with dignity.

Source: Adapted from Kendyl Depoali Middle School, STRIKE Committee, n.d.

Figure 6.9: Kennedy Middle School's matrix of expectations and rules for common settings.

continued ➜

	P **Productivity**	**R** **Respect**	**I** **Integrity**	**D** **Diligence**	**E** **Empathy**
	We are active, responsible participants in our education.	**We respect others and accept differences.**	**We do the right thing even when no one else is watching.**	**We are safe members of our school community.**	**We seek to understand the feelings of others.**
Bus or Vehicle Areas	Know your bus stop and bus number. Walk your bikes and scooters at all times. Lock your bike and materials securely. Be a role model for others.	Be patient with peers and drivers—look in all directions.	Follow the rules to promote safety. Be on time to buses.	Use safe routes and all crosswalks. Follow all bus rules and driver's instructions. Know your bus and bike lane rules. Take time to be safe.	Understand that there are many vehicles and students trying to get somewhere at the same time.
Home or Community	Do your homework daily. Attend school and be on time. Use resources to seek assistance. Check your grades and assignments.	Communicate with your family or community members. Be friendly to all.	Do the right thing when unsupervised. Make decisions that benefit you, your family, and your community.	Be a safe and positive community member. Apply your knowledge when in the community.	Recognize and strive to appreciate the efforts and struggles of your family and community members.

Tier One Practices for Teaching Expectations for Kennedy Middle School

For teaching the expectations, the leadership team outlined a teaching plan. The staff at Kennedy Middle School taught the schoolwide expectations from the PRIDE matrix during the first two weeks of school. Teachers received a universal presentation (called basic training) to use to introduce students to the expectations within their homeroom classes, which included taking students on a guided tour of the building and modeling and teaching the expectations within the various school settings listed on the matrix. The staff also reviewed other safety issues, such as the weapons policy and the dangers of prescription drugs, and the staff taught the students a specific strategy for dealing with bullying (Stop-Walk-Talk). Following the basic training, students participated in weekly focus lessons during their advisory class periods that focused on a specific skill within the matrix. The leadership team identified the focus skill each week and provided the staff with a lesson plan and activity to use to teach the focus skill (J. Ancina, personal communication, August 20, 2015). Kennedy Middle School created a website for staff as a means to communicate the focus lesson and to share materials (for instance, lesson plans or templates). As part of the weekly lessons, students identified goals from one specific area of the matrix, and students used their advisory period to share their goals and successes.

Tier One Practices for Reinforcing Expectations for Kennedy Middle School

Kennedy Middle School had a comprehensive reward system for their SWPBIS model. For high-frequency acknowledgments, students were given praise in the form of signatures based on meeting the school expectations (see figure 6.10). The staff were trained to verbally acknowledge the student's behavior and then provide signatures on the student's signature page, which they kept in their daily planners (each student enrolled at Kennedy Middle School received a planner). Teachers recorded the total number of signatures students earned within a grade book during each student's advisory periods.

	P Productivity We are active, responsible participants in our education.		R Respect We respect others and accept differences.		I Integrity We do the right thing even when no one else is watching.		D Diligence We are safe members of our school community.		E Empathy We seek to understand the feelings of others.	
	Date	Teacher Initial	Date	Teacher Initial	Date	Teacher Initial	Date	Teacher Initial	Date	Teacher Initial
Week One Total										
Initial										

Note: The planner had a row for each week of the school's term.

Source: Adapted from Kendyl Depoali Middle School, STRIKE Committee, n.d.

Figure 6.10: Example of high-frequency acknowledgment in the form of a signature (Kennedy Middle School).

Students could use the signatures as money at the school store each quarter as a form of long-term acknowledgment. Items in the store included pens, pencils, folders, a "front of the line" hall pass, an "early out" pass, highlighters, a PRIDE T-shirt, a one-day-late homework pass, and other items. For every ten signatures earned during a one-week time period, students also earned one ticket for a random drawing (they could earn several per week, however). If students earned five signatures per week, they were eligible for group acknowledgment, which included a pancake breakfast, an extended lunch period with popcorn or chips and salsa, and end-of-year events including a field trip or field day. Table 6.5 (page 180) illustrates the range of reward opportunities for students at Kennedy Middle School.

Tier One Practices for Managing Misbehavior for Kennedy Middle School

As part of their Tier One practices, the leadership team also developed a process for managing misbehavior among students. The staff and leadership team developed agreement on the behaviors that needed to be managed by the classroom teachers versus those to be managed by administration. The leadership team created a flowchart that illustrated minor versus major behaviors, the process for handling each incident, and responses that teachers could use (see figure 6.11, page 181).

Table 6.5: Kennedy Middle School's Reinforcement Plan

Type	Description	Criteria	Frequency
High Frequency	Students earn signatures for meeting schoolwide expectations	Displaying schoolwide expectations earns a signature.	Daily
Long Term	School store	Every signature is worth $1 at the school store.	Redeemed quarterly
	Random drawings	Every ten signatures per week earns students one ticket into a random drawing.	Weekly
	Positive referral	Teachers write positive referrals and send them to the office. Office/admin staff praise the student and notify the parent or guardian.	Intermittent
	Self-manager badge	Students displaying extended periods of the PRIDE expectations earn a sticker on their ID badge that allows additional privileges (headphones at lunch, having lunch in the courtyard, and so on).	Earned based on weekly performance
Group	Extended lunch	Students can earn an extended lunch with popcorn or chips and salsa as an appetizer. (Students must earn five signatures each week for admittance to group events.)	Midquarter and quarterly
	Pancake breakfast	A pancake breakfast is provided during the advisory period. (Students must earn five signatures each week for admittance to group events.)	Quarterly
	Dance/activity event	Students are invited to attend dances or various activities, such as game rooms, sports, movies, or computer games. (Students must earn five signatures each week for admittance to group events.)	Quarterly or end of year

Source: Adapted from Kendyl Depoali Middle School, STRIKE Committee, n.d.

Here is the process teachers used when managing behaviors that constituted minor referrals. This created consistency among the staff in their responses to problem behaviors.

- ▲ **First offense:** The teacher will state the expectation to student with a verbal cue.
- ▲ **Second offense:** The teacher will implement an intervention and complete a minor referral.
- ▲ **Third offense:** The teacher will implement an intervention, complete a minor referral, and contact a parent.

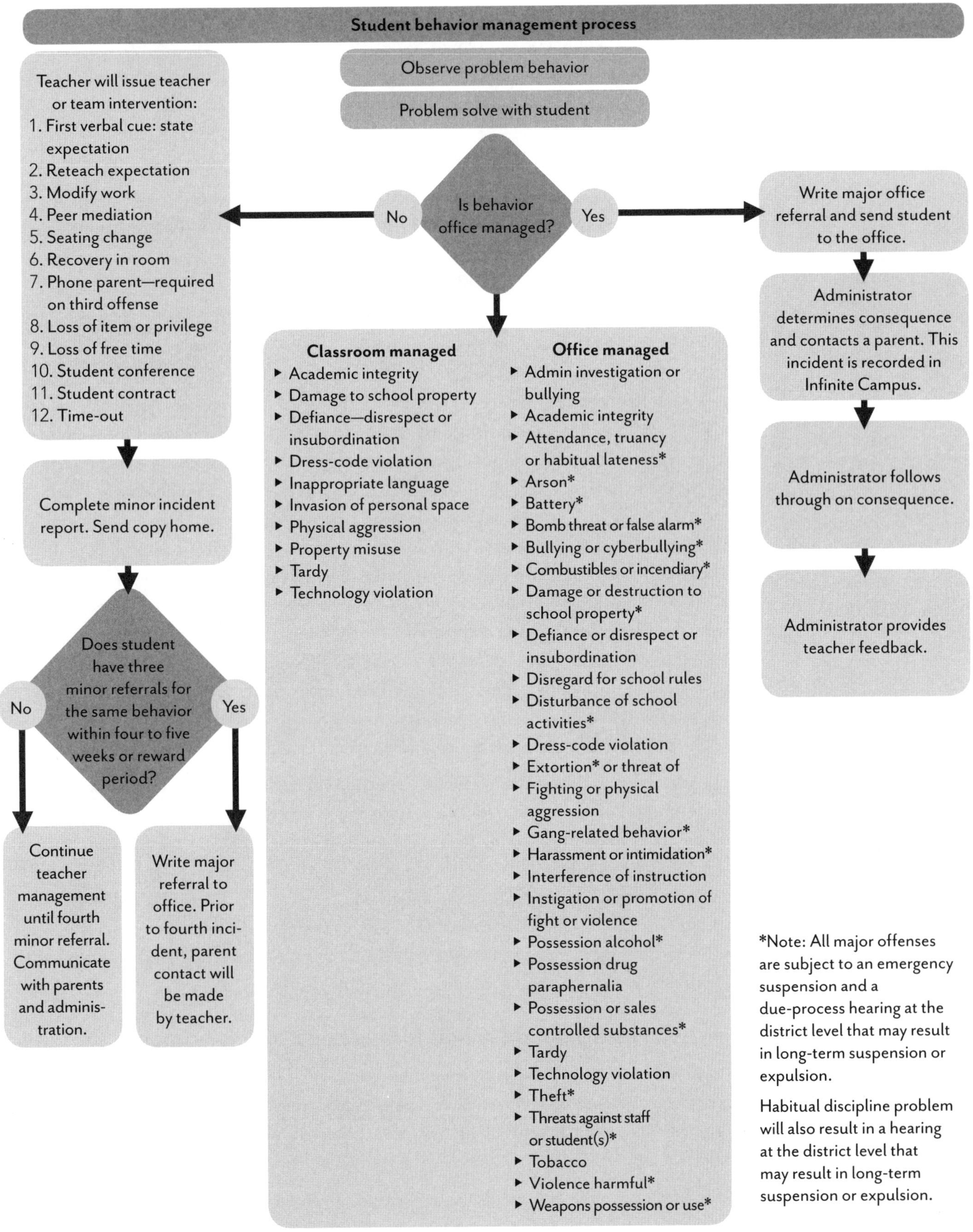

Student behavior management process

Observe problem behavior

Problem solve with student

Is behavior office managed?

No →

Yes →

Teacher will issue teacher or team intervention:
1. First verbal cue: state expectation
2. Reteach expectation
3. Modify work
4. Peer mediation
5. Seating change
6. Recovery in room
7. Phone parent—required on third offense
8. Loss of item or privilege
9. Loss of free time
10. Student conference
11. Student contract
12. Time-out

Complete minor incident report. Send copy home.

Does student have three minor referrals for the same behavior within four to five weeks or reward period?

No

Yes

Continue teacher management until fourth minor referral. Communicate with parents and administration.

Write major referral to office. Prior to fourth incident, parent contact will be made by teacher.

Classroom managed
▸ Academic integrity
▸ Damage to school property
▸ Defiance—disrespect or insubordination
▸ Dress-code violation
▸ Inappropriate language
▸ Invasion of personal space
▸ Physical aggression
▸ Property misuse
▸ Tardy
▸ Technology violation

Office managed
▸ Admin investigation or bullying
▸ Academic integrity
▸ Attendance, truancy or habitual lateness*
▸ Arson*
▸ Battery*
▸ Bomb threat or false alarm*
▸ Bullying or cyberbullying*
▸ Combustibles or incendiary*
▸ Damage or destruction to school property*
▸ Defiance or disrespect or insubordination
▸ Disregard for school rules
▸ Disturbance of school activities*
▸ Dress-code violation
▸ Extortion* or threat of
▸ Fighting or physical aggression
▸ Gang-related behavior*
▸ Harassment or intimidation*
▸ Interference of instruction
▸ Instigation or promotion of fight or violence
▸ Possession alcohol*
▸ Possession drug paraphernalia
▸ Possession or sales controlled substances*
▸ Tardy
▸ Technology violation
▸ Theft*
▸ Threats against staff or student(s)*
▸ Tobacco
▸ Violence harmful*
▸ Weapons possession or use*

Write major office referral and send student to the office.

Administrator determines consequence and contacts a parent. This incident is recorded in Infinite Campus.

Administrator follows through on consequence.

Administrator provides teacher feedback.

*Note: All major offenses are subject to an emergency suspension and a due-process hearing at the district level that may result in long-term suspension or expulsion.

Habitual discipline problem will also result in a hearing at the district level that may result in long-term suspension or expulsion.

Source: Kendyl Depoali Middle School, STRIKE Committee, n.d. Reprinted with permission.

Figure 6.11: Referral chart for minor versus major behaviors, Kennedy Middle School.

▲ **Fourth offense:** The student receives a major referral to the office for disciplinary action with the administration.

▲ **Office referrals:** All office referrals are subject to a three-hour detention on Friday or at Saturday School, in-school suspension to be served in a time-out room in the main office, or an out-of-school suspension.

The district had a standard referral form that teachers were to use for tracking minor and major behavior (see figure 6.12). The leadership team and staff used this form to gather some of the necessary data they needed to make decisions about their SWPBIS model.

Tier One Systems for Kennedy Middle School

Having defined the practices for Tier One for Kennedy Middle School, the leadership team also developed some clear systems to ensure that the school implemented the practices accordingly and gathered the data. To ensure appropriate oversight and expertise of the model, Kennedy Middle School had an internal coach (the assistant principal) who attended trainings that were provided by district-level coaches. This enabled the team to receive up-to-date information and regular oversight on SWPBIS. The leadership team also created a Summary Handbook that each teacher received. It included the SWPBIS expectations, steps to provide acknowledgment, a copy of the referral forms, the schoolwide matrix, the referral process for handling minor and major behaviors, and a link to the school website that contained information on teaching the expectations and ways to embed the expectations each week into various classes. New teachers received this document, and then a peer would review the handbook with them to ensure that the teacher was up to speed on the SWPBIS model. The school's handbook also included information on Tiers Two and Three, including a summary of Tier Two interventions, how students receive Tier Two, the matrix that matches interventions to functions of behavior, the referral process for Tier Three, and information on screeners used to identify students for additional supports.

To ensure that data screening occurred, Kennedy Middle School set aside approximately fifteen minutes of school time twice a year during which the staff completed screening measures to identify students who might need additional support; during this time, students worked independently on academic content. Department-level teams also had an early release every other Wednesday that was designated time to use for discussions and problem solving related to, among other things, SWPBIS. These are just a few of the systems that the leadership team developed as a means to ensure that their staff could both implement the practices as intended and have time to gather the necessary data.

Tier Two Practices and Systems for Kennedy Middle School

At Kennedy Middle School, a separate team from the Tier One team managed Tier Two. Once formed, the team identified two systems-level outcomes: (1) that at least 80 percent of students should be successful with each of the interventions that they use, and (2) that students receive that support within five school days of identification.

The Tier Two team consisted of six members: sixth-, seventh-, and eighth-grade regular education teachers, the assistant principal, the school counselor, and the school psychologist. The team first identified a few interventions that they would use to address common

Referral Form	Location of Event	
Student Name: _____	☐ Restroom	☐ Library
Staff: _____	☐ Cafeteria or commons	☐ Locker room
Grade: _____	☐ Classroom	☐ Office
Date: _____	☐ Gymnasium	☐ Parking lot
Time: _____	☐ Hallway	☐ Playground
School: _____	☐ Other: _____	

Minor Behavior	Response and Intervention	Possible Motivation
☐ Academic integrity	☐ Intervention _____	☐ Avoid adults
☐ Damage to school property	☐ Reteach expectation or behavior	☐ Avoid peers
☐ Defiance or insubordination	☐ Adjust prompts or cues	☐ Avoid task or activity
☐ Disrespect	☐ Student conference	☐ Obtain adult attention
☐ Dress-code violation	☐ Adjust instruction, differentiate	☐ Obtain peer attention
☐ Inappropriate language	☐ Extra time or practice on task	☐ Obtain item or activity
☐ Invasion of personal space	☐ Seating change	☐ Unknown
☐ Physical aggression	☐ Referral to intervention team	**Others Involved**
☐ Property misuse	☐ Loss of item or privilege	☐ Peers
☐ Tardy	☐ Detention	☐ Staff member
☐ Technology violation	☐ Parent conference	☐ Substitute
☐ Other: _____	☐ Other: _____	☐ Other: _____

Major Behavior		Response and Intervention
☐ Academic integrity	☐ Tardy	☐ Referral to intervention team
☐ Attendance or truancy	☐ Technology violation	☐ Tier Two intervention
☐ Damage to school property	☐ Theft	☐ Tier Three intervention
☐ Defiance or insubordination	☐ Threat to staff	☐ Parent conference
☐ Disrespect	☐ Threat to students	☐ Restitution
☐ Disturbance of school activities	☐ Other: _____	☐ Detention
☐ Dress-code violation		☐ In-school suspension
☐ Fighting or physical aggression		☐ Out of school suspension
☐ Gang-related behavior		☐ Saturday school
☐ Possession of drugs or alcohol		☐ After-school intervention
☐ Possession of weapon		☐ Other: _____
☐ Sale of drugs or alcohol		

Signatures		
_____ Student	_____ Administrator	_____ Parent or Guardian

Figure 6.12: Kennedy Middle School's minor and major ODR form.

*Visit **MarzanoResearch.com/reproducibles** to download a free reproducible version of this figure.*

behavioral issues they identified in students (by examining their ODR data). As seen in table 6.6, the team selected three Tier Two interventions that addressed different functions of behavior, thereby allowing them flexibility in matching students' needs. This team managed all of the interventions, and the Tier Two coordinator was the eighth-grade regular education teacher who tracked all students using the school's database system. This data system also was used to analyze fidelity and progress-monitoring data. The team met every week to either discuss students, the impact of the system, or issues with systems or processes of Tier Two.

Table 6.6: Kennedy Middle School's Tier Two Interventions

Intervention	Description	Function and Behaviors
Check In–Check Out	Student will check in each day with an adult to review his or her goals and progress on his or her Check In–Check Out sheet. The adult will provide positive feedback and reinforcement for progress toward meeting the goal and exhibiting desired behaviors. A copy of the Check In–Check Out sheet will be provided to the student to take home to his or her parent or guardian.	Attention seeking and externalizing behaviors
Social or School Success Skills Advisory	Students will be provided direct instruction during advisory class to improve their social skills and school success skills.	Avoid adult, peers, and tasks or activities and internalizing behaviors Low academic achievement, peer rejection, lying, cheating
Peer Mentoring	Students will be placed with a positive peer role model within their classes. Their peers will provide support in maintaining a focus on tasks. The peers will also ignore misbehavior and instead report all unwanted behavior to the classroom teacher.	Obtain peer attention, avoid a task or activity Poor impulse control, hyperactivity, high levels of aggression

Source: Adapted from Kendyl Depoali Middle School, STRIKE Committee, n.d.

To identify students for Tier Two, Kennedy Middle School used ODRs, a request-for-assistance form, and a screening instrument (the Student Risk Screening Scale; Drummond, 1994). The data sources and thresholds points for Tier Two consideration are in table 6.7.

To check if the Tier Two supports were effective, the Tier Two team at Kennedy Middle School used data that differed based on the intervention they used. For Check In–Check Out, each student had a goal of reaching at least 80 percent of his or her daily points each day (see figure 6.13). The school implemented Check In–Check Out for twenty days, and once a student met the 80 percent goal for ten days, he or she would exit the intervention. If the student did not reach that goal, the Tier Two team would examine the intervention and adjust it accordingly or refer the student for Tier Three services. Implementation of

Table 6.7: Data Used for Tier Two Identification for Kennedy Middle School

Data	Criterion
Minor ODRs	Three or more within a quarter period
Major ODRs	Two or more within a quarter period
Student Risk Screening Scale	High-risk score in categories related to internalizing or externalizing behaviors.
Teacher Nomination	Approval by Tier Two team

Source: Adapted from Kendyl Depoali Middle School, STRIKE Committee, n.d.

the intervention was measured by checking whether or not the teacher had assigned points on the student's card at the designated times. A percentage was calculated to indicate if the student was receiving the intervention (for example, if the teachers assigned points for twelve out of twenty-four opportunities, the fidelity score for that day was 50 percent; see the bottom row of figure 6.13).

PRIDE Check In–Check Out		**Period**							
Student name: _____ Date: _____		**Adv**	1	2	3	4	5	6	7
Productivity	Completed classwork and homework; full participation	2	2	2	2	2	2	2	2
	Completed homework or classwork; some participation	1	1	1	1	1	1	1	1
	No work or participation	0	0	0	0	0	0	0	0
Diligence and Integrity	Followed rules and worked honestly and safely	2	2	2	2	2	2	2	2
	One instance or reminder to comply or work safely	1	1	1	1	1	1	1	1
	Less than one instance or reminder to comply or work safely	0	0	0	0	0	0	0	0
Respect and Empathy	Worked well with others	2	2	2	2	2	2	2	2
	One instance of not working well with others	1	1	1	1	1	1	1	1
	More than one instance of not working well with others	0	0	0	0	0	0	0	0
Teacher initials									
Earn less than eighty percent (fourty-eight points)?		48			YES	NO			
Fidelity percentage (out of twenty-four total opportunities)		____ /24 = ____%							

Adv = Advisory period

Source: Adapted from Kendyl Depoali Middle School, STRIKE Committee, n.d.

Figure 6.13: Check In–Check Out card for Kennedy Middle School.

To monitor social skills and school success, the Tier Two team monitored minor and major ODRs, and they also required the students to complete the class and meet the objectives outlined within the class. A student needed fewer than three minors and one major referral within a quarter to exit the intervention. The team measured fidelity by collecting attendance data.

Monitoring of the peer-mentoring intervention varied depending on the targeted behavior the student was working on. For off-task behavior, the team gathered data on the percentage of assignments completed, with a goal of at least 80 percent of all assignments for twenty days. For disruptive behavior in class, the student had to earn at least forty-three points (90 percent) on his or her daily behavior card (see figure 6.13; note that this intervention also used the Check In–Check Out daily behavior card). It measured fidelity by either analyzing attendance data or examining the fidelity percentage on the daily behavior card.

To measure fidelity of SWPBIS, the Tier Two team worked with the leadership team to administer the Benchmarks for Advanced Tiers (Anderson et al., 2012). It then reviewed the results with teams and developed action plans as needed to ensure that implementation was successful with Tier Two elements.

For students who were not successful in the Tier Two interventions (in other words, not meeting their goal or earning at least 80 percent of their daily points), the Tier Two team either analyzed the situation to modify or change the intervention or referred the student for possible Tier Three services.

Tier Three Practices and Systems for Kennedy Middle School

The Tier Three practices and systems at Kennedy Middle School were coordinated by a separate Tier Three team; however, this team had overlapping members with the leadership team. Consequently, Kennedy Middle School had a three-team structure for SWPBIS: a leadership team, a Tier Two team, and a Tier Three team. The Tier Three team included the school psychologist, the school counselor, the assistant principal, the principal, a special education teacher, and a regular education teacher.

The outcomes identified at Tier Three were similar to those at Tier Two in that leadership and the Tier Three team wanted at least 80 percent of students to be successful with their supports. The team also wanted to ensure that students who received Tier Three actually needed Tier Three, so it identified an outcome of at least 90 percent accuracy with referrals. To check this outcome, the team would examine the number of students referred to the Tier Three team each month and compare it to the number of students who actually received Tier Three supports. The team viewed this as a fidelity and quality outcome, as it wanted to ensure that if it were evaluating referrals, it was for students who had either received previous Tier Two interventions with fidelity or had scored very high on screening assessments.

The Tier Three team considered students for Tier Three support through a referral by the Tier Two team. Often the Tier Two team would refer based on a student's lack of progress in Tier Two, but the team could examine a student's scores on screening measures and make a decision to refer. Upon receiving a referral for a student to receive Tier Three supports, the Tier Three team would ensure that the student's Tier Two supports were implemented with fidelity and that the student was not making progress. For students who scored high on screening measures and were referred for that reason, the Tier Three team would examine the student's history and data from other sources to ensure that Tier Three was appropriate and reasonable for the student. The Tier Three team would conduct the FBA, and then after reviewing results, the team would invite the students' teachers and parents or guardians to the conversation to design a comprehensive BSP. It developed BSPs using the

Prevent-Teach-Reinforce framework (Dunlap et al., 2010). This process uses a team-based approach that identifies the different components of a BSP that we discussed in chapter 4.

Summary

Within this chapter, we provided two case summaries of SWPBIS in an elementary school and a middle school, respectively. Our goal was to illustrate the four key elements at two different types of schools. Even though the specific application of the elements may have varied between the schools, each school had to identify the outcomes they wanted to achieve with SWPBIS, the practices to put in place to reach those outcomes, the systems to ensure that the staff could implement those practices, and the data to gather to inform those outcomes. We didn't discuss the use of the PSM by either school explicitly, but the teams at the schools used the PSM as an organizing framework to identify and solve problems that arose, all of which took into consideration the four key elements we discussed.

Epilogue

SWPBIS is a model that aligns with a Multi-Tiered System of Supports framework designed to improve the overall school climate within a school. Schools use it to provide structure for decision making, resulting in improvements in the behavioral and social functioning of students. This in turn impacts academic outcomes (Bradshaw et al., 2010; Horner et al., 2009; Muscott et al., 2008). Additionally, SWPBIS implementation has been shown to correlate with improved staff morale and perception of effectiveness (Ross et al., 2012). School teams implement SWPBIS by understanding the four key elements—(1) outcomes, (2) practices, (3) systems, and (4) data—and then building those elements for each tier, beginning with Tier One. As teams implement SWPBIS, they'll generally progress through four developmental stages: (1) consensus building, (2) infrastructure, (3) implementation, and (4) sustainability.

Creating a school culture where there is common agreement on language, vision, and values increases the likelihood that all members will successfully integrate into the community. This creates a standard for all to know what it means when they walk in the front doors of the school. We agree that when SWPBIS is implemented well, it is immediately obvious from the moment someone steps into the front office of the school and is evident throughout the building. Students and staff alike clearly exhibit the expectations, and the focus on prosocial expected behaviors is visually and verbally evident. Coauthor Billie Jo Rodriguez shares her experience at her daughter's school:

> When attending kindergarten orientation at my daughter's school this spring, SWPBIS was evident not only by the posters on the wall stating expectations to be safe, respectful, responsible, and kind, but it was also evident as the principal handed out to students positive compliments and tangible tickets that were placed on a wall to earn a whole school extra recess. It was evident in the kind language students used with one another in their classrooms, the respect they showed to computer equipment, in the students' behaviors as they walked on the right side of the hall, and when students used the restroom quickly and quietly. This is refreshing because it was clear even after a short visit that the school community values safety, respect, responsibility, and kindness—the adults obviously teach and model those behaviors, and students are confident in meeting the expectations.

"PBIS has served as the platform for establishing a positive culture within our school setting. It gives students the opportunity to interact positively in a safe learning environment. It also provides the staff the opportunity to collaborate to develop a common plan to implement schoolwide with input and buy-in, where they believe in the outcome of a positive and nurturing environment for all. Our culture here at Depoali MS has been molded by the PBIS system, and the system gives all stakeholders a common ground to communicate and work in partnership to treat each other with mutual respect. The rapport that our staff has built with the students and the families through this process has allowed us to reach a high level of achievement in academics and behavior schoolwide and contributed to awards such as our [2016] Blue Ribbon Award."

—Joye Ancina, principal, Depoali Middle School, Reno, Nevada (personal communication, January 18, 2017)

Within this book, we have provided the theoretical background, research support, and practical application of SWPBIS. It is our hope that this book and its content will show schools how straightforward and powerful the use of SWPBIS can be in creating that positive school culture where common values of respect and positive behaviors are encouraged.

Tier Two Interventions Template

This template can be used to list all of the available Tier Two interventions at a school. Include the description of the intervention, information on the outcomes (which are the behaviors that it aims to increase and decrease), the setting or location of the intervention, the duration of each session, the behavior functions that are appropriate to use with the intervention (for example, what is the function of the problem behavior), and progress monitoring frequency and decision rules. Examples are included in the table.

Blank Template of Menu of Tier Two Interventions

Intervention	Description	Outcome (behaviors to increase and/or behaviors to decrease)	Intervention setting or location	Duration of each intervention session	Behavior function(s) of problem behavior that intervention targets	Progress monitoring and decision rules		
Example: Check In–Check Out	To provide feedback on expectations throughout the day	Increase use of schoolwide expectations and decrease minor behaviors, such as off-task and disruption	Occurs in classroom and at the Check In–Check Out coordinator's office	Check In–Check Outs are a few minutes; feedback during day provided to student is brief (for example, one minute)	Adult attention (can be modified for additional functions of problem behavior)	Data is gathered daily on point card. Reviewed weekly. If less than 80 percent of daily points for one week, adjust goal. After three weeks of 80 percent of daily points or more, can fade intervention.		
Academic Intervention	To increase missing academic skills so student does not need to escape work	Increase engagement and work completion; decrease off-task or disruptive behavior related to avoidance of work	Varies; location designated by team	Sessions are three times a week for thirty minutes each; can vary based on skill being targeted	Avoidance of work	Academic progress monitoring occurs once/week with review every three to four weeks; make adjustments if three consecutive data points below aim line; fade intervention when four to six consecutive points above the aim line.		

*Potential purposes for the intervention include:

Obtain adult attention
Obtain peer attention
Obtain preferred activities
Academic skill deficit
Academic fluency deficit

Avoid adult attention
Avoid peer attention
Avoid academic task or other activity
Social behavior skill deficit
Social behavior fluency deficit

Functional Behavior Assessment Interview

Teams can use this brief functional behavior assessment (FBA) interview to help them understand the function of a student's behavior, including its possible environmental triggers. Team members interview staff members and observe the student's behavior to identify the function of the particular behavior. As mentioned, each FBA should result in a summary statement that not only predicts the problem behavior but also provides a detailed summary of when and where the behavior occurs.

Brief Functional Behavior Assessment Interview

1. What is the behavior of concern? Please describe the behavior in concrete, observable, and measurable terms.
2. How often does the behavior occur daily? Circle one.
   a. <1
   b. 1–3
   c. 4–6
   d. 7–9
   e. 10–12
   f. >13

Antecedents

Think of the things that occur before the behavior and respond to the following questions. If the answer to a question is yes, further describe the behavior or situation.

1. Does the behavior occur during a certain type of task?
2. Does the behavior occur more often during easy tasks?
3. Does the behavior occur more often during difficult tasks?
4. Does the behavior occur more often during certain subjects?
5. Does the behavior occur more often during new subject material?
6. Does the behavior occur more often when a request is made to stop an activity?
7. Does the behavior occur more often when a request is made to start an activity?
8. Does the behavior occur more often during transition times?
9. Does the behavior occur more often when a request has been denied?
10. Does the behavior occur more often when a specific person is in the room?
11. Does the behavior occur more often when a specific person is absent from the room?
12. Are there other behaviors that precede the behavior?
13. Are there events at home that seem to precede the behavior?
14. Does the behavior occur more in certain settings? Circle all that apply.
    a. Large group
    b. Small group
    c. Independent work
    d. One-on-one interaction
    e. Common areas
    f. Lunch or cafeteria
    g. Other:

Consequences

Think of the things that occur after the behavior and respond to the following questions. If the answer to a question is yes, further describe the behavior or situation.

1. Does the student receive access to a preferred activity?
2. Does the student receive access to a preferred object?
3. Does the task the student was given stop?
4. Is the student's behavior ignored?
5. Is the student removed from the setting (that is, given time alone)?
6. Does the student receive attention from classmates or peers?
7. Does the student receive teacher attention in the form of
   a. Praise?
   b. Redirection?

page 1 of 2

    c.   Interrupting the teacher?

    d.   A reprimand?

8.   Is there any task that you stopped presenting to the student as a result of the behavior?

9.   Does the student receive any sort of positive benefits or attention from the behavior?

Strategies attempted:

☐ Teach desired behavior	☐ Provide extra support: what support? _____	☐ Self-management program
☐ Five to one positives	☐ Modified assignment: how? _____	☐ Behavior contract
☐ Preferential seating		☐ Other: _____
☐ Precorrection	☐ Clarify rules	
☐ Proximity praise	☐ Practice expected behaviors	
☐ Prompts/signals	☐ Breaks	
☐ Class discussion		

Positive Rewards	Other Consequences
☐ Increase tangible rewards and tokens ☐ Use group contingencies ☐ All stars ☐ Hoorays!!! How many? _____ ☐ Systematic feedback about behavior ☐ Other: _____	☐ Reprimands ☐ Removal of privileges ☐ Time-outs ☐ Owed time ☐ Apology/self-reflection ☐ Individual meeting with student ☐ Contact parent—how many calls? _____ ☐ Meeting with parents—how many? _____ ☐ Office referrals—how many? _____ ☐ Other: _____

Source: Adapted from Steege, M. W., & Watson, T. S. (2009). Conducting school-based functional behavioral assessments: A practitioner's guide *(2nd ed.).* New York: Guilford Press.

References and Resources

Abbott, M., Wills, H., Kamps, D., Greenwood, C. R., Dawson-Bannister, H., Kaufman, J., et al. (2008). The Kansas Reading and Behavior Center's K–3 prevention model. In C. Greenwood, T. Kratochwill, & M. Clements (Eds.), *Schoolwide prevention models: Lessons learned in elementary schools* (pp. 215–265). New York: Guilford Press.

Advancement Project and Civil Rights Project. (2000). *Opportunities suspended: The devastating consequences of zero tolerance and school discipline.* Washington, DC: Authors. Accessed at http://civilrightsproject.ucla.edu/research/k-12-education /school-discipline/opportunities-suspended-the-devastating-consequences-of-zero-tolerance-and-school-discipline- policies/crp-opportunities-suspended-zero-tolerance-2000.pdf on December 2, 2014.

AIMSweb. (2010). *Behavior: Administration and technical manual.* Bloomington, MN: NCS Pearson.

Akin-Little, K. A., Eckert, T. L., Lovett, B. J., & Little, S. G. (2004). Extrinsic reinforcement in the classroom: Bribery or best practice. *School Psychology Review, 33*(3), 344–362.

Alberto, P. A., & Troutman, A. C. (2013). *Applied behavior analysis for teachers* (9th ed.). Boston: Pearson.

Algozzine, B., Barrett, S., Eber, L., George, H., Horner, R. H., Lewis, T., et al. (2017). *SWPBIS Tiered Fidelity Inventory: Version 2.1.* Accessed at www.pbisapps.org/Resources/SWIS%20Publications/SWPBIS%20Tiered%20Fidelity%20 Inventory%20(TFI).pdf on February 24, 2017.

Algozzine, B., Cooke, N., White, R., Helf, S., Algozzine, K., & McClanahan, T. (2008). The North Carolina Reading and Behavior Center's K–3 prevention model: Eastside Elementary School case study. In C. Greenwood, T. Kratochwill, & M. Clements (Eds.), *Schoolwide prevention models: Lessons learned in elementary schools* (pp. 173–214). New York: Guilford Press.

Algozzine, B., Newton, J. S., Horner, R. H., Todd, A. W., & Algozzine, K. M. (2012). Development and technical characteristics of a team decision-making assessment tool: Decision observation, recording, and analysis (DORA). *Journal of Psychoeducational Assessment, 30*(3), 237–249.

Algozzine, B., Wang, C., White, R., Cooke, N., Marr, M. B., Algozzine, K., et al. (2012). Effects of multi-tier academic and behavior instruction on difficult-to-teach students. *Exceptional Children, 79*(1), 45–64.

Allday, R. A., Hinkson-Lee, K., Hudson, T., Neilsen-Gatti, S., Kleinke, A., & Russell, C. S. (2012). Training general educators to increase behavior-specific praise: Effects on students with EBD. *Behavioral Disorders, 37*(2), 87–98.

American Psychological Association Zero Tolerance Task Force. (2008). Are zero tolerance policies effective in the schools? *American Psychologist, 63*(9), 852–862.

Anderson, C., & Borgmeier, C. (2010). Tier II interventions within the framework of school-wide positive behavior support: Essential features for design, implementation, and maintenance. *Behavior Analysis in Practice, 3*(1), 33–45.

Anderson, C., Childs, K., Kincaid, D., Horner, R. H., George, H. P., Todd, A. W., et al. (2012). *Benchmarks for advanced tiers (BAT).* Accessed at www.pbisapps.org/Resources/SWIS%20Publications/BAT%20Guide.pdf on February 24, 2017.

Anderson, C., Horner, R. H., Rodriguez, B. J., & Stiller, B. (2013). Building systems for successful implementation of function-based support in schools. *International Journal of School and Educational Psychology*, *1*(3), 141–153.

Anderson, C., & Scott, T. M. (2009). Implementing function-based support within schoolwide positive behavior support. In W. Sailor, G. Dunlap, G. Sugai, & R. H. Horner (Eds.), *Handbook of positive behavior support* (pp. 705–728). New York: Springer.

Anhalt, K., McNeil, C. B., & Bahl, A. B. (1998). The ADHD classroom kit: A whole-classroom approach for managing disruptive behavior. *Psychology in the Schools*, *35*(1), 67–79.

Baer, D. M., Wolf, M. M., & Risley, T. R. (1968). Some current dimensions of applied behavior analysis. *Journal of Applied Behavior Analysis*, *1*(1), 91–97.

Balfanz, R., & Byrnes, V. (2012). *The importance of being in school: A report on absenteeism in the nation's public schools*. Baltimore: Johns Hopkins University.

Bambara, L. M., & Kern, L. (2005). *Individualized supports for students with problem behaviors: Designing positive behavior plans*. New York: Guilford Press.

Barrish, H. H., Saunders, M., & Wolf, M. M. (1969). Good behavior game: Effects of individual contingencies for group consequences on disruptive behavior in a classroom. *Journal of Applied Behavioral Analysis*, *2*(2), 119–124.

Beaman, R., & Wheldall, K. (2000). Teachers' use of approval and disapproval in the classroom. *Educational Psychology*, *20*(4), 431–446.

Benazzi, L., Horner, R. H., & Good, R. H. (2006). Effects of behavior support team composition on the technical adequacy and contextual fit of behavior support plans. *Journal of Special Education*, *40*(3), 160–170.

Bohanon, H., Fenning, P., Borgmeier, C., Flannery, B., & Mallory, J. (2009). Finding a direction for high school positive behavior supports. In W. Sailor, G. Dunlap, G. Sugai, & R. H. Horner (Eds.), *Handbook of positive behavior support* (pp. 581–601). New York: Springer.

Bohanon, H., Fenning, P., Carney, K. L., Minnis-Kim, M. J., Anderson-Harriss, S., Moroz, K. B., et al. (2006). Schoolwide application of positive behavior support in an urban high school: A case study. *Journal of Positive Behavior Interventions*, *8*(3), 131–145.

Bohanon, H., & Wu, M. (2014). Developing buy-in for positive behavior support in secondary settings. *Preventing School Failure*, *58*(4), 1–7, 223–229.

Bowen, J. M., Jenson, W. R., & Clark, E. (2004). *School-based interventions for students with behavior problems*. New York: Kluwer Academic.

Boyd, R. J., & Anderson, C. (2013). Breaks are better: A tier II social behavior intervention. *Journal of Behavioral Education*, *22*(4), 348–365.

Bradshaw, C. P., Koth, C. W., Bevans, K. B., Ialongo, N., & Leaf, P. J. (2008). The impact of school-wide positive behavioral interventions and supports (PBIS) on the organizational health of elementary schools. *School Psychology Quarterly*, *23*(4), 462–473.

Bradshaw, C. P., Mitchell, M. M., & Leaf, P. J. (2010). Examining the effects of schoolwide positive behavioral interventions and supports on student outcomes: Results from a randomized controlled effectiveness trial in elementary schools. *Journal of Positive Behavior Interventions*, *12*(3), 133–148.

Bradshaw, C. P., Koth, C. W., Thornton, L. A., & Leaf, P. J. (2009). Altering school climate through school-wide positive behavioral interventions and supports: Findings from a group-randomized effectiveness trial. *Prevention Science*, *10*(2), 100–115.

Bradshaw, C. P., Waasdorp, T. E., & Leaf, P. J. (2012). Effects of school-wide positive behavioral interventions and supports on child behavior problems. *Pediatrics*, *130*(5), e1136–e1145.

Brophy, J. (1981). Teacher praise: A functional analysis. *Review of Educational Research*, *51*(1), 5–32.

Brophy, J. E., & Good, T. L. (1986). Teacher behavior and student achievement. In M. C. Wittrock (Ed.), *Handbook of research on teaching* (3rd ed., pp. 328–375). New York: Macmillan.

Brown-Chidsey, R., & Steege, M. W. (2010). *Response to intervention: Principles and strategies for effective practice* (2nd ed.). New York: Guilford Press.

Bruner, C., Discher, A., & Chang, H. (2011). *Chronic elementary absenteeism: A problem hidden in plain sight.* Accessed at www.attendanceworks.org/wordpress/wp-content/uploads/2010/04/ChronicAbsence.pdf on February 24, 2017.

Buffum, A., Mattos, M., & Weber, C. (2009). *Pyramid response to intervention: RTI, professional learning communities, and how to respond when kids don't learn.* Bloomington, IN: Solution Tree Press.

Caldarella, P., Shatzer, R. H., Gray, K. M., Young, K. R., & Young, E. L. (2011). The effects of school-wide positive behavior support on middle school climate and student outcomes. *RMLE Online, 35*(4), 1–14.

Cameron, J., & Pierce, W. D. (1994). Reinforcement, reward, and intrinsic motivation: A meta-analysis. *Review of Educational Research, 64*(3), 363–423.

Campbell, A., Rodriguez, B. J., Anderson, C., & Barnes, A. (2013). Effects of a Tier 2 intervention on classroom disruptive behavior and academic engagement. *Journal of Curriculum and Instruction, 7*(1), 32–54.

Carr, E. G. (1997). Invited commentary: The evolution of applied behavior analysis into positive behavior support. *Journal of the Association for Persons with Severe Handicaps, 22*(4), 208–209.

Carr, E. G., Dunlap, G., Horner, R. H., Koegel, R. L., Turnbull, A. P., Sailor, W., et al. (2002). Positive behavior support: Evolution of an applied science. *Journal of Positive Behavior Interventions, 4*(1), 4–16, 20.

Carter, D. R., Carter, G. M., Johnson, E. S., & Pool, J. L. (2012). Systematic implementation of a Tier 2 behavior intervention. *Intervention in School and Clinic, 48*(4), 223–231.

Cavell, T. A., & Henrie, J. L. (2010). Deconstructing serendipity: Focus, purpose, and authorship in lunch buddy mentoring. *New Directions for Youth Development,* 126, 107–121.

Celio, C. I., Durlak, J., & Dymnicki, A. (2011). A meta-analysis of the impact of service-learning on students. *Journal of Experiential Education, 34*(2), 164–181.

Centers for Disease Control and Prevention. (2009). *School connectedness: Strategies for increasing protective factors among youth.* Atlanta, GA: U.S. Department of Health and Human Services. Accessed at www.cdc.gov/healthyyouth /protective/pdf/connectedness.pdf on February 24, 2017.

Chard, D. J., & Harn, B. A. (2008). Project CIRCUITS: Center for Improving Reading Competence Using Intensive Treatments Schoolwide. In C. Greenwood, T. Kratochwill, & M. Clements (Eds.), *Schoolwide prevention models: Lessons learned in elementary schools* (pp. 143–172). New York: Guilford Press.

Chard, D. J., Harn, B. A., Sugai, G., Horner, R. H., Simmons, D. C., & Kame'enui, E. J. (2008). Core features of multi-tiered systems of reading and behavioral support. In C. Greenwood, T. Kratochwill, & M. Clements (Eds.), *Schoolwide prevention models: Lessons learned in elementary schools* (pp. 31–60). New York: Guilford Press.

Cheney, D., Lynass, L., Flower, A., Waugh, M., Iwaszuk, W., Mielenz, C., et al. (2010). The Check, Connect, and Expect Program: A targeted, Tier 2 intervention in the schoolwide positive behavior support model. *Preventing School Failure, 54*(3), 152–158.

Cheney, D., Stage, S. A., Hawken, L. S., Lynass, L., Mielenz, C., & Waugh, M. (2009). A 2-year outcome study of the Check, Connect, and Expect intervention for students at risk for severe behavior problems. *Journal of Emotional and Behavioral Disorders, 17*(4), 226–243.

Childs, K., Kincaid, D., & George, H. P. (2009). *Positive behavior support implementation checklist (PIC).* Unpublished instrument, University of South Florida, Tampa, FL.

Christ, T. (2008). Best practices in problem analysis. In A. Thomas & J. Grimes (Eds.), *Best practices in school psychology V* (pp. 159–176). Bethesda, MD: National Association of School Psychologists.

Cook, C. R., Rasetshwane, K. B., Truelson, E., Grant, S., Dart, E. H., Collins, T. A., et al. (2011). Development and validation of the student internalizing behavior screener: Examination of reliability, validity, and classification accuracy. *Assessment for Effective Intervention, 36*(2), 71–79.

Cooper, J. O., Heron, T. E., & Heward, W. L. (2007). *Applied behavior analysis* (2nd ed.). Upper Saddle River, NJ: Pearson.

Costenbader, V., & Markson, S. (1998). School suspension: A study with secondary school students. *Journal of School Psychology, 36*(1), 59–82.

Crone, D. A., Hawken, L. S., & Horner, R. H. (2010). *Responding to problem behavior in schools: The behavior education program* (2nd ed.). New York: Guilford Press.

Crone, D. A., & Horner, R. H. (2003). *Building positive behavior support systems in schools: Functional behavioral assessment.* New York: Guilford Press.

Cummings, K. D., Kaminski, R. A., & Merrell, K. W. (2008). Advances in the assessment of social competence: Findings from a preliminary investigation of a general outcome measure for social behavior. *Psychology in the Schools, 45*(10), 930–946.

Curtis, R., Van Horne, J. W., Robertson, P., & Karvonen, M. (2010). Outcomes of a school-wide positive behavioral support program. *Professional School Counseling, 13*(3), 159–164.

Darch, C. B., & Kame'enui, E. J. (2004). *Instructional classroom management: A proactive approach to behavior management* (2nd ed.). Upper Saddle River, NJ: Merrill.

Drummond, T. (1994). *The Student Risk Screening Scale (SRSS).* Grants Pass, OR: Josephine County Mental Health Program.

DuBois, D. L., Holloway, B. E., Valentine, J. C., & Cooper, H. (2002). Effectiveness of mentoring programs for youth: A meta-analytic review. *American Journal of Community Psychology, 30*(2), 157–197.

Dunlap, G., Iovannone, R., Kincaid, D., Wilson, K., Christiansen, K., Strain, P. S., et al. (2010). *Prevent-teach-reinforce: The school-based model of individualized positive behavior support.* Baltimore, Maryland: Brookes Publishing.

Durlak, J. A., Weissberg, R. P., Dymnicki, A. B., Taylor, R. D., & Schellinger, K. B. (2011). The impact of enhancing students' social and emotional learning: A meta-analysis of school-based universal interventions. *Child Development, 82*(1), 405–432.

Dymond, S. K., Chun, E. J., Kim, R. K. & Renzaglia, A. (2013). A validation of elements, methods, and barriers to inclusive high school service-learning programs. *Remedial and Special Education, 34*(5), 293–304.

Dymond, S. K., Renzaglia, A., & Chun, E. (2007). Elements of effective high school service learning programs that include students with and without disabilities. *Remedial and Special Education, 28*(4), 227–243.

Fairbanks, S., Sugai, G., Guardino, D., & Lathrop, M. (2007). Response to intervention: Examining classroom behavior support in second grade. *Exceptional Children, 73*(3), 288–310.

Fenton Community High School. (n.d.). *The be REAL initiative.* Accessed at www.fenton100.org/content/be-real-initiative on February 24, 2017.

Feuerborn, L. L., Wallace, C., & Tyre, A. D. (2013). Gaining staff support for schoolwide positive behavior supports: A guide for teams. *Beyond Behavior, 22*(2), 27–34.

Filter, K. J., McKenna, M. K., Benedict, E. A., Horner, R. H., Todd, A. W., & Watson, J. (2007). Check In–Check Out: A post-hoc evaluation of an efficient, secondary-level targeted intervention for reducing problem behaviors in schools. *Education and Treatment of Children, 30*(1), 69–84.

Fixsen, D., Naoom, S., Blase, K., Friedman, R., & Wallace, F. (2005). *Implementation research: A synthesis of the literature.* Tampa: University of South Florida, Louis de la Parte Florida Mental Health Institute, National Implementation Research Network.

Fixsen, D., Naoom, S., Blase, K., & Wallace, F. (2007). Implementation: The missing link between research and practice. *APSAC Advisor, 19*(1 & 2), 4–10.

Flora, S. R. (2000). Praise's magic reinforcement ratio: Five to one gets the job done. *Behavior Analyst Today, 1*(4), 64–69.

Fox, L., & Hemmeter, M. L. (2009). A programwide model for supporting social emotional development and addressing challenging behavior in early childhood settings. In W. Sailor, G. Dunlap, G. Sugai, & R. H. Horner (Eds.), *Handbook of positive behavior support* (pp. 177–202). New York: Springer.

Franzen, K., & Kamps, D. (2008). The utilization and effects of positive behavior support strategies on an urban school playground. *Journal of Positive Behavior Interventions, 10*(3), 150–161.

Frey, A. J., Boyce, C. A., & Tarullo, L. B. (2009). Integrating a positive behavior support approach within Head Start. In W. Sailor, G. Dunlap, G. Sugai, & R. H. Horner (Eds.), *Handbook of positive behavior support* (pp. 125–149). New York: Springer.

Gable, R. A., & Shores, R. E. (1980). Comparison of procedures for promoting reading proficiency of two children with behavioral and learning disorders. *Behavioral Disorders, 5*(2), 102–107.

George, H. (2009, June). Schoolwide positive behavioral interventions and supports training. In-service provided at Washoe County School District, Reno, NV.

George, H. P., Kincaid, D., & Pollard-Sage, J. (2009). Primary-tier interventions and supports. In W. Sailor, G. Dunlap, G. Sugai, & R. H. Horner (Eds.), *Handbook of positive behavior support* (pp. 375–394). New York: Springer.

Good, R. H., Gruba, J., & Kaminski, R. (2002). Best practices in using Dynamic Indicators of Basic Early Literacy Skills (DIBELS) in an outcomes-driven model. In A. Thomas & J. Grimes (Eds.), *Best practices in school psychology IV* (4th ed., pp. 679–699). Bethesda, MD: National Association of School Psychologists.

Goodman, R. (1997). The strengths and difficulties questionnaire: A research note. *Journal of Child Psychology and Psychiatry, 38*(5), 581–586.

Gottfried, A. E. (1983). Intrinsic motivation in young children. *Young Children, 39*(1), 64–73.

Greenwood, C., Kratochwill, T., & Clements, M. (Eds.). (2008). *Schoolwide prevention models: Lessons learned in elementary schools.* New York: Guilford Press.

Gregus, S. J., Craig, J. T., Rodriguez, J. H., Pastrana, F. A., & Cavell, T. A. (2015). Lunch buddy mentoring for children victimized by peers: Two pilot studies. *Journal of Applied School Psychology, 31*(2), 167–197.

Gresham, F. M. (2002). Teaching social skills to high-risk children and youth: Preventive and remedial strategies. In M. R. Shinn, H. M. Walker, & G. Stoner (Eds.), *Interventions for academic and behavior problems II: Preventive and remedial approaches* (pp. 403–432). Bethesda, MD: National Association of School Psychologists.

Gresham, F. M., & Elliott, S. N. (2008). *Social skills improvement system rating scales.* Boston: Pearson.

Gresham, F. M., Van, M. B., & Cook, C. R. (2006). Social skills training for teaching replacement behaviors: Remediating acquisition deficits in at-risk students. *Behavioral Disorders, 31*(4), 363–377.

Grossman, J. B., & Tierney, J. P. (1998). Does mentoring work?: An impact study of the Big Brothers Big Sisters program. *Evaluation Review, 22*(3), 403–426.

Handler, M. W., Rey, J., Connell, J., Their, K., Feinberg, A., & Putnam, R. (2007). Practical considerations in creating school-wide positive behavior support in public schools. *Psychology in the Schools, 44*(1), 29–39.

Hanh, T. N. (1991). *Peace is every step: The path of mindfulness in everyday life.* New York: Bantam Books.

Haring, N. G. (1988). A technology for generalization. In N. G. Haring (Ed.), *Generalization for students with severe handicaps: Strategies and solutions* (pp. 5–12). Seattle: University of Washington Press.

Harlacher, J. E. (2011, June). *Tier 1 school-wide positive behavior support.* In-service provided at 2011 PBS Nevada and Washoe County School District Summer Training Institute, Reno, NV.

Harlacher, J. E. (2015). *Designing effective classroom management.* Bloomington, IN: Marzano Research.

Harlacher, J. E., Potter, J. B., & Weber, J. M. (2015). A team-based approach to improving core instructional reading practices within response to intervention. *Intervention in School and Clinic, 50*(4), 210–220.

Harlacher, J. E., Roberts, N. E., & Merrell, K. W. (2006). Classwide interventions for students with ADHD: A summary of teacher options beneficial for the whole class. *Teaching Exceptional Children, 39*(2), 6–12.

Harlacher, J. E., Sakelaris, T. L., & Kattelman, N. M. (2014). *Practitioner's guide to curriculum-based evaluation in reading.* New York: Heidelberg.

Harlacher, J. E., Sanford, A., & Walker, N. N. (n.d.). *Distinguishing between Tier 2 and Tier 3 instruction in order to support implementation of RTI.* Accessed at http://rtinetwork.org/essential/tieredinstruction/tier3/distinguishing-between-tier -2-and-tier-3-instruction-in-order-to-support-implementation-of-rti?utm_source=newsletter_may_15_2014&utm _medium=email&utm_content=text&utm_campaign=rtiactionupdate on February 24, 2017.

Hawken, L. S., Adolphson, S. L., MacLeod, K. S., & Schumann, J. (2009). Secondary-tier interventions and supports. In W. Sailor, G. Dunlap, G. Sugai, & R. H. Horner (Eds.), *Handbook of positive behavior support* (pp. 395–420). New York: Springer.

Hawken, L. S., MacLeod, K. S., & Rawlings, L. (2007). Effects of the Behavior Education Program (BEP) on office discipline referrals of elementary school students. *Journal of Positive Behavior Interventions, 9*(2), 94–101.

Hawken, L. S., O'Neill, R. E., & MacLeod, K. S. (2011). An investigation of the impact of function of problem behavior on effectiveness of the Behavior Education Program (BEP). *Education and Treatment of Children, 34*(4), 551–574.

Hawkins, S. M., & Heflin, L. J. (2011). Increasing secondary teachers' behavior-specific praise using a video self-modeling and visual performance feedback intervention. *Journal of Positive Behavior Interventions, 13*(2), 97–108.

Horner, R. H., & Day, H. M. (1991). The effects of response efficiency on functionally equivalent competing behaviors. *Journal of Applied Behavior Analysis, 24*(4), 719–732.

Horner, R. H., Kincaid, D., Sugai, G., Lewis, T., Eber, L., Barret, S., Dickey, C. R., et al. (2014). Scaling up school-wide positive behavioral interventions and supports: Experiences of seven states with documented success. *Journal of Positive Behavior Interventions, 16*(4), 197–208.

Horner, R. H., Lewis-Palmer, T., Sugai, G., & Todd, A. W. (2005). *School-wide evaluation tool (SET) v 2.1.* Accessed at www.pbis.org/resource/222/school-wide-evaluation-tool-set-v-2–1 on April 28, 2017.

Horner, R. H., & Sugai, G. (2015). School-wide PBIS: An example of applied behavior analysis implemented at a scale of social importance. *Behavior Analysis in Practice, 8*(1), 80–85.

Horner, R. H., Sugai, G., & Anderson, C. (2010). Examining the evidence base for school-wide positive behavior support. *Focus on Exceptional Children, 42*(8), 1–14.

Horner, R. H., Sugai, G., & Lewis, T. (2015). *Is school-wide positive behavior support an evidence-based practice?* Accessed at www.pbis.org/research on February 27, 2015.

Horner, R. H., Sugai, G., Smolkowski, K., Eber, L., Nakasato, J., Todd, A. W., et al. (2009). A randomized, wait-list controlled effectiveness trial assessing school-wide positive behavior support in elementary schools. *Journal of Positive Behavior Interventions, 11*(3), 133–144.

Horner, R. H., Sugai, G., Todd, A. W., & Lewis-Palmer, T. (2005). Schoolwide positive behavior support. In L. M. Bambara & L. Kern (Eds.), *Individualized supports for students with problem behaviors: Designing positive behavior plans* (pp. 359–390). New York: Guilford Press.

Hosp, J. L. (2008). Best practices in aligning academic assessment with instruction. In A. Thomas & J. Grimes (Eds.), *Best practices in school psychology V* (pp. 363–376). Bethesda, MD: National Association of School Psychologists.

Houghton-Portage Township Schools. (n.d.). *GRIT.* Accessed at www.hpts.us/highschool/grit on February 27, 2017.

Howell, K. W., & Nolet, V. (2000). *Curriculum-based evaluation: Teaching and decision making.* Belmont, CA: Wadsworth/ Thomason Learning.

Irvin, L. K., Tobin, T. J., Sprague, J. R., Sugai, G., & Vincent, C. G. (2004). Validity of office discipline referral measures as indices of school-wide behavioral status and effects of school-wide behavioral interventions. *Journal of Positive Behavior Interventions, 6*(3), 131–147.

January, A. M., Casey, R. J., & Paulson, D. (2011). A meta-analysis of classroom-wide interventions to build social skills: Do they work? *School Psychology Review, 40*(2), 242–256.

Jenson, W. R., Evans, C., Morgan, D., & Rhode, G. (2006). *The tough kid principal's briefcase: A practical guide to schoolwide behavior management and legal issues.* Longmont, Colorado: Sopris West Educational Services

Jimerson, S. R., Burns, M. K., VanDerHeyden, A. M. (2007). *Handbook of response to intervention: The science and practice of assessment and intervention*. New York: Springer.

Kaminski, R., Cummings, K. D., Powell-Smith, K. A., & Good, R. H. (2008). Best practices in using dynamic indicators of basic early literacy skills for formative assessment and evaluation. In A. Thomas & J. Grimes (Eds.), *Best practices in school psychology V* (pp. 1181–1204). Bethesda, MD: National Association of School Psychologists.

Kazdin, A. E. (1975). The impact of applied behavior analysis on diverse areas of research. *Journal of Applied Behavioral Analysis, 8*(2), pp. 213–229.

Kendyl Depoali Middle School, STRIKE Committee. (n.d.). *Depoali Middle School STRIKE*. Accessed at www.washoe schools.net/cms/lib08/NV01912265/Centricity/Domain/342/Progressive%20Discipline%20Plan%2013_14.pdf on February 24, 2017.

Kern, L., Choutka, C. M., & Sokol, N. G. (2002). Assessment-based antecedent interventions used in natural settings to reduce challenging behavior: An analysis of the literature. *Education and Treatment of Children, 25*(1), 113–130.

Kern, L., & Clarke, S. (2005). Antecedent and setting event interventions. In L. M. Bambara & L. Kern (Eds.), *Individualized supports for students with problem behaviors: Designing positive behavior plans* (pp. 201–236). New York: Guilford Press.

Kern, L., Gallagher, P., Starosta, K., Hickman, W., & George, M. (2006). Longitudinal outcomes of functional behavioral assessment-based intervention. *Journal of Positive Behavior Interventions, 8*(2), 67–78.

Kern, L., White, G. P., & Gresham, F. M. (2007, March/April). Educating children with behavioral challenges. *Principal*, 56–59.

Kincaid, D., Childs, K., & George, H. (2010). *School-wide benchmarks of quality (revised)*. Unpublished instrument, University of South Florida, Tampa, FL.

Knoster, T., Villa, R., & Thousand, J. (2000). A framework for thinking about systems change. In R. Villa & J. Thousand (Eds.), *Restructuring for caring and effective education: Piecing the puzzle together* (pp. 93–128). Baltimore: Paul H. Brookes Publishing Co.

Kovaleski, J. F., Marco-Fies, C. M., & Boneshefski, M. J. (n.d.). *Treatment integrity: Ensuring the "I" in RTI*. Accessed at www.rtinetwork.org/getstarted/evaluate/treatment-integrity-ensuring-the-i-in-rti on February 27, 2017.

Kraemer, E. E., Davies, S. C., Arndt, K. J., & Hunley, S. (2012). A comparison of the mystery motivator and the *Get 'Em On Task* interventions for off-task behaviors. *Psychology in the Schools, 49*(2), 163–174.

Kratochwill, T., Elliott, S. N., & Callan-Stoiber, K. (2002). Best practices in school-based problem-solving consultation. In A. Thomas & J. Grimes (Eds.), *Best practices in school psychology IV* (pp. 583–608). Bethesda, MD: National Association of School Psychologists.

Kratochwill, T., & Shernoff, E. S. (2004). Evidence-based practice: Promoting evidence-based interventions in school psychology. *School Psychology Review, 33*(1), 34–48.

Lane, K. L., Wehby, J., Menzies, H. M., Doukas, G. L., Munton, S. M., & Gregg, R. M. (2003). Social skills instruction for students at risk for antisocial behavior: The effects of small-group instruction. *Behavioral Disorders, 28*(3), 229–248.

Lane, K. L., Wehby, J., Menzies, H. M., Gregg, R. M., Doukas, G. L., & Munton, S. M. (2002). Early literacy instruction for first-grade students at-risk for antisocial behavior. *Education and Treatment of Children, 25*(4), 438–458.

Langland, S., Lewis-Palmer, T., & Sugai, G. (1998). Teaching respect in the classroom: An instructional approach. *Journal of Behavioral Education, 8*(2), 245–262.

Lehr, C. A., Sinclair, M. F., & Christenson, S. L. (2004). Addressing student engagement and truancy prevention during the elementary school years: A replication study of the Check and Connect model. *Journal of Education for Students Placed at Risk, 9*(3), 279–301.

Lenski, S. (2011). What RTI means for content area teachers. *Journal of Adolescent and Adult Literacy, 55*(4), 276–282.

Lewis, T. J. (n.d.). *Positive behavioral interventions & supports: A framework for addressing the social and emotional behavioral needs of all students*. Accessed at www.pbis.org/common/cms/files/pbisresources/Lewis_Keynote.ppt on September 18, 2017.

Lewis, T. J., Hudson, S., Richter, M., & Johnson, N. (2004). Scientifically supported practices in emotional and behavioral disorders: A proposed approach and brief review of current practices. *Behavioral Disorders, 29*(3), 247–259.

Lewis, T. J., Powers, L. J., Kely, M. J., & Newcomer, L. L. (2002). Reducing problem behaviors on the playground: An investigation of the application of schoolwide positive behavior supports. *Psychology in the Schools, 39*(2), 181–190.

Lippitt, M. (1987). *The managing complex change model.* Palm Harbor, FL: Enterprise Management.

Litow, K., & Pumroy, D. K. (1975). A brief review of classroom group-oriented contingencies. *Journal of Applied Behavior Analysis, 8*(3), 341–347.

Loman., S. L., Rodriguez, B. J., & Borgmeier, C. (2014). Critical features for identifying function-based supports: From research to practice. *Research and Practice in the Schools, 2*(1), 9–20.

Luiselli, J. K., & Downing, J. N. (1980). Improving a student's arithmetic performance using feedback and reinforcement procedures. *Education and Treatment of Children, 3*(1), 45–49.

Lynass, L., Tsai, S., Richman, T. D., & Cheney, D. (2012). Social expectations and behavioral indicators in school-wide positive behavior supports: A national study of behavior matrices. *Journal of Positive Behavior Interventions, 14*(3), 153–161.

Mace, F. C., Hock, M. L., Lalli, J. S., West, B. J., Belfiore, P., Pinter, E., et al. (1988). Behavioral momentum in the treatment of noncompliance. *Journal of Applied Behavior Analysis, 21*(2), 123–141.

Mandinach, E. B. (2012). A perfect time for data use: Using data-driven decision making to inform practice. *Educational Psychologist, 47*(2), 71–85.

Marchant, M. R., Solano, B. R., Fisher, A. K., Caldarella, P., Young, K. R., & Renshaw, T. L. (2007). Modifying socially withdrawn behavior: A playground intervention for students with internalizing behaviors. *Psychology in the Schools, 44*(8), 779–794.

Mass-Galloway, R. L., Panyan, M. V., Smith, C. R., & Wessendorf, S. (2008). Systems change with school-wide positive behavior supports: Iowa's work in progress. *Journal of Positive Behavior Interventions, 10*(2), 129–135.

Maynard, B. R., Kjellstrand, E. K., & Thompson, A. M. (2014). Effects of Check and Connect on attendance, behavior, and academics: A randomized effectiveness trial. *Research on Social Work Practice, 24*(3), 296–309.

McDaniel, S. C., Flower, A., & Cheney, D. (2011). Put me in, Coach!: A powerful and efficient Tier 2 behavioral intervention for alternative settings. *Beyond Behavior, 20*(1), 18–24.

McIntosh, K., Filter, K. J., Bennett, J. L., Ryan, C., & Sugai, G. (2010). Principles of sustainable prevention: Designing scale-up of school-wide positive behavior support to promote durable systems. *Psychology in the Schools, 47*(1), 5–21.

McIntosh, K., Frank, J. L., & Spaulding, S. A. (2010). Establishing research-based trajectories of office discipline referrals for individual students. *School Psychology Review, 39*(3), 380–394.

McIntosh, K., & Goodman, S. (2016). *Integrated multi-tiered systems of support: Blending RTI and PBIS.* New York: Guilford Press.

McIntosh, K., Horner, R. H., Chard, D. J., Boland, J., & Good, R. H. (2006). The use of reading and behavior screening measures to predict nonresponse to school-wide positive behavior support: A longitudinal analysis. *School Psychology Review, 35*(2), 275–291.

McIntosh, K., Horner, R. H., & Sugai, G. (2009). Sustainability of systems-level evidence-based practices in schools: Current knowledge and future directions. In W. Sailor, G. Dunlap, G. Sugai, & R. H. Horner (Eds.), *Handbook of positive behavior support* (pp. 327–352). New York: Springer.

McIntosh, K., MacKay, L. D., Hume, A. E., Doolittle, J., Vincent, C. G., Horner, R. H., et al. (2011). Developmental and initial validation of a measure to assess factors related to sustainability of school-wide positive behavior support. *Journal of Positive Behavior Interventions, 13*(4), 208–218.

McKevitt, B. C., & Braaksma, A. (2008). Best practices in developing a positive behavior support system at the school level. In A. Thomas & J. Grimes (Eds.), *Best practices in school psychology V* (pp. 735–747). Bethesda, MD: National Association of School Psychologists.

Merrell, K. W., Ervin, R. A., & Peacock, G. G. (2012). *School psychology for the 21st century: Foundations and practices* (2nd ed.). New York: Guilford Press.

Metzler, C. W., Biglan, A., Rusby, J. C., & Sprague, J. R. (2001). Evaluation of a comprehensive behavior management program to improve school-wide positive behavior support. *Education and Treatment of Children, 24*(4), 448–479.

Missouri Schoolwide Positive Behavior Support. (n.d.a). *Tier 2 resources.* Accessed at http://pbismissouri.org/teams/tier-2-workbook on February 27, 2017.

Missouri Schoolwide Positive Behavior Support. (n.d.b). *Using existing school data to identify students at risk.* Accessed at http://pbismissouri.org/wp-content/uploads/2012/05/Using_Existing-School_Data_08.30.12.pdf on February 27, 2017.

Mitchell, B. S., Stormont, M., & Gage, N. A. (2011). Tier two interventions implemented within the context of a tiered prevention framework. *Behavioral Disorders, 36*(4), 241–261.

Muscott, H. S., Mann, E. L., & LeBrun, M. R. (2008). Positive behavioral interventions and supports in New Hampshire: Effects of large-scale implementation of schoolwide positive behavior support on student discipline and academic achievement. *Journal of Positive Behavior Interventions, 10*(3), 190–205.

Musser, E. H., Bray, M. A., Kehle, T. J., & Jenson, W. R. (2001). Reducing disruptive behaviors in students with serious emotional disturbance. *School Psychology Review, 30*(2), 294–304.

National Technical Assistance Center on Positive Behavioral Interventions and Supports. (n.d.). *What is school-wide PBIS?* Accessed at www.pbis.org/school on February 27, 2017.

National Technical Assistance Center on Positive Behavioral Interventions and Supports. (2010). *PBIS frequently asked questions.* Accessed at www.pbis.org/common/cms/files/pbisresources/PBIS_Q&A.pdf on February 27, 2017.

Nelson, J. R., Hurley, K. D., Synhorst, L., Epstein, M., Stage, S., & Buckley, J. (2009). The child outcomes of a behavior model. *Exceptional Children, 76*(1), 7–30.

Netzel, D. M., & Eber, L. (2003). Shifting from reactive to proactive discipline in an urban school district: A change of focus through PBIS implementation. *Journal of Positive Behavior Interventions, 5*(2), 71–79.

Newton, J. S., Horner, R. H., Algozzine, R. F., Todd, A. W., & Algozzine, K. M. (2009). Using a problem-solving model to enhance data-based decision making in schools. In W. Sailor, G. Dunlap, G. Sugai, & R. H. Horner (Eds.), *Handbook of positive behavior support* (pp. 551–580). New York: Springer.

Newton, J. S., Todd, A. W., Algozzine, K. M., Horner, R. H., & Algozzine, B. (2009). *Team-initiated problem solving training manual.* Eugene: University of Oregon, Educational and Community Supports.

Noell, G. H., Duhon, G. J., Gatti, S. L., & Connell, J. E. (2002). Consultation, follow-up, and implementation of behavior management interventions in general education. *School Psychology Review, 31*(2), 217–234.

O'Neill, R. E., Horner, R. H., Albin, R. W., Sprague, J. R., & Storey, K. (1997). *Functional assessment and program development for problem behavior: A practical handbook* (2nd ed.). Pacific Grove, CA: Brooks/Cole.

Ott, T. (2010). *As schools' gym classes and recesses disappear, districts must get creative to help fight childhood obesity.* The Plain Dealer. Accessed at http://www.cleveland.com/fighting-fat/index.ssf/2010/06/as_schools_gym_class_and_recess_disappear_districts_must_get_creative_to_help_fight_childhood_obesit.html on July 23, 2017.

Payton, J., Weissberg, R. P., Durlak, J. A., Dymnicki, A. B., Taylor, R. D., Schellinger, K. B., et al. (2008). *The positive impact of social and emotional learning for kindergarten to eighth-grade students: Findings from three scientific reviews.* Chicago: Collaborative for Academic, Social, and Emotional Learning. Accessed at www.casel.org/wp-content/uploads/2016/08/PDF-4-the-positive-impact-of-social-and-emotional-learning-for-kindergarten-to-eighth-grade-students-executive-summary.pdf on February 28, 2017.

PBISApps. (n.d.). *2013–14 SWIS summary national data sample.* Accessed at www.pbisapps.org/Resources/SWIS%20Publications/SWIS%20Data%20Summary%202013-14.pdf on February 27, 2017.

PBISApps. (2016, August). *SWIS summary.* Accessed at www.pbisapps.org/Resources/SWIS%20Publications/SWIS%20 Data%20Summary%202015-16.pdf#search=Data%20for%20Major%20ODRs%2C%202015%E2%80%9316 on May 29, 2017.

PBIS Center, U.S. Department of Education, Office of Special Education. (n.d.). *4 PBS elements.* Retrieved from PBIS Center, U.S. Department of Education, Office of Special Education on June 22, 2017.

PBIS Maryland. (n.d.). Elementary and middle school examples. Accessed at www.pbismaryland.org/schoolexamples.htm on February 28, 2017.

Peace Power Tools. (n.d.). Accessed at www.peacepower.info/modules/RespectStrucRec.pdf on February 28, 2017.

Peacock, G. G., Ervin, R. A., Daly, E. J., & Merrell, K. W. (Eds.). (2010). *Practical handbook of school psychology: Effective practices for the 21st century.* New York: Guilford Press.

Petscher, E. S., Rey, C., & Bailey, J. S. (2009). A review of empirical support for differential reinforcement of alternative behavior. *Research in Developmental Disabilities, 30*(3), 409–425.

Pisacreta, J., Tincani, M., Connell, J. E., & Axelrod, S. (2011). Increasing teachers' use of a 1:1 praise-to-behavior correction ratio to decrease student disruption in general education classrooms. *Behavioral Interventions, 26*(4), 243–260.

Pool, J. L., Carter., D. R., & Johnson, E. S. (2013). Tier 2 team processes and decision-making in a comprehensive three-tiered model. *Intervention in School and Clinic, 48*(4), 232–239.

Pyle, N., & Vaughn, S. (2012). Remediating reading difficulties in a response to intervention model with secondary students. *Psychology in the Schools, 49*(3), 273–284.

Quinn, M. M., Kavale, K. A., Mathur, S. R., Rutherford, R. B., & Forness, S. R. (1999). A meta-analysis of social skill interventions for students with emotional or behavioral disorders. *Journal of Emotional and Behavioral Disorders, 7*(1), 54–64.

Rathel, J. M., Drasgow, E., Brown, W. H., & Marshall, K. J. (2014). Increasing induction-level teachers' positive-to-negative communication ratio and use of behavior-specific praise through e-mailed performance feedback and its effect on students' task engagement. *Journal of Positive Behavior Interventions, 16*(4), 219–233.

Rathvon, N. (2008). *Effective school interventions: Evidence-based strategies for improving student outcomes* (2nd ed.). New York: Guilford Press.

Reinke, W. M., Herman, K. C., & Stormont, M. (2013). Classroom-level positive behavior supports in schools implementing SW-PBIS: Identifying areas for enhancement. *Journal of Positive Behavior Interventions, 15*(1), 39–50.

Reschly, D. J. (2008). School psychology paradigm shift and beyond. In A. Thomas & J. Grimes (Eds.), *Best practices in school psychology V* (pp. 3–15). Bethesda, MD: National Association of School Psychologists.

Rodriguez, B. J. (2015, November). *Tier 1 school-wide positive behavior support meetings.* In-service provided at 2015 Springfield Public Schools Maple Elementary PBIS team. Springfield, OR.

Rodriguez, B. J., & Anderson, C. (2014). Integrating a social behavior intervention during small group academic instruction using a total group criterion intervention. *Journal of Positive Behavior Interventions, 16*(4), 234–245.

Rodriguez, B. J., Campbell, A., Falcon, S., & Borgmeier, C. (2015). Examination of critical features and lessons learned for implementation of a tier 2 intervention system for social behavior. *Journal of Educational and Psychological Consultation, 25,* 224–251.

Rodriguez, B. J., Loman, S. L., & Borgmeier, C. (2016). Tier 2 interventions in positive behavior support: A survey of school implementation. *Preventing School Failure, 60*(2), 94–105.

Rollin, S. A., Kaiser-Ulrey, C., Potts, I., & Creason, A. H. (2003). A school-based violence prevention model for at-risk eighth grade youth. *Psychology in the Schools, 40*(4), 403–416.

Ross, S., Horner, R. H., & Stiller, B. (n.d.). *Bully prevention in positive behavior support.* Accessed at www.pbis.org/common /cms/files/pbisresources/bullyprevention_ES.pdf on February 28, 2017.

Ross, S., Romer, N., & Horner, R. H. (2012). Teacher well-being and the implementation of school-wide positive behavior interventions and supports. *Journal of Positive Behavior Interventions, 14*(2), 118–128.

Sailor, W., Dunlap, G., Sugai, G., & Horner, R. H. (Eds.). (2009). *Handbook of positive behavior support.* New York: Springer.

Scott, T. M. (2001). A schoolwide example of positive behavioral support. *Journal of Positive Behavior Interventions, 3*(2), 88–94.

Scott, T. M., Anderson, C., Mancil, R., & Alter, P. (2009). Function-based supports for individual students in school settings. In W. Sailor, G. Dunlap, G. Sugai, & R. H. Horner (Eds.), *Handbook of positive behavior support* (pp. 421–442). New York: Springer.

Scott. T. M., & Barrett, S. B. (2004.) Using staff and student time engaged in disciplinary procedures to evaluate the impact of school-wide PBS. *Journal of Positive Behavior Interventions, 6(1),* 21–27. Accessed at http://www.nhcebis. seresc.net/document/filename/355/Time_and_Cost_analysis_of_PBIS.pdf on May 17, 2017.

Severson, H., Walker, H. M., Hope-Doolittle, J., Kratochwill, T., & Gresham, F. M. (2007). Proactive, early screening to detect behaviorally at-risk students: Issues, approaches, emerging innovations, and professional practices. *Journal of School Psychology, 45*(2), 193–223.

Shinn, M. R. (2008a). Best practices in curriculum-based measurement and its use in a problem-solving model. In A. Thomas & J. Grimes (Eds.), *Best practices in school psychology V* (pp. 243–262). Bethesda, MD: National Association of School Psychologists.

Shinn, M. R. (2008b). RTI at the secondary level. In S. L. Fernley, S. D. LaRue, & J. Norlin (Eds.), *What do I do when . . . : The answer book on RTI.* Horsham, PA: LRP.

Shinn, M. R., Walker, H. M., & Stoner, G. (Eds.). (2002). *Interventions for academic and behavior problems II: Preventive and remedial approaches.* Bethesda, MD: National Association of School Psychologists.

Simonsen, B., Eber, L., Black, A. C., Sugai, G., Lewandowski, H., Sims, B., et al. (2012). Illinois statewide positive behavioral interventions and supports: Evolution and impact on student outcomes across years. *Journal of Positive Behavior Interventions, 14*(1), 5–16.

Simonsen, B., Fairbanks, S., Briesch, A., Myers, D., & Sugai, G. (2008). Evidence-based practices in classroom management: Considerations for research to practice. *Education and Treatment of Children, 31*(3), 351–380.

Simonsen, B., & Myers, D. (2015). *Classwide positive behavior interventions and supports: A guide to proactive classroom management.* New York: Guilford Press.

Simonsen, B., Myers, D., & Briere, D. E. (2011). Comparing a behavioral check-in/check-out (CICO) intervention to standard practice in an urban middle school setting using an experimental group design. *Journal of Positive Behavior Interventions, 13*(1), 31–48.

Sinclair, M. F., Christenson, S. L., Lehr, C. A., & Anderson, A. R. (2003). Facilitating student engagement: Lessons learned from Check and Connect longitudinal studies. *The California School Psychologist, 8*(1), 29–41.

Sinek, S. (2009, September). *Simon Sinek: How great leaders inspire action* [Video file]. Accessed at www.ted.com/talks /simon_sinek_how_great_leaders_inspire_action on February 28, 2017.

Skinner, B. F. (1953). *Science and human behavior.* New York: Macmillan.

Skinner, B. F. (1976). *About behaviorism.* New York: Vintage Books.

Smith, C., Bicard, S. C., Bicard, D. F., & Casey, L. B. (2012). Decreasing in-school suspensions with function-based interventions. *Kappa Delta Pi Record, 48*(4), 174–177.

Smith, D. D., & Rivera, D. P. (1993). *Effective discipline* (2nd ed.). Austin, TX: PRO-ED.

Sprague, J. R., & Horner, R. H. (1999). Low-frequency high-intensity problem behavior: Toward an applied technology of functional assessment and intervention. In A. C. Repp & R. H. Horner (Eds.), *Functional analysis of problem behavior: From effective assessment to effective support* (pp. 98–116). Belmont, CA: Wadsworth.

Springfield Public Schools. (n.d.). Accessed at www.springfield.k12.or.us on February 28, 2017.

Steege, M. W., & Watson, T. S. (2009). *Conducting school-based functional behavioral assessments: A practitioner's guide* (2nd ed.). New York: Guilford Press.

Stormont, M., Reinke, W. M., Herman, K. C., & Lembke, E. S. (2012). *Academic and behavior supports for at-risk students: Tier 2 interventions.* New York: Guilford Press.

Sugai, G., & Horner, R. H. (2006). A promising approach for expanding and sustaining school-wide positive behavior support. *School Psychology Review, 35*(2), 246–259.

Sugai, G., & Horner, R. H. (2009). Defining and describing schoolwide positive behavior support. In W. Sailor, G. Dunlap, G. Sugai, & R. H. Horner (Eds.), *Handbook of positive behavior support* (pp. 307–326). New York: Springer.

Sugai, G., Horner, R. H., Lewis-Palmer, T., & Dickey, C. R. (2014). *Team implementation checklist.* Accessed at www.pbisapps.org/Applications/Pages/PBIS-Assessment-Surveys.aspx#sas on February 28, 2017.

Sugai, G., Horner, R. H., & Todd, A. W. (2009). *Self-assessment survey (SAS).* Accessed at www.pbisapps.org/Applications/Pages/PBIS-Assessment-Surveys.aspx#sas on February 28, 2017.

Sutherland, K. S., & Wehby, J. H. (2001). Exploring the relationship between increased opportunities to respond to academic requests and the academic and behavioral outcomes of students with EBD: A review. *Remedial and Special Education, 22*(2), 113–121.

Sutherland, K. S., Wehby, J. H., & Copeland, S. R. (2000). Effect of varying rates of behavior-specific praise on the on-task behavior of students with EBD. *Journal of Emotional and Behavioral Disorders, 8*(1), 2–8.

Swann, W. B., & Pittman, T. S. (1977). Initiating play activity of children: The moderating influence of verbal cues on intrinsic motivation. *Child Development, 48*(3), 1128–1132.

Taylor-Greene, S., Brown, D., Nelson, L., Longton, J., Gassman, T., Cohen, J., et al. (1997). School-wide behavioral support: Starting the year off right. *Journal of Behavior Education, 7*(1), 99–112.

Theodore, L. A., Bray, M. A., Kehle, T. J., & Jenson, W. R. (2001). Randomization of group contingencies and reinforcers to reduce classroom disruptive behavior. *Journal of School Psychology, 39*(3), 267–277.

Thomas, D. R., Becker, W. C., & Armstrong, M. (1968). Production and elimination of disruptive classroom behavior by systematically varying teacher's behavior. *Journal of Applied Behavior Analysis, 1*(1), 35–45.

Thorndike, R. M., & Thorndike-Christ, T. M. (2010.) *Measurement and evaluation in psychology and education* (8th ed.). London, England: Pearson.

Tilly, W. D. (2008). The evolution of school psychology to science-based practice: Problem solving and the three-tiered model. In A. Thomas & J. Grimes (Eds.), *Best practices in school psychology V* (pp. 17–35). Bethesda, MD: National Association of School Psychologists.

Tobin, T. J., & Sugai, G. (1999). Using sixth-grade school records to predict school violence, chronic discipline problems, and high school outcomes. *Journal of Emotional and Behavioral Disorders, 7*(1), 40–53.

Tobin, T., Sugai, G., & Colvin, G. (1996). Patterns in middle school discipline records. *Journal of Emotional and Behavioral Disorders, 4*(2), 82–94.

Todd, A. W., & Horner, R. H. (2006). *Referral form examples: Version 4.0.* Accessed at http://www.pbis.org/common/cms/files/newteam/data/referralformexamples.pdf on June 22, 2017.

Todd, A. W., Horner, R. H., & Tobin, T. (2006). *Referral form definitions: Version 4.0.* Accessed at www.pbis.org/common/cms/files/NewTeam/Data/ReferralFormDefinitions.pdf on December 2, 2014.

Todd, A. W., Newton, J. S., Horner, R. H., Algozzine, B., & Algozzine, K. (2010). *Team-initiated problem solving trainer-of-trainers manual.* Eugene: University of Oregon, Educational and Community Supports.

Turtura, J. E., Anderson, C., & Boyd, R. J. (2014). Addressing task avoidance in middle school students: Academic behavior check-in/check-out. *Journal of Positive Behavior Interventions, 16*(3), 159–167.

University of Minnesota. (n.d.). *About Check and Connect.* Accessed at http://checkandconnect.umn.edu/model/ on February 28, 2017.

University of Oregon. (2011, April). *School wide information system facilitator training manual.* Training session presented at University of Oregon, Eugene.

VanDerHeyden, A. M., Witt, J. C., & Gilbertson, D. (2007). A multi-year evaluation of the effects of a response to intervention (RTI) model on identification of children for special education. *Journal of School Psychology, 45*(2), 225–256.

Vaughn, S., Cirino, P. T., Wanzek, J., Wexler, J., Fletcher, J. M., Denton, C. D., et al. (2010). Response to intervention for middle school students with reading difficulties: Effects of a primary and secondary intervention. *School Psychology Review, 39*(1), 3–21.

Vaughn, S., Linan-Thompson, S., & Hickman, P. (2003). Response to instruction as a means of identifying students with reading/learning disabilities. *Exceptional Children, 69*(4), 391–409.

Vaughn, S., Wanzek, J., Woodruff, A. L., & Linan-Thompson, S. (2007). Prevention and early identification of students with reading disabilities: A research review of the three-tier model. In D. Haager, J. Klingner, & S. Vaughn (Eds.), *Evidence-based reading practices for response to intervention* (pp. 11–27). Baltimore: Brookes.

Vavrus, F., & Cole, K. (2002). "I didn't do nothin'": The discursive construction of school suspension. *Urban Review, 34*(2), 87–111.

Walker, H. M. (1979). *The acting–out child: Coping with classroom disruption.* Boston: Allyn & Bacon.

Walker, H. M., Ramsey, E., & Gresham, F. M. (2004). *Antisocial behavior in schools: Evidence-based practices* (2nd ed.). Belmont, CA: Wadsworth.

Walker, H. M., Small, J. W., Severson, H. H., Seeley, J. R., & Feil, E. G. (2014). Multiple-gating approaches in universal screening within school and community settings. In R. J. Kettler, T. A. Glover, C. A. Albers, & K. A. Feeney-Kettler (Eds.), *Universal screening in educational settings: Evidence-based decision making for schools* (pp. 47–75). Washington, DC: American Psychological Association.

Watson, J. B. (1913). Psychology as the behaviorist views it. *Psychological Review, 20*(2), 158–177.

Wesley, K. (2008). *A sample systematic process for fading CICO.* Unpublished manuscript.

White, M., George, H., Childs, K., & Martinez, S. (2009). *Tier 1 PBS walkthrough.* Unpublished instrument, University of South Florida, Tampa, FL.

Wilder, D. A., Harris, C., Reagan, R., & Rasey, A. (2007). Functional analysis and treatment of noncompliance by preschool children. *Journal of Applied Behavior Analysis, 40*(1), 173–177.

Wolery, M. (2011). Intervention research: The importance of fidelity measurement. *Topics in Early Childhood Special Education, 31*(3), 155–157.

Wolery, M., Bailey, D. B., & Sugai, G. (1988). *Effective teaching: Principles and procedures of applied behavior analysis with exceptional students.* Boston: Allyn & Bacon.

Wright, R. A., & McCurdy, B. L. (2012). Class-wide positive behavior support and group contingences: Examining a positive variation of the good behavior game. *Journal of Positive Behavior Interventions, 14*(3), 173–180.

Yong, M., & Cheney, D. A. (2013). Essential features of Tier 2 social-behavioral interventions. *Psychology in the Schools, 50*(8), 844–861.

Index

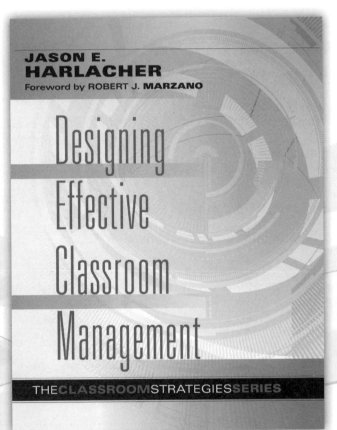

Create an encouraging, productive school culture

 Signature PD Service

An Educator's Guide to Schoolwide Positive Behavioral Interventions and Supports

This workshop will guide your school or district through every step of implementing Schoolwide Positive Behavioral Interventions and Supports (SWPBIS).

- Learn the foundational tenets and salient features of SWPBIS.

- Understand the four key elements of SWPBIS and what they look like in practice.

- Examine Tiers One, Two, and/or Three in depth, respectively, and be ready for implementation.

- Apply the Problem-Solving Model (PSM) to answer questions about the implementation of and the impact of SWPBIS.

- Examine how each key element interacts with the PSM to support student learning and social behavior outcomes.

Learn more
MarzanoResearch.com/SWPBIS